Bahamian Memories

Florida A&M University, Tallahassee
Florida Atlantic University, Boca Raton
Florida Gulf Coast University, Ft. Myers
Florida International University, Miami
Florida State University, Tallahassee
University of Central Florida, Orlando
University of Florida, Gainesville
University of North Florida, Jacksonville
University of South Florida, Tampa
University of West Florida, Pensacola

Olga Culmer Jenkins . . . .

University Press of Florida

GAINESVILLE · TALLAHASSEE · TAMPA · BOCA RATON

PENSACOLA · ORLANDO · MIAMI · JACKSONVILLE · FT. MYERS

Bahamian Memories

Island Voices of the Twentieth Century

Copyright 2000 by the Board of Regents of the State of Florida
Printed in the United States of America on acid-free paper
All rights reserved

05 04 03 02 01 00   6   5   4   3   2   1

LIBRARY OF CONGRESS CATALOGING-IN-PUBLICATION DATA
Jenkins, Olga Culmer.
Bahamian memories : island voices of the Twentieth Century /
Olga Culmer Jenkins.
p. cm.
Includes bibliographical references and index.
ISBN 0-8130-1779-3 (alk. paper)]
1. Bahamas—Social life and customs—20th century.
2. Oral history. I. Title.
F1654.J46   2000
972.96—dc21   00-023469

The University Press of Florida is the scholarly publishing
agency for the State University System of Florida, comprising
Florida A&M University, Florida Atlantic University, Florida
Gulf Coast University, Florida International University, Florida
State University, University of Central Florida, University
of Florida, University of North Florida, University of South
Florida, and University of West Florida.

University Press of Florida
15 Northwest 15th Street
Gainesville, FL 32611
http://www.upf.com

To my mother and all Bahamians who matured
during the first half of the twentieth century—

in the hope that their struggles to survive
will be remembered and valued by future generations.

Contents

Map of the Bahamas

The Bahamas consist of seven hundred islands and cays, twenty-two of which have permanent residents. The archipelago extends from approximately fifty miles off the southern coast of Florida to sixty miles off Cuba, with a total land area of approximately 5,400 square miles. Islands previously called Out Islands now have the more positive designation of Family Islands. These include all of the Bahamas except New Providence and Grand Bahama. Narrators in this book include persons born on the following islands:

Abacos—a group of islands in the northeast Bahamas. Area = 650 square miles. Population = 7,271.

Andros—largest of the Bahama islands. Area = 2,300 square miles. Population = 8,187.

Bimini—leading game-fishing island. Area = 9 square miles. Population = 1,639.

Cat Island—contains Mount Alvernia, the highest point in the Bahamas. Area = 150 square miles. Population = 1,698.

Eleuthera—110 miles long and approximately 2 miles wide. Area = 200 square miles. Population = 10,631.

Exuma—a major group of Bahamian islands. Area = 72 square miles. Population = 3,670.

Grand Bahama—location of Freeport/Lucaya, nation's second most populous city. Area = 530 square miles. Population = 40,898.

Harbour Island—spectacular pink sand beaches. Area = 1 square mile. Population = 1,004.

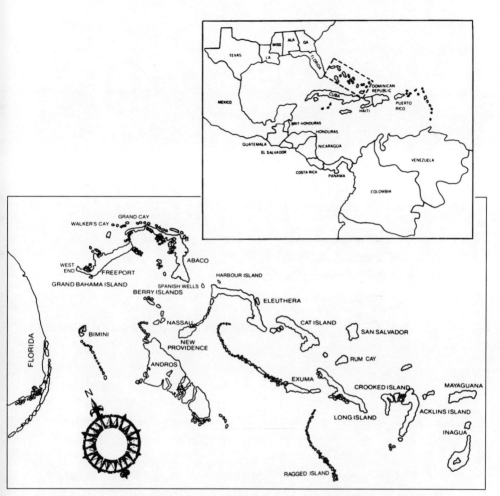

Map courtesy of The Counsellors, Ltd., Nassau, The Bahamas. Reproduced with permission.

Inagua—two islands, Great and Little, in the southern Bahamas. Area = 645 square miles. Population = 924.

Long Island—64 miles long and just over 3 miles wide at its widest point. Area = 173 square miles. Population = 2,954.

New Providence—location of Nassau, capital of the Bahamas and the city with the largest population. Area = 80 square miles. Population = 172,196.

San Salvador—most frequently described as site of Columbus's first landfall. Formerly known as Watling's Island. Area = 63 square miles. Population = 518.

Turks and Caicos—linked formally to the Bahamas until 1848. Area = 200 square miles. Population = 9,983.

Distribution of Population by Islands

Year	Total Population	New Providence (%)	Grand Bahama (%)	Family Islands (%)
1901	53,735	23.33	3.31	73.36
1911	55,944	24.23	3.26	72.51
1921	53,031	24.47	3.20	72.33
1931	59,828	33.02	3.75	63.23
1943	68,846	42.69	3.39	53.92
1953	84,841	54.37	4.83	40.80
1963	130,220	62.13	6.32	31.55
1970	168,812	60.13	15.32	24.55
1980	209,505	64.65	15.80	19.55
1990	254,685	67.35	16.11	16.54

Foreword

The Bahamas in the Twentieth Century: An Overview

Gail Saunders

At the beginning of the twentieth century, the Bahamas could have been considered rural. The majority—that is, 73 percent—of the population lived on the Out Islands (now known as the Family Islands), which were isolated and more rural in character than New Providence.

Most people engaged in agriculture, and even much of New Providence was under agricultural cultivation. Nassau, the chief town and a mini-metropolis, served as the market for produce brought from the outlying district of New Providence and also by boat from the other islands. The most populous islands outside of New Providence, where about a quarter of the population lived (10,914), were Eleuthera (7,358), Cat Island (5,244) and Andros (4,589).[1]

Out Island settlements were usually self-contained and isolated, and they might have had more contact with Nassau for trade purposes than with a neighbouring village. Just as each island was quite a distance from another, so, too, was each settlement. In the early 1900s, intercommunication was very difficult. There was a lack of good roads—except in Nassau—and the means of transportation between the distant settlements was by foot, horse, small sailboat or schooner.

The Bahamas benefitted from worldwide advances in scientific and technological research in the late nineteenth and early twentieth centuries. Especially significant were new developments in the fields of electricity, communication and transportation. Cable communication was established between Nassau and Jupiter, Florida, in 1892. The more modern wireless telegraphy, which supplied an efficient service between Nassau, Miami and England, brought even more up-to-date world news.

Another innovative step in communications was taken in 1906 with the passing of the Telephone Act. In the following year a telephone system was installed in downtown Nassau. Although it only marginally affected Nassauvians, by 1912 the telephone system had expanded and many more stations had been installed, not only in the city but also in the eastern and western suburbs.[2]

Electricity was introduced in Nassau in 1909, although the Electric Light Act had been passed two years before. It would take a number of years for the labouring class and Out Islanders to benefit from electricity, some Out Islands not receiving electrical supplies until late in the twentieth century.

The motor car made its advent in Nassau in about 1905. However, it was not until well into the middle of the century that ordinary working Bahamians could afford to purchase a motor vehicle.

Economically, although there were longstanding industries in nineteenth- and early twentieth-century Bahamas, such as sponge-fishing and pineapple, sisal, citrus and tomato farming, these one by one failed for various reasons, and agriculture was never put on a sound scientific basis. Gradually, but especially after the First World War and the Prohibition years between 1919 and 1933, when Nassau was used as a transshipment port to smuggle liquor into the United States, agriculture was superceded by land booms, building booms and the development of the fledgling tourist industry, which provided lucrative jobs. The Out Islanders, mainly peasant farmers, flocked to Nassau. In 1921, 24.4 percent of the entire population lived in New Providence. By 1943, it had attracted nearly 43 percent, an increase of over 126 percent in 22 years. Post–World War II years witnessed a continuation of this process and by the 1990s, over 65 percent of the population lived in Nassau. Modern tourism in the Bahamas is built on the foundation of the earlier development.

The growth of tourism during and after the 1920s and 1930s, which stimulated the expansion and improvement of the infrastructure and the building of hotels, gave Nassau a reputation as a tourist destination and a seasonal resort for the wealthy. Whereas the tourist industry in the '20s, '30s and '40s was seasonal and catered to the happy few, today the Bahamas and the Caribbean cater to large numbers of tourists. In 1994, of the 13.7 million Caribbean tourists, about 3.5 million visited the Bahamas. The change from elite tourism to mass tourism means that the Bahamas now compete with the rest of the Caribbean, which has embraced tourism in light of declining staple industries such as sugar, oil and agriculture.[3]

It was during the 1930s that the Bahamas first became known internationally as a tax haven, attracting foreign investment not only in Nassau, the capital, but also on several of the Out Islands. Owing to its loose tax structure, there were no income, profits, capital gains or real-estate taxes; many investors were drawn to Nassau to escape taxation in North America and Britain. The Bahamas are now a leading financial center, attracting more than 400 banks and trust companies to their shores. Offshore banking and finance, the number two industry in the Bahamas behind tourism, accounts for approximately 15 percent of the country's gross domestic product (GDP). Nassau ranks highly among the top ten offshore jurisdictions worldwide.

The expansion of tourism in the post–World War II years, with its ancillary spinoffs in construction, finance, real estate and foreign investment, generated many jobs, especially in Nassau, and contributed greatly to a high level of prosperity and optimism.

Despite Freeport's many problems—not least of which was that it was a foreign outpost—its development (under the Hawksbill Creek Agreement in 1955) as an industrial complex and luxury hotel and residential area over the central third of Grand Bahama has assisted in uplifting the Bahamian economy. Generally, wages paid in the Bahamas were considerably higher than those paid in the British West Indies. The cost of living in the Bahamas was the highest in the Caribbean.[4]

Fundamentally, the social structure based on the three-tier class racial structure present in the Caribbean generally until the 1940s survived in the Bahamas until at least the early 1960s. In the Bahamas, an intermediate coloured class developed in Nassau and expanded by the late 1950s, but it was weaker than its West Indian counterparts, who gained their place in economic social and political development.

Colin Hughes posits that certain facts such as the relatively high percentage of whites (always over ten percent), the proximity of the United States with its segregation practices, and the close cultural ties between white and black Bahamians and the United States, made for more antagonistic race relations in the Bahamas. Wealth was also important; it attracted power and authority. Therefore, in the Bahamas, racial difference was linked to economic relationships.[5]

The essentially mercantile-based economy primarily benefitted the white merchant elite, which absorbed a large proportion of the total profits in the export and import trade. The elite also devoted much time and energy to public affairs and ensured that the benefits from the healthy economy largely accrued to themselves and their relatives and friends, thus creating private wealthy empires.[6]

The small black and coloured intermediate class and a growing white middle class—both of which comprised professionals, civil servants, small-business people and shop clerks—also benefitted, but to lesser degree. The majority of the working population, mainly blacks, profited least; as a result, poverty persisted. Urban blacks and Out Islanders suffered, receiving much less than the average income. Until the early 1960s, the majority of people lived in poverty, while a small percentage, mainly whites, had enormous wealth. As Gordon Lewis succinctly stated, "In effect, the Bahamas government was deliberately kept a poor government in a rich economy."[7]

This uneven distribution of wealth was reflected in the rapid development of downtown Nassau and the neglect of the black urban section of Over-the-Hill (Nassau), which was deteriorating into a slum. There was also an increasing division between the colony's capital and the neglected Out Islands.

Significant but guarded progress was also made on the race issue. As noted, racial prejudice permeated Bahamian society even in the 1950s. In Nassau and the Out Islands, white communities sought to preserve their racial integrity by isolating themselves from coloureds and blacks as much as possible. Racial tension had been an underlying cause of the first mass riot in 1942 (known as the Burma Road riot), as the Duke of Windsor and the American vice-consul admitted privately. Coloured and black leaders felt indignant about the severe discriminatory practices in Nassau, which barred nonwhites from all hotels, some restaurants, movie houses and certain schools. Indeed, some had tried to stop such practices through various organizations such as the Citizens Committee and the House of

Assembly. However, it was not until after two embarrassing incidents involving prominent black West Indians stranded in Nassau that the issue of
discrimination was brought to a head.[8]

Progress was made in 1956, when Etienne Dupuch, editor of the *Tribune* and representative in the House of Assembly of the Eastern District,
brought a resolution concerning discrimination in public places and asked
for a Commission of Inquiry to be appointed to investigate all matters
pertaining to discrimination.[9] The first part of the resolution was accepted
but not the second. Racial discrimination generally persisted in the Bahamas well into the 1970s and, some would argue, beyond that. Although
there were few race-related incidents after the resolution, tension in fact
increased, especially during pre-election periods, when the populist party,
the Progressive Liberal Party (PLP) led by Sir Lynden O. Pindling, used
the race factor to its advantage. In 1992, after twenty-five years in power,
the PLP lost the election to the Free National Movement, led by Hubert
Ingraham.

Constitutionally, the Bahamas—like Barbados and Bermuda—retained the old representative system. Although in theory the colonial gov-
ernors wielded much power, the Bahamian House of Assembly (the lower
house) controlled the purse; it raised revenue and authorized expenditures. The outmoded board system, which directed departments of the
government, was controlled by the members of the House of Assembly, the
majority of whom represented Bay Street. The reactionary Assembly used
its traditional obstructionist tactics to delay social, political and constitu-
tional change.

Political representation did not dramatically change in ethnic terms
until 1967. In 1890, six nonwhites sat in the House of Assembly, yet in 1956,
in spite of the introduction of the secret ballot, there were only eight.
However, significant political change followed the Taxi-Cab Union General Strike in 1958, which was supported by the PLP. The latter—the first
successful political party—was established in 1953. The strike stirred the
usually complacent colonial office into action. Lennox Boyd, secretary of
state for the colonies, visited the Bahamas following the strike. His recommendations accelerated change and had a significant impact on constitu-
tional and political development.[10]

Significant electoral reforms were incorporated in the General Assembly Election Act of 1959.[11] Male suffrage was introduced, giving all men
over twenty-one years of age the right to vote; the company vote was
abolished, and the plural vote, which allowed one person to vote in every

constituency, was limited to two. To bring the constituencies into line with the movement of population, four additional seats in New Providence (two in the south and two in the east) were created, with provision to be made for by-elections as soon as possible. Lennox Boyd, strongly influenced by his discussion with the PLP, made these latter recommendations in an attempt to redress the imbalance of representation between Nassau and the Out Islands. Although Lennox Boyd saw no need or evidence of widespread demand for granting women the vote, his visit highlighted the women's suffrage movement, which had existed in the Bahamas since the mid 1950s. The movement was mobilized, and after some agitation women were enfranchised in 1961. They voted for the first time in the 1962 general elections.[12]

The gains made in 1958 created optimism and hope for the black majority. A new constitution was introduced in 1964, establishing the ministerial system, with Sir Roland Symonette as premier. The Bahamas were granted internal self-government, which led finally to independence in 1973. Six years earlier during a period of sustained prosperity, the predominantly black PLP, led by Sir Lynden O. Pindling, had defeated the United Bahamian Party (UBP), which represented the interests of Bay Street, in what is known as the Quiet Revolution. Majority rule had begun. Independence came in 1973. Although it brought a new feeling of national pride, it also revealed a number of problems posed by disease, drugs, crime, illegal immigration and the need to diversify the economy.

Bahamianization was encouraged, secondary education was made free, and the College of the Bahamas (COB) was established in 1974. In the social sphere, a national insurance scheme was introduced and health care was expanded. An extensive housing scheme for low- and medium-income workers was introduced.

The last five decades of the twentieth century saw unprecedented growth in the economy and achievements and changes in almost every aspect of life. The commercially oriented economy, based mainly on tourism, flourished, assisted by improved air communications. Ties with the United States strengthened, and the Bahamas increasingly identified with America. Massive migration of Out Islanders, some of whom had worked on the overseas project after the 1942 riot in Nassau, put a strain on the fragile infrastructure of the capital. Immigrants from the Out Islands into New Providence especially exacerbated the already crowded conditions in the predominantly black Over-the-Hill district in Nassau.

Soon after the country's independence, the Bahamas government set up a diplomatic corps virtually from scratch, joining important organizations such as the United Nations Educational, Scientific and Cultural Organization (UNESCO) that came under the umbrella of the United Nations. It delayed its membership in the Organization of American States (OAS) for almost a decade and delayed its membership in the Caribbean Community (CARICOM) even longer, perhaps because some of these countries (particularly Jamaica, under Michael Manley) were thought to be dangerously left-leaning, if not, like Cuba and Guyana, actually socialist.[13]

In this respect, the Bahamas exhibited their ideological correlation with the United States as well as their dependence on American tourists, investors and military protection in the event of a foreign attack. Their continued fidelity to the ideal of the Commonwealth and to some British institutions, such as the legal system and symbols (particularly the monarchy), was similarly practical.[14] Indeed, the Bahamas hosted Her Majesty Queen Elizabeth II five times (1966, 1975, 1977, 1985 and 1994) and sundry lesser royals on other occasions. Nassau was the meeting place of the Commonwealth heads of government in 1985, and the Bahamas also hosted important CARICOM (1991) and OAS (1992) plenary sessions.

The Bahamas played a significant part in the evolution of a new Law of the Sea in the mid 1970s, formed a Defence Force in 1976, and were involved in a serious international incident of the sinking of the HMBS *Flamingo* by Cuban war planes in 1980, when four Bahamian marines drowned.

A serious problem facing the Bahamas in post-independence years was the drug traffic in cocaine and marijuana, which had been escalating in the mid to late 1970s—and by 1983 had reached staggering proportions. The Commission of Inquiry into illegal use of the Bahamas and the transshipment of dangerous drugs destined for the United States revealed that drugs posed one of the most serious social problems. Drug corruption pervaded every level of society and government. Even more problematic, the drugs themselves had become so readily available and relatively cheap in the islands that many Bahamians were addicted, thus attracting the wrong type of visitor to the islands. Drug-related profits distorted the economy, and the easy and ill-gotten wealth upset the material and moral values of Bahamians. Fortunately, by 1990, the cocaine traffic had diminished considerably and had slowed to a trickle.[15]

The Bahamas also suffered during the mid 1980s and 1990s from a serious economic recession highlighted by the loss of drug money, a situation not helped by the government's mismanagement and alleged corruption. The Free National Movement (FNM) was elected on August 19, 1992. Although it encountered many unforeseen problems, including the islands' being hit by Hurricane Andrew two days after the party came to power, the FNM promised a complete turnabout and succeeded in revitalizing tourism, attracting new foreign investment and improving the infrastructure. It was reelected in 1997.

A negative spinoff from the drug trafficking trade was an increase in violent crime. Despite their historical involvement in international lawlessness, including piracy, buccaneering, privateering, blockade running, and various other types of smuggling, Bahamians have always regarded themselves as a relatively law-abiding and peace-loving people, a perception borne out by the colonial crime statistics. However, in the second half of the twentieth century, the situation changed dramatically, so that the Bahamas (and, above all, Nassau) came to be near the top in world tables of serious crimes per capita. Much of the escalating crime was blamed on drugs, but it could equally be attributed to unemployment, the disappointment of rising expectations and the effects of U.S. patterns so readily displayed in the media. Blame could also be associated with the breakdown of the traditional family and other unfortunate features of modernization in the Bahamian context.

Another serious problem facing the Bahamas was illegal immigration into their territory, particularly by Haitian nationals. The Bahamas have had connections with Haiti since the seventeenth century. The early French émigrés into the Bahamas, such as Stephen Dillet, actually made a great contribution to Bahamian society. Although Bahamians tend to disclaim any Haitian provenance, undoubtedly there was a great influx between 1791 and 1804 of Haitian slave owners and their slaves, which accounts for the prevalence of French surnames among modern Bahamians. There was trade between Haiti and the Bahamas in the late nineteenth and early twentieth centuries, especially between Inagua and Port de Paix and Cap Haitian. Some Bahamians even educated their children in Haitian schools.

However, the situation changed in the 1950s and substantially from the 1970s on. As Haiti's economy declined and political oppression took hold, the Bahamas became increasingly prosperous, and more and more Haitian nationals made their homes in the Bahamas, many illegally. By 1970, the numbers of Haitians were estimated to be about 20 percent of the population. Haitian migrants usually worked as labourers on farms, and for Bahamian individuals as gardeners and casual labourers.

Bahamians did not deny that Haitians performed an essential economic function in taking jobs that Bahamians no longer wanted. However, Bahamians generally despised Haitians and resented their drain on the health, social and educational systems. Moreover, unemployed Bahamians claimed that Haitians—by working for lower wages—were squeezing them out of jobs.

Most Bahamian children attended school in the twentieth century. However, in the early 1900s most received only a basic primary education in small, badly equipped schools staffed by untrained or poorly trained teachers.

The majority of children did not attend secondary schools, which catered mainly to the upper class and some of the coloured middle class. Secondary schools, operated primarily by the Anglican, Methodist, Baptist and, after 1890, Roman Catholic churches, offered a high school education for those of its members who could afford modest fees.

The government did not provide secondary education until 1925, when the Government High School was established. It charged 10.10.0 (1 guinea) per annum. Queens College, the premier secondary school at that time, drew a rigid colour line. The Government High School quickly became a prestigious and predominantly black school, and it was crucial in the growth of the coloured and black middle class. It produced many future political and civic leaders, including Lynden Pindling (prime minister, 1967–92); Kendal Isaacs (leader of the opposition, 1972, 1982 and 1987); and Orville Turnquest (attorney general and minister of foreign affairs, 1992–94). He was appointed governor-general in 1994.

Since the 1960s, however, the government made a concerted effort to improve educational conditions and to provide secondary education for the majority of the population. Education began to receive the lion's share of the national budget, and government secondary schools increased dramatically between the late 1960s and the end of the twentieth century.

Moreover, the College of the Bahamas, opened in 1975, made great strides, and by the 1990s it was offering four-year degree courses in selected subjects. It achieved much in its first twenty years of existence, despite major problems and chronic underfunding. By the late 1990s, it had greatly expanded and improved its facilities, gained semiautonomy by legislation in 1994, and is now well on the road to being elevated into a national university of the Bahamas in the twenty-first century.

The Bahamas in the twentieth century was a Christian nation. The church played a significant role in the spiritual and secular lives of Bahamians. The major denominations in the early twentieth century were Anglican, Baptist and Methodist. Established in 1880s in the Bahamas, the Roman Catholic Church, through its educational efforts and supply of missionaries—who catered to the poor and black—made significant inroads by the 1950s.

The Baptist faith, known for its spiritual democracy, attracted the majority of the black labouring classes in New Providence and on the majority of Out Islands. By 1953, it was the largest denomination in the Bahamas, and for the rest of the century it remained so. The next largest congregation at the end of the century was the Anglican Church. Not only did the Baptist Church increase in membership, but it also developed a more educated and respected leadership; most of the new leaders were being educated mainly in the southern United States. Division within the Baptist Church continued, though after 1942 all the main Baptist groups combined (at least temporarily) under the title Bahamas Baptist Mission and Educational Convention to plan an educational system. A Baptist high school was established in 1961 and a community college in the 1990s.

Similar in doctrine and American in origin, but not as widespread as the Baptist denomination, was the Church of God, which also attracted blacks. Akin to the ancient African Episcopal Methodist Church or Shouter Chapel established in Nassau in the mid-nineteenth century, the Church of God was a branch of the American institution of the same name.

Other North American churches established themselves in the Bahamas in the late nineteenth century, including the Brethren Church and the Seventh-Day Adventists. By the end of the century, the Methodists, plagued by serious internal splits, had fallen in popularity, and by 1990 they were outnumbered by the adherence to both Pentecostalism and the Church of God.

Expansion of tourism and dominant North American culture greatly influenced the Bahamian sports psyche. Modern Bahamians are attracted to baseball, softball, volleyball, tennis, and track and field events. A remarkable number of Bahamians—with the help of athletic scholarships in the United States—are attending American colleges and universities.

Many have reached world-class levels in athletics. This includes the silver-medalist Olympians in the 4 x 100 relay, Fynes, Sturrup, Clarke, Davis and Smith in 1996, and world champions Fynes, Smith, Davis, Clarke and Sturrup in the same event in 1999. These successes are a culmination of highly impressive performances at the Caribbean, Pan-American and Commonwealth Games over the past three decades.

Though the Bahamas has had a weak literary tradition, since independence there has been an expanding nucleus of Bahamian writers, especially poets and playwrights. A wealth of plays, comic and serious, by Bahamians was produced by a variety of drama groups, especially in the repertory season at the Dundas Centre of the Performing Arts from the 1970s on. During this same period, Bahamian musicality, the impulse toward dramatic storytelling, and the growth of national self-expression were borne out.

Such productions as the opera *Sammy Swain,* written and produced by Clement Bethel (1975), and the nationalist opera epic *Our Boys* by Winston Saunders, Philip Burrows and Cleophas Adderley (1987) were inspired by the Flamingo incident of 1980. Bahamian artists such as Brent Malone, Max Taylor, Amos Ferguson, Eddie Minnis, Alton Lowe and Antonius Roberts have blossomed since the 1960s, and their work has been not only nationalistic but also versatile. Accomplished painters emerged so rapidly that by 1990 scarcely a month went by without a new show displaying yet another remarkable talent.

There has also developed an interest in preservation, as manifested in the establishment of the Bahamas Archives in 1971 and the establishment of an Antiquities, Monuments and Museum Corporation in 1998.

The quincentennial activities in 1992 saw the creation of the nucleus of a national institution, such as a national museum and art gallery housed in the former slave Vendue House on Bay Street—named after Pompey, a slave rebel. Consultant Winston Saunders also spearheaded the establishment of the National Dance Company, headed by Robert Bain and Shirley Hall Bass; the National Youth Choir, headed by Cleophas Adderley; the National Youth Orchestra, headed by Duke Errol Strachan; and the National Children's Choir, headed by Patricia Bazard.

Traditional customs and culture underwent some weakening as a result of the impact of the large immigrant population on cultural life. However, Bahamian crafts such as boat building, quilting, straw weaving and woodcarving—as demonstrated on the Washington National Mall in 1994—showed that much had been retained and preserved.

Strong superstitious beliefs in the supernatural forces of Obeah, the practice of herbal medicine, and the musical forms of the anthems and rhyming spirituals, so popular during the sponging era, survived but in a weakened form. Death rituals, the tradition of holding wakes, and the observation of other death rites and Rushing meetings were common in the 1950s and 1960s and are still practiced in some communities today. Customary dances, including the fire dance, jumping dance and ring play were kept alive in performances at local nightclubs (for the benefit of tourists) and in folk operas such as *Sammy Swain*.

The largest and most important Bahamian festival (particularly in Nassau) is Junkanoo. Despite various bans on all public gatherings especially after the 1942 riot, there was a resurgence of Junkanoo. Its spirit could not be crushed. It was increasingly touted as a tourist attraction offering prize money, and today it is still the premier festival in the Bahamas. It comprises huge groups with splendid costumes and huge music and dancing sections. A variety of theories is offered as to its origins in West Africa, but we know it was celebrated in some form in the Bahamas from the early nineteenth century, when slaves took advantage of the traditional three-day holiday at Christmas to let off steam and assert their independence. Music is essential to the festival. The most popular instruments associated with Junkanoo are cowbells, horns, whistles and goombay drums.

Modern Junkanoo is more sophisticated and often organized by government agencies. Costumes must be made primarily from bright-coloured paper fringe, and large, fiercely competitive groups vie for first place. Despite the enormous changes in Junkanoo throughout the years, the roots of this musical tradition remain Bahamian. Previously a black working-class festival, Junkanoo is now universally accepted and practiced regardless of class and colour.[16] The spirit of Junkanoo is truly the soul of the Bahamian.

Notes

1. Gail Saunders, "The Social History of the Bahamas" (Ph.D. dissertation, University of Waterloo, 1985), 505.

2. Ibid., 186.

3. Gail Saunders, "The Changing Face of Nassau: The Impact of Tourism on Bahamian Society in the 1920s and 1930s," *New West Indian Guide,* 71, nos. 1, 2 (1997): 36.

4. Gail Saunders, "The 1958 General Strike in Nassau: A Landmark in Bahamian History," *Journal of Caribbean History,* 27: 1, 83.

5. Colin Hughes, *Race and Politics in the Bahamas* (St. Lucia, Queensland [Australia] and London: University of Queensland Press, 1981), 22.

6. Gordon Lewis, *Growth of the Modern West Indies* (New York: Monthly Review Press, 1968), 320. See also Pridie to Luke, November 12, 1950. CO23/888.

7. Ibid., 320.

8. Gail Saunders, "The 1958 General Strike in Nassau."

9. "Bahamas Voices of the House of Assembly," May 17 and November 17, 1956, *Nassau Guardian,* 286.

10. Gordon Lewis, *Growth of the Modern West Indies,* 320–21.

11. The House of Assembly Election Act, 39 of 1959. *Statute Law of the Bahama Islands,* vol. 1, 157–271.

12. Gail Saunders, "The 1958 General Strike in Nassau."

13. Michael Craton and Gail Saunders, *Islanders in the Stream: A History of the Bahamian People,* vol. 2 of *From the Ending of Slavery to the Twenty-First Century* (Athens: University of Georgia Press, 1998), 368.

14. Ibid., 368.

15. Ibid., 384.

16. Ibid., 408–418, 444–450, 466–491.

Preface

My sister, Eloise, and I received our first lessons on Bahamian culture in the kitchen of our family's second-floor apartment on the corner of Seventeenth Street and Fountain Avenue in North Philadelphia. The lessons took place on rainy days in the 1930s and early 1940s. Since the weather prevented us from going outside to play, our mother entertained Eloise and me by describing her experiences growing up in Governor's Harbour, Eleuthera and Nassau. When I was four or five, she used to describe the physical beauty of the Bahamas—the white sand; the ocean water so calm and clear you could see sea shells resting on the sandy bottom; the palm trees, the fronds of which we used on Palm Sunday. Later, her stories dealt with growing up in a family of eight siblings, her three years of schooling and the games she played as a child. When we were trying to learn to cook, she described the foods she missed, from guava duff to fried plantain. Mother was unaware that she was following the oral traditions of our African ancestors in order to develop in her daughters an awareness of our heritage.

In later years, my father used our evening dinners and our fishing trips to Wildwood, New Jersey, to pass on knowledge of his struggles to obtain an education and to earn a living in Palmetto Point, Eleuthera and

Nassau. His stories always had a moral. He valued education, honesty, loyalty and respectability. He was a lay philosopher who repeatedly told us, "Girls, you have to know where your family came from to know who you are." He described fishing for conch and crawfish, and the taste of Eleutheran pineapples, sugar apples, land crabs and rice. Once a week, during the summer, he brought a mango home from Reading Terminal, our local farmers' market. As he sliced the fruit, our mouths watered. Dividing one mango among four people is no easy task; my sister and I received the two side slices, and Mother always ended up eating the fruit that remained on the seed. Again, in that urban setting so far away, my parents managed to pass on the rich traditions of their islands.

My family was too poor ever to consider a return visit home, so I never met my grandparents. Until I was an adult, I had seen their native land only through the eyes of my parents. My first trip to the Bahamas occurred in the mid 1950s, and the natural beauty of New Providence overwhelmed me. I learned more about Nassau—the capital of the Bahamas, located on New Providence—from my aunt and uncle, Olga and Eddie Dillet, and my cousin Leo Davis. They showed me the beauty of bougainvillea, hibiscus and croton. Casuarina trees, exotic seashells and wonderful big green fruit called sour sop became part of my world.

With Aunt Olga, I attended teas and Anglican church services, where we wore hats and white gloves. Uncle Eddie provided an introduction to another part of Bahamian culture. We rode all over the island in his green pickup truck. Most of the floor had rusted out on the passenger's side, so I had to be very careful where I placed my feet. We ate conch salad seasoned with hot peppers and drank rum punch served in jelly coconuts. Leo introduced me to the politics of the Bay Street Boys and to native clubs, where calypso musicians played and sang about life. One night at a local nightclub, Rama, Queen of the Jungle, induced a trancelike state and rolled in broken glass without receiving either scratches or cuts. That event is still a vivid memory. Other members of my family patiently explained local customs and history.

As a youngster in Philadelphia, I often felt that if my parents loved the Bahamas so much, they should have stayed there. What did I know of class structures and impossible dreams? Nor did I realize the lack of opportunities on the Family Islands when they were growing up. After visiting their birthplaces, I became captivated with the people who had chosen either to remain or to leave and return. The seed of a desire to document their lives began to germinate in me.

I have attempted this project to capture the remembrances of typical Bahamians' lives because of my love for my parents and because I recognized that few records of the lives of "ordinary" people exist. Indeed, it is an unfortunate reality that this set of memories may prove to be one of the few documents describing the lives of average Bahamians who grew up during the early years of the twentieth century.

Acknowledgments

Dozens of people were instrumental in the completion of this book. They made it possible. I thank them all.

A very special thank you is due my cousin Iris Dillet Knowles, and my son, Alan Jenkins. Without their encouragement and support in a multitude of ways, I never would have been able to accomplish this undertaking. To both of them, I offer my appreciation for their faith.

From the beginning, Dr. Gail Saunders, Director of the Archives Department of the Ministry of Education, has been my mentor. Not only did she encourage me; Dr. Saunders offered valuable suggestions and contacts. She has also given freely of her time. I am indebted to her.

Dr. Saunders and Ms. Knowles were able to obtain financial support for my travel to and expenses on Long Island, the Bahamas, from the Historical Society of the Bahamas and the Zonta Club of Nassau. I am grateful for their assistance.

A heartfelt thank you to the Bahamians who, not knowing me, were willing to be interviewed and to provide memories that are irreplaceable. Each person who shared a narrative provided a wonderful gift. My trips have given me a view of the Bahamas that has become a beautiful montage.

Introduction

As my objectives for this undertaking began to crystallize, Dr. Gail
Saunders, Director of the Department of Archives in the Ministry of Education, furnished guidance concerning how to proceed, which questions
to ask and what form the finished product should take. During the summer of 1988, my cousin Iris Dillet Knowles and I conducted a pilot study.
We visited Eleuthera and Harbour Island to conduct interviews with
people who would not view me as Bahamian. To my delight, most individuals were open, glad to discuss their memories and happy to have been
chosen to be interviewed. I was so nervous on my first interviews that I
forgot to ask half the questions Dr. Saunders had suggested.

It was not until I began to review the twentieth-century history of the
Bahamas in juxtaposition with the interviews that I realized certain important issues had not been considered. Consequently, I returned to the
Bahamas during the next few years to conduct additional interviews. A
variety of people who had worked as farmers, fishermen, government employees, businesspeople and homemakers living on Abaco, Andros, Cat
Island, Grand Bahama, Long Island and New Providence shared their
narratives.

The individuals with whom I spoke were identified for me in two ways. Most were suggested by school principals, commissioner's office employees, and guest house or hotel managers once I had arrived on each island. Several names were obtained in advance from Dr. Saunders or from acquaintances in Nassau. Each participant was interviewed once. The talks lasted from two to five hours, depending on when we felt we had finished.

Each meeting began with an introduction of myself and a description of where my parents had grown up. This background information seemed necessary so that the individuals would recognize that I had Bahamian roots. I explained that the interviews were for the Archives Department of the Ministry of Education and, more generally, to preserve their memories of their island's history. The project was described as an effort to record what life was like during the early part of the twentieth century. Typically, my first question was: "What was life like when you were growing up?" This query was followed by others dealing with education, employment and family life that built on the response to the initial question. My final question was: "How does your life now compare to when you were young?" When other topics were introduced by the person, we discussed those also. A number of people mentioned politics, drugs and health problems. Later, I wrote to the participants, explaining that I would like to include their stories in a book. Some sent additional information or names of other people they felt I should contact. Usually, people were completely willing to have their names and interviews included; others requested anonymity; and a few did not want to be included. I have respected each of those requests.

Many interviews were conducted in private homes, which provided an opportunity to observe family members, photographs, keepsakes and the surrounding community. Initially, my interest was in the early experiences, beliefs, values and occupations of each person. But as I became more familiar with the culture, I realized that other topics were equally important. Some perceptions and descriptions by the narrators differed from those contained in the Colonial Reports and/or historical texts. I have used my introductions to each topic to provide facts as professionally recorded. I hope that the content selected will give readers some insights about the lives of average Bahamians during the twentieth century.

Narrations in the chapters are organized chronologically, so that the oldest person's description of a given subject appears first. In addition, interviews are segmented by topic. My aim, in using this format, is to give

XXXI . . . INTRODUCTION

readers an opportunity to compare and contrast perceptions of common experiences as described by a variety of individuals.

My initial intention was to interview the oldest people who were verbal and willing to talk about their experiences during the first half of this century on a few of the Family Islands. Whenever possible, I talked with those born prior to 1920, because I felt that their stories would be lost if they were not recorded quickly. In several instances, the individuals I planned to interview died before I could meet them; in those circumstances, I spoke with the nearest relative who was amenable. The following table indicates the age distribution of the narrators:

Year of Birth	Number of Narrators
1900–1909	7
1910–1919	11
1920–1929	9
1930–1939	7

A second intention was to interview black working-class people living on the Family Islands whose stories had not been recorded. As the project continued, however, other groups were added. Descendants of two ethnic groups comprise the bulk of the population: African and European. Some Bahamians are of mixed ancestry. Several of those who appeared mixed seemed uncomfortable with the question of race and quickly changed the subject. In those cases, I did not ask for a further explanation.

None of the people who suggested other persons to be interviewed mentioned those individuals' race. A number of those suggested appeared to be white. Some looked mixed. At no time did I ask narrators to categorize themselves racially. Asking them to do this might have interfered with the rapport I wished to develop. The following groupings are based strictly on my observations:

Black	Mixed	White
21	9	4

Fifty-nine percent of these narrators were men. In many settlements, the names suggested for interviews were all male. In most cases, when a couple was present, the wife deferred to the husband when a question was asked. The gender distribution of interviewees was as follows:

Female   Male
14   20

Certain Family Islanders are legendary in their own and neighbouring settlements. Their fame is based on such criteria as longevity, occupational skill, sexual prowess and/or wisdom. Since I was primarily interested in "average" people, I did not interview doctors, lawyers, or other professionals. In many cases, their stories have already been recorded.

Half of the people I interviewed can be described as working class based on their occupations, housing and speech patterns. Although most of them have little or no formal education, they are intelligent and verbal. The other half are middle class, have successfully completed their education and, with one exception, either own their own businesses or are/have been government employees. Their verbalizations are characterized by a larger vocabulary, explicit descriptions and "standard" speech.

Early interviews took place on Eleuthera and Harbour Island in 1988. I began in Eleuthera because both of my parents and most of my relatives were born there. I wanted to build on the stories I had heard from my parents. I found, however, that those interviews were not as rich as I had hoped, probably because of my inexperience as an interviewer. Therefore, I did not include this material.

Subsequent trips to Abaco and Andros were more profitable. Dr. Saunders then suggested that I might find the residents of Cat Island and Long Island interesting. These two islands had been exposed to fewer tourists and seem more typical of what life had been like in the early part of this century.

As I developed an increased understanding of the Bahamas, I realized that most people on the Family Islands had relatives in Nassau or Grand Bahama. In order to add that perspective, I interviewed one or two people, from each age category, who were living in New Providence.

Financial constraints limited the number of islands I was able to visit. I believe that those of Bahamian ancestry have a responsibility to preserve and honor their history for future generations. It is my hope that I have made a small contribution toward this goal and that younger Bahamians will be interested in continuing to record the traditional lifestyles of senior citizens.

Brief Chronology of
the Twentieth Century

These dates pertain specifically to topics discussed by narrators and/or the author.

1900–1910

Major exports are sisal, sponge, pineapples.

Steamers from New York en route to Gulf ports and Mexico call at the southern Bahamian islands of Inagua and Long Cay to hire railway workers, stevedores and laborers.

Queens College, Nassau Grammar School, St. Francis Xavier's Academy and a school at Governor's Harbour offer secondary education to white Bahamian students for a fee.

1903   World price of sisal, which had been introduced in the Bahamas in 1845, begins to fall. Bahamian sisal producers are unable to compete with those in the Philippines, India and East Africa.

1905   Truck System Act attempts to force outfitters to pay fishermen in money rather than credit or goods. The law is frequently violated.

1911–1920

Tomatoes are a rapidly growing industry.

Sisal and sponge prices continue to drop.

Tuberculosis is rampant among the poor.

1913   Over 100 steam vessels stop at Inagua or Long Cay to hire almost 3,000 stevedores and railroad and lumber-camp workers for employment in Cuba, Central or South America.

1914   Family Islands lose their position as main producers of foodstuffs and livestock used in the Bahamas.

1914   At the outbreak of World War I, all steamships cease to call.

1919   Volstead Act (the 18th Amendment to the U.S. Constitution) is passed. It prohibits the manufacture, importation or selling of intoxicating liquors in the United States. Prohibition in the United States causes a boom in the Bahamian economy.

1920   Bahamas pass the Immigration Act of 1920—no immigrant is allowed to enter the colony without the permission of the Governor in Council.

1921–1930

Sponge beds are being depleted from hurricane damage and overfishing.

Nassau Harbour is dredged to accommodate larger ships.

1921   Colonial Hotel burns down on March 31.

1921   Blue-gray fly destroys almost all of the citrus trees.

1923   New Colonial Hotel opens in February.

1924   Greek immigrants establish themselves in the sponge trade as buyers and exporters.

1926   Every island is struck by at least one of three serious hurricanes, temporarily crippling both the sponge and sisal industries.

1927   The Bahamas begin to rigorously enforce the Immigration Act to reduce influx of foreign businessmen.

1928   The Bahamas further restrict immigrants.

1929   One-fourth of the total population is now living on New Providence.

1929   Pan American Airways commences seaplane service between Miami and Nassau.

1931–1940

Major exports are tortoiseshell, sponge and tomatoes.

All of the sisal factories begin closing. As a result, the production of sisal becomes a cottage industry.

1933   United States repeals the 18th Amendment, causing many Bahamians to return to subsistence farming.

1938   In November and December, a microscopic fungus attacks sponge beds and wipes out the sponge industry. Thousands of spongers lose their livelihood and must depend on subsistence farming.

1939 The secret ballot is introduced in New Providence but not on the other Bahamian islands.

1939 Dr. Axel Wenner-Gren purchases the Lynch estate on Hog Island (later known as Paradise Island).

1939 Britain declares war on Germany on September 3.

1940 His Royal Highness the Duke of Windsor becomes Royal Governor.

1941–1950

Major exports are pineapples, crawfish and lumber.

A Lend Lease Agreement between Britain and the United States provides 50 destroyers to Britain in return for 4 United States bases in the Bahamas.

1941 Pan American Airways commences airplane service to Nassau.

1942 A major disturbance occurs because of unequal salaries for Bahamian and U.S. workers building air bases on New Providence.

1942 An agreement between the British and American governments provides Bahamian workers for agricultural labor in the United States. Workers refer to this employment as "the Contract" or "the Project."

1942 Tourism ceases because of World War II.

1943 Sir Harry Oakes, a huge investor in the Bahamas, is murdered on July 7. His eldest daughter's husband, Count de Marigny, is accused and acquitted of the murder, which remains unsolved.

1944 Hurricane reconnaissance by aircraft is introduced.

1945 Air conditioning arrives in Nassau.

1945 Crawfishing becomes the main occupation of many Bahamians.

1945 World War II ends on August 14.

1946 The secret ballot is introduced on all of the islands.

1947 Bahamas Airways commences regular flights to Eleuthera.

1951–1960

Sponge beds are reopened for fishing. Sponge from Abaco, Andros and Long Island is exported to Israel, Canada and Great Britain.

Pineapples are no longer exported.

Sisal is now used only for local crafts.

Three lobster-tail processing plants are located in Nassau. The tails are exported to the United States.

Cuba is closed to U.S. tourists.

Tourism and the building trade are booming.

1953   The Progressive Liberal Party (PLP) is formed.

1955   Hawksbill Creek Agreement is signed, making the creation of Freeport possible.

1956   Father Jerome (John Hawes) dies at St. Francis Hospital in Florida at eighty years of age.

1956   Sir Etienne Dupuch succeeds in getting an antidiscrimination resolution accepted by the Assembly, opening all public places to every citizen.

1958   United Bahamian Party (UBP) is formed.

1958   General Strike affects tourism and government.

1958   Pan American Airlines introduces jet service to Nassau.

1961–1970

Abaco, Andros and Grand Bahama have large enterprises exporting tomatoes.

1961   Huntington Hartford purchases a large area of Hog Island (Wenner-Gren's estate), intending to build a resort. He has the island's name changed to Paradise Island.

1962   The Progressive Liberal Party (PLP) appeals to the United Nations, because in the previous election the United Bahamian Party (UBP) won 19 of 33 House seats, having received less than 37 percent of the vote. Although the PLP obtained 44 percent of the vote, they won only eight seats.

1962   Women vote for the first time on November 26.

1964   Colony of the Bahamas gains internal self-government. The premier is Sir Roland Symonette.

1965   Lynden O. Pindling throws the House of Assembly's mace, the symbol of authority, out the window into the square below on April 27 to protest the lack of justice in the government of the Bahamas.

1967   Progressive Liberal Party wins the majority of seats in the House of Assembly when Randol Fawkes and Alvin Braynen align themselves with the PLP. The new premier is Lynden O. Pindling.

1967   Dr. Doris Johnson is appointed the first female Bahamian senator.

1969   The Bahamian constitution is revised. The colony becomes a commonwealth. Sir Lynden O. Pindling becomes prime minister.

1970   The Bahamian and Haitian governments sign a treaty to limit illegal immigration of Haitians to the Bahamas.

1971–1980

Bahama Islands are used for the transshipment of marijuana and cocaine from South America to the United States. Some Bahamians provide landing strips, storage depots and distribution routes to drug traffickers. Because of the availability of drugs, addiction and drug-related offenses have become problems in the Bahamas.

1972   Free National Movement (FNM) political party is formed when the United Bahamian Party and the Free PLP, a splinter of the PLP, combine forces.

1972   PLP wins 61 percent of the popular vote and 29 of the 33 seats in the House.

1973   On July 10, complete independence is granted to the Bahamas. The official lowering of the Union Jack and the raising of the Bahamian flag take place on Fort Charlotte. Independence provides for complete control of government functions. The Bahamas is a member of the Commonwealth of Nations.

1973   Sir Milo Butler becomes the first governor-general. He serves as Queen Elizabeth II's representative.

1973   The Bahamas become a member of the United Nations.

1974   Government introduces first national social insurance program.

1978   Sir Gerald Cash becomes governor-general.

1981–1990

The bulk of government revenue continues to be tied to customs duties (indirect taxation on international trade) and direct taxes on hotel rooms and casino gambling.

Number of tourists declines as a result of the United States' recession.

1980   Cuban military aircraft sink a Bahamian Royal Bahamas Defence Force patrol boat, killing four.

1982   The Bahamas join the Organization of American States.

1983   The Bahamas oppose the United States' invasion of Granada.

1984   Sale and use of cocaine are serious problems.

1985   Bahamian and Haitian governments sign a second treaty, hoping to limit illegal migration.

1985   The United States classifies the Bahamas as an upper middle-income developing country and ranks the Bahamas among the wealthiest nations in the Caribbean region.

1986   Legislation is introduced that provides heavy penalties for drug runners.

1986   Unemployment is at 17–22 percent.

1988   Sir Henry Milton Taylor becomes acting governor-general.

1990   Three-hundred-million-dollar Crystal Palace Resort and Casino opens on Cable Beach.

1990   Over 3,628,500 tourists visit the Bahamas.

1991—PRESENT

1992   Hurricane Andrew causes unprecedented economic devastation in northern Eleuthera on August 23 and in the southern Berry Islands early on the August 24.

1992   Bahamas celebrates the 500th anniversary of the landing of Columbus.

1992   Family Islands continue to receive less than 20 percent of tourists to the Bahamas.

1992   The Free National Movement (FNM) wins 31 seats in the 49-member parliament on August 19. The new prime minister is Hubert A. Ingraham.

1994   Sir Orville Turnquest becomes governor-general.

1995   Junkanoo Expo, a permanent display of costumes, crafts and artifacts, opens at Prince George Wharf.

1997   The FNM is reelected.

C h a p t e r / . . . .

Early Lifestyles

This chapter contains a journey through some of the islands of the Bahamas during the first half of the twentieth century. The narrators were born between 1900 and 1927. Coming of age on one of the Family Islands (or the Out Islands, as the Bahamian islands, except New Providence, were known at that time) was becoming, as it is today, a vastly different experience than growing up in the capital city, Nassau—or, for that matter, anywhere on the island of New Providence.

While these narrators were becoming adults, the Bahamas were undergoing vast changes. During the first decade of the century, the Colonial Reports explain that prices for exported farm goods began to fall because of competition from the Philippines, India and East Africa, resulting in reduced earnings by Bahamian farmers.

The second and third decades of the century brought additional changes. Yet the developments that would most gravely affect the future of the Family Islands were the out-migration of residents to New Providence and beyond, and the loss of the Family Islands' position as the main producers of food and livestock used in the Bahamas.

By 1940, two-fifths of the total population of the Bahamas was living on New Providence, up from less than one-fourth in 1901. Two of the problems of the Family Islands were that sisal plantations had failed and that natural disasters had destroyed the citrus fruit industry. (Sisal is a natural fiber in the leaves of agave rigida sisalana plants.) Accordingly, from 1910 until the beginning of World War II, the Family Islands experienced severely depressed economies.

It should be explained that the narrators have used two forms of the English language. Generally, those with some formal education used standard English. Others spoke in Bahamian dialect. Following the examples in I Could Talk Old-Story Good (Crowley, 6), I have transcribed the narrations primarily using standard English spelling and have elected not to change the patterns of speech or word order of the narrators. Some of their phrases are so lovely and descriptive that I wanted to retain them. When a word or term was strictly a Bahamian expression, I have placed an equivalent word in brackets to make the meaning clearer. A glossary is included on pages 265–70.

Clementina Adderley, born on October 15, 1900, Lower Deadman's Cay, Long Island

Mrs. Adderley is the oldest person I interviewed. Her mind is clear and her memory excellent. Mrs. Adderley was sitting in her rocking chair shelling pigeon peas (reddish-brown beans) when I knocked on her kitchen door on a warm January afternoon in 1991. She proudly told me that she was ninety-one years old and that, except for some trouble with her knees, she felt fine. She lives next door to one of her sons and is a great-great grandmother. Mrs. Adderley has lived on Long Island in the Deadman's Cay area her entire life. As she *reminisced about her diet in the old days when she was growing up, I mentally contrasted it to our "balanced meals." Although, by comparison, her diet was severely lacking, she is healthy, does not wear glasses and has her own teeth!*

Long Island is seventy-six miles long and no more than four miles wide. Because the ocean is not visible from the main road, it seemed to be much wider than it actually is. Long Island has a population of approximately 3,500. Clarence Town is the capital of Long Island.

When we was growing up here on Long Island, we had to weed. We had to cut sisal, strip sisal and tote it and put it in the sea and clean it. We had to plant corn, potatoes, cassava, pineapples and peas. In between that, we had to go to school.

I stayed right home with my mother. I stayed until after I got married. Then I was on my own. Mind, I never went nowhere. But after my sons grow up and go to the United States, in between times, I go over there. But I didn't like over there. I stay right here in Long Island. I cut bush. I plant corn. I plant sisal. I stay up here right to today and I in my ninety-one [year].

Was no cars in them days. All of these things you see them used to now, so much of this, that and the other, in our days, when we was children, we didn't know nothing at all about them. We eat pigeon peas, guinea corn [small ears with black and white kernels], Indian corn [large ears with red kernels], beans, potatoes. That's what you used to eat. A piece of pork now and then. The people just started raising sheep and goats when we was grown women and men. And when we was children, we didn't know nothing about that. We never used to hardly have no meat. We had plenty of fruit and plenty of fish. It was so cheap. Ain't like today. You coulda take a quarter and go out here when the men come back from fishing or you coulda take two loads of corn and trade them. But you can't do that no more.

When we used to work on the farm, I used to go to bed at five or six at night and get up at three in the morning. When I go in, my children go in. And I make them get down to sleep. When I wake, I wake them up, catch the early morning. That's how we live in those days. Not like now [laughter].

N. Granville M. Major, born in 1904, Burrow's Harbour, Long Island

Mr. Major's joy and sense of humor were extraordinary. At eighty-seven, he had many recollections of his education and career as a teacher. His love of learning and his respect and concern for his students were obvious. Every one of his ex-students with whom I spoke praised him. None of Mr. Major's brothers and sisters were able to receive an education because there were no schools near Burrow's Harbour. The facts that "my sister was married to Mr. John Wells," who lived at Buckley's," where there was a school nearby, and that "she needed someone from Burrow's Harbour to keep her company" changed Mr. Major's life. It became possible for him to receive an education and to enrich the lives of hundreds of his students.

Burrow's Harbour, Mr. Major's birthplace, is located at the southern-most tip of Long Island but is not identified on most maps.

I was born on Long Island in the deep south at a place called Burrow's Harbour. Hardly anyone living there now. It's a bit on the east side, near the sea. Going on this road, it is as far south as you can go. It'll take you to a place called Gordon's. From Gordon's you go this way as far as you can. I was born in 1904.

I had eight brothers and six sisters. My mother liked plenty people around her [laughter]. Even with all of those, she kept one or two who weren't hers. We lived right near the sea. And my father and the boys could use the boat to get fish to feed all of us. My parents had people working for them, getting the farms ready. They used to have people working every day. Get up early, go fishing and have fish for breakfast. They used to have pigs out in the yard and they kept three or four dogs. When the pigs were old enough and they want one slaughtered, take the dogs and get one. My father kept large corn, beans. They always had something.

None of my brothers or sisters went into teaching. The problem with them was there was no school where they lived. The nearest school was seven miles. I went to school here at Deadman's Cay. My sister was married to Mr. John Wells, who lived at Buckley's. She needed someone from Burrow's Harbour to keep her company. So she brought me down here just after the 1908 hurricane. Water was still in the road as I rode behind the horse to get down here. They built a new school in 1910. And I went to that school the first day it started. It was an all-age school and we had a gallery. It was like a balcony upstairs. The teacher could see us from downstairs. That's where we started from.

In 1915, I was made a monitor [a pupil who teaches younger students]. And I began to teach. I was—what's the word—I was precocious [laughter]. At that time, the highest grade was grade five. And there were only two of us in grade five, D. H. Burroughs and myself. They only needed one. But we two couldn't be chosen from—so much equality that they used both of us and divided the salary: two bob [two shillings; 48 cents U.S.— laughter]. We were glad of it. Money was scarce. And that's how I started my career of teaching.

Joanna Alexandria Wilchcombe Bethel, born on March 15, 1908, West End, Grand Bahama

Mrs. Bethel is the only narrator who grew up on Grand Bahama. I doubt there is anyone in the Bahamas who could have painted a more enjoyable or superior picture of early life in West End than she did. Mrs. Bethel sacrificed a great deal to provide the best possible education for her children. She glowed with pride as she discussed their accomplishments. At eighty- four, she lives alone in South Beach on New Providence.

Grand Bahama is the fourth larg- est Bahamian island. One-third of

*its people live in settlements outside the Freeport area. West End is lo-
cated on the island's western edge, twenty-eight miles from Freeport.
Eight Mile Rock is eight miles of rocky land east and west of Hawksbill
Creek.*

My parents were Claudius and Jestina Wilchcombe. I lived on West End
until I was eight years old and then I wanted to go to school. I came to
Nassau with my father once. Somebody promised to send me to school if
I could stay, and so I stayed here with them. But they didn't send me to
school. I stayed here four years, off and on. I went home and came back.
They still wanted me to stay on, you know, but I couldn't. I wanted to go
to school. I really was hungry for education. I seen all the children going
to school and I can't go. So I went back home. I was twelve years old then.

My mother had a good education. She receive her education at Eight
Mile Rock. She had lived at Eight Mile Rock before she married. She
hadn't taught her children because she liked to farm. She was very busy
round the farm and garden.

I put up with that [trying to get an education] until my husband came
around and I got married. I was nineteen years old. My husband was from
Governor's Harbour, Eleuthera. He was working in Grand Bahama as a
wireless operator. He went to school at Eleuthera. He learned a lot up
there at Governor's Harbour. The government was sending him around to
different stations and, in 1927, he came to Grand Bahama.

Eight Mile Rock was the oldest community on Grand Bahama. West
End had very few inhabitants when I was a child, just about four or five
homes. There was a little place called Rocker Town. All of that was a part
of West End. A few houses were there. Then you skip from there and you
go up to my uncle's house and then you go to my aunt. And then you go to
my cousin's house. It was way down. It was so scattered, you know?

Everyone in West End was a member of my family. That's why I was
so glad my husband came as a telegraph operator [laughter]. That's why
I moved my children too. Some of my cousins were interested in my
children. That's what happens when you get to Spanish Wells and I didn't
want that to happen. We lived like brothers and sisters. All this thing I
hear going on now with family [having sexual relations] is terrible. That's
strange to us. Always trust ourselves with our cousins. People used to
go to Eight Mile Rock and other settlements to find someone to marry.
That's where my father found (*met*) my mother. And even at that, you find
family in the different settlements. The Smiths, they're my family also. My

grandmother was from Smith's Point. My grandfather found her in Smith's Point and he brought her to West End. All her family was still in Smith's Point, so they were our cousins. In recent years they've been having family reunions just so that the kids would know who they're related to. I have family scattered all over Grand Bahama. I don't know the young set. That's why I went to the reunion last year. My mother was a Barr. One of my grandmothers was a Smith and the other was a Perpall. She was from Nassau.

My grandfather on my father's side, his father was from Wales. He was the first Wilchcombe—Richard Thomas Wilchcombe. I think he came here after the Boer War. Many years later, there was a Wilchcombe who came from Wales and was working in Grand Bahama. First Wilchcombe other than us. He found out that there was this one set of Wilchcombes in Grand Bahama—the only set in the Bahamas. When he found that out, he searched for us. My mother told me that he keep looking for us. My great-grandfather's name was Richard Thomas and he named his oldest son Richard Thomas. My uncle named his eldest son Richard Thomas. So when the visitor found us, he said, "Oh my God, this where Richard Thomas come? We lost him and we couldn't find him. We thought he was dead." After that, she said they couldn't get rid of him. He was so happy to see them and to know that he found out where that man went. Sometimes it's good to name the son after the father because then you can trace it. My cousin Richard Thomas didn't have any sons, so it ended right there. He had three daughters. So you never know; we have roots all around.

I have stories after stories. My mother used to tell me stories about Eight Mile Rock. How they lived. They had to get up in the morning and milk the cows before they go to school. Do their tasks, clean, whatever they have to do. Their father died and left them at an early age. They had it rough. My mother, when she lived at West End, used to collect fish, corn them [salt them] and send them up there [to Eight Mile Rock] to help out.

My sister Lillian went up there [to Eight Mile Rock] to go to school. But my uncle must have whipped her. She was living with my grandmother. He did something to hurt her and she walked from Eight Mile Rock clean to West End, eight miles. [Walked] all alone, only on sandy beach. There wasn't any street. They never got her to go back. She had a little education. She had gone as far as grade six. But she never went back. My brother was up there, but he left because things was too rough.

It was so tough that people would leave from Eight Mile Rock in the morning and walk to West End to sell milk. Sometimes they drink half of the milk and fill it up with water from the ponds [laughter]. They would bring it and sell it to you. You could see the water on it. You had to boil it, you know? Sometimes the children would come down and you would ask them, "Have you had anything to eat this morning?" Oh, they looked so sad. They had to get back so they could go to school. They had to walk so far to school. You should have seen those kids. Every time, after I got married, they used to come to us to sell these things. As I told you, they looked so sad. I'd give them breakfast.

So Eight Mile Rock was very, very hard. They had to live mostly on the farm. And in dry weather like this drought, the farm isn't doing very much. They had to come down to West End to get what we call the relish. That's fish and conchs [gastropod with a foot and a large shell]. They were all the way on the south side and the water was kind of rough and deep at Hawks-bill Creek. They had to go way out the ocean way to fish. West End is on the bank area. And it's on the edge of the Gulf Stream as well. You could walk out from where we lived and pick up the conchs. It's not the same now. You have to go way out to get conchs.

The people who lived at Eight Mile Rock couldn't even move to West End. There wasn't any accommodations for them. They had property up there already and cows. They had cattle and stuff. Sometimes they bring a cow to West End and they kill it. In the bootleggin' days [the years known as the Prohibition period, when it was illegal for U.S. citizens to have alcoholic liquor within the borders of the U.S.], they mostly used to bring cows down there and sell. Get some money. They had it tough, very tough. My mother, she used to do a lot of helping. Everybody who came from Eight Mile Rock used to stop at my mother's house. She would prepare a meal for them, even if it was just dry food. Give them a little sugar with it because they were so hungry. Everybody used to stop there. Sometimes we used to be mad with her, too. Strangers used to come and she would squeeze them in.

Growing up, children liked to go fishing. Girls and boys used to go out fishing. They just used to hang around and play [laughter]. The older children took care of the younger children all day. Sometimes the girls would learn to sew, make embroidery, crochet, and hand work, mostly for the Red Cross. You got your own supplies even if your settlement was poor. West End was poor, money wise. But food, if you can grow your own things, you don't have to starve. We had a lot of seafood. We raised our own chicken, pigs and cows. A lot of cows were in Grand Bahama, you know. You could ship them to Nassau and get a sale. That's how we get a little money. We would ship them alive on the boat. We had to do lots of things to help ourselves. When there was a killing at West End they would send around and take an order from each one. How much you want of it [laughter]? Especially us—the wireless operator, the commissioner, the teachers—we got first choice. If they have chicken to sell, they come from Water Cay or some other place near Eight Mile Rock with a box of chicken. And sometime we only have to pay a shilling each. We would buy the whole box and put them in the chicken coop. We had the chicken coop full of chicken all the time. My family never starved. They used to get things in from the mailboat from Abaco, fruits and stuff. They were sent for us to sell. Sugar cane syrup was canned up in these big five-gallon cans. They send it to us to sell for them and send the money back to them.

You had your little farms, but there was this community spirit. In those days, we lived like one big family. We never used to sell the fish and things. Only after the bootleggin' start and people got money and [only a] few people [still] go out fishing. They would come in and sell the fish very cheap. Other than that, in our neighbourhood, someone go out fishing, we go there and could get a meal. Sometimes you don't have to ask them. My father used to say, "Put a sign up on the door so everybody come." That's how we lived. We got along very well.

In the evenings, the families would come together, mostly to our house. We had the biggest house [laughter]. We would sit on the porch with plenty mosquitoes [laughter]. Make a big fire and smoke away the mosquitoes. We would sit on the porch and watch the children playing biddy, biddy, hold fast or ring. The children would sit down with their hands behind their backs and somebody would get a stone, you know? And they go along. Biddy, biddy, hold fast. They pass the stone behind their back. Someone is in the middle of the ring and that person got to guess who has the stone. If he guesses right, that person is called to the center. The ring, well, we also call it jump dance. Someone would be in a circle and start to shimmy and shake [laughter]. "Tell me who you love? I love nobody." And they walking all around [laughter]. Whoever you put your hand on to touch, that person comes into the ring. We had a lot of fun out of that. Boys and girls [laughter]. We used to have fun.

It wasn't any gas stoves. If you could get a kerosene stove, that was a luxury [laughter]. It was wood stoves. We used to cut wood from the button wood tree and cut it into short pieces, make little bundles, a penny a bundle. Sent a hundred bundles to Nassau. Grown-ups did that part. We had a mailboat about once or twice a month. The weather had to be very good to get that because our boats were sailing boats. There wasn't any motor in those days. And twice a month we get the mailboat. That's how we get the news from Nassau and everything else.

West End got a telegraph station in about 1924. That was in the bootleggin' days. And the telephone only got there since I left. The mailboat would take people from West End up to Sweeting's Cay [on the eastern end of Grand Bahama], making stops. We had other boats also, sponge boats, shell boats and so on, that come back and forth.

My husband and I had all of our children when we came to Nassau, so that was ten [laughter]. I came to Nassau because of school again. I wanted my children to get a higher education. I always wanted education for myself and I didn't get what I wanted, so I thought try to give it to my children. I discussed it with my husband, Leonard. He was quite happy living in Grand Bahama. But I said, "Look, our children are growing up. They're getting up to fourteen and they have to leave school. What they going to do then?" He agreed with me. Well then, Joan was studying for the test to go to Government High. So he said to me—this was shortly after I had my last child—"When Joan going in for the exam, you go along with her and see if you can find a home in Nassau and you can come back and get the children." Before the day was out, when he went to work, he had a different thought again. I had a good friend up here [Nassau] by the name of Annie Archer. He said, "Ask Annie to look around so when you go with Joan, you can take all the children." And he was rushing me. He did that for our children.

Houses around here were very, very scarce. You couldn't find a good home, but Annie did find a place in Nassau Street, Mrs. Bowen's, and she claimed that for us. We telegrammed the money to her and she had that for us. Boy, now let me tell you, that was hell. Three little rooms—we had to have a kitchen, and two of the rooms were bedrooms [laughter]. The children were like sardines. I had cots and things that opened up to beds. And afterwards Mrs. Bowen got the other two rooms from the man who was in there. She put him out and let us have the whole house. But it still wasn't a healthy thing for us.

Just about all the children were in school. Only one I had home with me. Joan sat for Government High and she got it. And I just was in time to get Jackie and Susan into St. John's College [a private primary-secondary school]. I was almost late, but Father Holmes [an Anglican priest] helped me get the papers through. He helped me very much. The other little ones, I got in public school. Leander and Lois, I sent them to a private school up on the hill. They were very young and the private school wasn't very far. Mrs. Wright was right up the hill. So I sent them up there. Things were rough for us. It wasn't easy, but I didn't mind. Susan, Jackie, Leander and Lois, I had to pay for. But Joan won a scholarship to Government High.

By the time we moved to Nassau, Tellis, my oldest son, was out of school. He was working at Pine Ridge, Grand Bahama. That was the lumber farm. He and his father spoke to the director, Pelecanos, and had Tellis come into Nassau with us because he was quite young. Tellis start working when he was fourteen. Pelecanos taught him his trade. And he was good at it. Tellis came and that was another squeeze for us [laughter]. We were paying a pound [$4.80 U.S.] a week for the house. Leonard wasn't getting much more than that. We bought a piece of property. We wasn't finished paying for that. So we finished paying for the property at Fort Fincastle. My husband had some property up in Eleuthera and he sold it so we can start building. After we got the house half-finished, we moved. It was much better, much easier for us because we had space [laughter]. We had space and we had water right in the yard. We didn't have it in the house, not yet. The house wasn't finished.

In the little house where we lived before, there was no water in the yard. We had to bring water from Beasley. When the children come from school, they would fill up everything for the next morning, 'cause they had to have their baths. I'm telling you, it wasn't no picnic.

One good thing was we always had enough to eat. My husband stuck with me. And my sons helped. Things, food was much cheaper in those days. Sometimes Father Holmes stopped by there and he saw the children eating butter and bread. And he said, "Butter and bread? I only get a quarter a pound for my ration." Yeah, but I had to have butter for my children.

I was used to eating good. When I was home in Grand Bahama I used to raise my chickens. Sometime we had goats. Sometime we had sheep. And then when Mother was farming, I would get produce from her. Fish, conch, crawfish, you didn't have to buy. So when I came here I continued very well. I didn't come here to play or to do stupidness. I came here for one purpose: to get my children educated. I spent the money for the education. I told them how to be careful with the clothing, you know? Sometime when I was in Grand Bahama I make the underclothes. Sometimes I make a dress for them to wear around the yard or something [laughter]. But the clothes, I used to order. I used to do a lot of ordering from America. We had agents here and you used to order oxfords, the children's shoes, from England. They was strong. Oh, we had to work our heads to keep them [the children] going. I don't regret it, you know [laughter].

Then we decided to move from Fort Fincastle Hill. All the families used to come from America and they would say, "Oh, you got a big house." And Leonard said, "Nobody helped me to get this" [laughter]. And as they come to live, you have to furnish food and everything. They come unaware to you. They don't write and say anything. When you look, you see the taxi stop in front of your house. They take you for granted. No, my children don't like that. So that's how we moved here to South Beach.

My husband always said that instead of us coming out here [to South Beach], we should have gone back to Grand Bahama. He didn't want to go to Eleuthera, I don't think. The people loved him in Grand Bahama. They honored him. Highly esteemed him, you know, that's what he liked. They were very friendly to him. He enjoyed that very much.

Rafaleta "Goddie" Williams, born on August 7, 1908,
Fresh Creek, Andros

> *Mrs. Williams was referred to me by Mona Birch at Small Hope Bay Lodge. Ms. Birch suggested I talk to Goddie because she is one of the oldest people living in Fresh Creek. Mrs. Williams is eighty-four and blind. Her memories of the poverty of her youth and how she and her siblings survived are marvelous. Her adult family members have either died or moved away, but fortunately two grandchildren live with her, and members of the church and community provide assistance as needed.*
>
> *Andros is the largest of the Bahamian islands and the third most populous. Mrs Williams' settlement, Fresh Creek, is near the Androsia factory where Bahamian batik is created and fashioned into attractive informal clothing.*

These days is no days at all. You all days now is dog days. Now we didn't have anything much. We didn't have money or clothes, no job like how they got jobs now. Well, right in the government road, you go weed the grass and every six month, they give the womens a job and they call it one and six a day [one shilling and sixpence, 30 cents U.S.]. Now you don't know nothing about the one and six, hay? That's what you used to get a day.

Tomorrow now, if I live, bring me a gift. I'm eighty tomorrow if I live to see. 'Cause I could go directly. I could go tonight. I getting pension, $100 a month. Momma was getting 10 shillings [$2.40 U.S.] for her age and when she was dead, she was 110. She was living in the back, this way. You see them high place over there? All in the back there, was houses then. They wasn't living on the range in the front like how we are now. You had to walk through the bush to go to the houses then. But [now] you got road right through from one to another [the range to the back]. As I was telling you, but when you go to the shop with eight shilling, two dollar, you bring a load! You could get a lot for that. My dear, a yard of cloth, threepence. When you get threepence a yard cloth, that's wedding dress! Wedding, they're making for bride. I'm telling you. The only other older person could tell you like that is Aggie Bullard. That the onliest one could explain like I could 'cause we the two oldest. 'Cause living in this district, they old, but not as old as we, 'cause I a little bit older.

What I crave when I young? I like to go to church. And in my young days, I used to like to go to dance. Oh, great God! I used to like to go to dance when I was young. And you keep party until you hear about concerts and things they have out here. And ain't no much of a bar been round here, not one. When time to go to dance, I go to dance. When time to go to church, I go to church. Ain't serving two master one time, no how. But I just enjoying my early days. So when it time to go to church, I put away the dancing in my mind and turn to God and what they telling me up there. When I get old, I wouldn't depart from it. I can't depart from what they teach me in them old days. Got to go to church, 'cause the parents ain't going to let you be home. No, you goin' to church.

In our days, we had nothing, nothing, daughter. Sometimes, when Saturday come, you gotta go wash your Sunday gown, hang it out and press that on Saturday night. Wash your tennis, old tennis [shoes], to put to your foot. And you walk barefoot until you get up to Meeting House Hill. You wash your foot in one water hole. You dry 'em off. You got your cloth. You dry 'em off. You put on your thick socks. You put them on, black or white, any one. When you come home, you take them off. You can't even afford to wear them goin' into the yard. The shoes, how you do now, sit down in the house? We couldn't do that. One pair of tennis. You may find someone who could hand you one old gown. Thems be short. Very few of them. Now, today, people could give you bales of clothes, bales of shoes. Sometimes they come, they shove one dollar in your hand, right so. Sometimes when you look, one box of groceries come right so. But it wasn't like that in our days. We go out in the pine yard rooting, daughter, for wild yam. You don't know. Many day, it's just pigeon peas. What we can raise, plenty of them, in the black land. It richer than white land 'cause it full of rotted leaves and stuff. When the morning, to go to school, we had to boil them [pigeon peas]. That's my breakfast, with salt. Go along the bay and pick the white coca plum. You may see them down there. You pick them and eat them sometime in class, in the daytime.

I got two sisters now living. They older than me. But one of them, the one I'm next to, you would think she is a baby to me. The oldest sister now, I don't know when I see her. Years now since I grab eyes on [have seen] her, 'cause I can't go to Nassau. She can't come. She live in Nassau. Her property in Nassau. The other two in Nassau, 'cause their husbands had property over there. You see, I didn't admire [envy her], I could have been over there too. But I didn't admire, I stayed with Momma. Only me one this way. Her only daughter this way and the other two over there in Nassau. See, there was four of us. There was four daughters. She had a couple—five or six—boys. All died. All my brothers died. Got no brothers living. All die when they grown up. All after they married. Every one. Good couple of years after they were married. They left big children when they died.

I didn't have children. But you know, I have to tell you the truth, I catch [became pregnant] with one and lost it. After that, I ain't take care of myself. I ain't catch no more. I catch with that before marriage and after that I didn't had any. I ain't catch with any; I ain't try. Left it alone and depend on God. My husband been in grave forty years now. He died when I was in my prime. I coulda both worked and do straw work [make goods from palm fronds]. You could say, I coulda jump over the moon. I ain't care about nothing then. And me and him wasn't together. He was plenty older than me. I was his second wife. He get in a way—lost his nature [became impotent], you know what I mean? And I was young. So I rather pull out and leave and let him be to his people and I be to my people up this way. I come back home. I was working out there to Small Hope Bay; that's where I take sick. That's where my first sickness in these legs come from. And now you can see how I is.

Carrie Lunn, born in November 1909, Turks and Caicos Islands

"Aunt Carrie" was my mother's best friend when they were in their early twenties. Mrs. Lunn tells wonderful stories. Her descriptions of her husband's courtship and her trip to Turks and Caicos were so vivid I

*could almost see the events. She is a lovely woman who is not easily for-
gotten. On the day I visited, her nails were painted and her hair was
freshly dyed and styled. She lives in Nassau with her granddaughter's
family and has regular telephone contact with a variety of friends.*

*Turks and Caicos Islands, where Mrs. Lunn was born, are two sepa-
rate archipelagos covering an area of over 5,000 miles of the Bahamas
chain. They were linked formally to the Bahamas until 1848, when their
supervision was transferred to Jamaica. Since 1976, they have had internal self-government.*

I had three brothers and one sister. They are all gone. I'm the only one
living. I was the baby.

Do you want to know where I met my husband [laughter]? Well, I met
him after the First World War. I met him in his mother's home because my
sister was friendly with one of his sisters. One day she took me there with
her. His mother introduced me to him. She said, "This is my youngest
son." That's how I met him. They liked me. That is, his mother told me
from the first day she saw me, she loved me. When her son told her he
loved me, and he wanted to become engaged, she was so happy. She said,
"Well, I know I will have a loving daughter-in-law." That's what the old lady
said to me.

And it happened so on one day. My sister and I, we went to the market.
We used to go to the market to buy our vegetables and different things. We
had this horse and buggy. It had a dickey seat and a nice seat in front. I was
sitting and holding the reins while my sister went in to get her packages.
While sitting there, child, I felt this jerk on the carriage. So I looked
around, and as I looked, there he was. He had rode up and put his foot
right up. He was on his bicycle. He put his foot right up on the step of the
carriage, which gave that jolt. As I looked round, I saw him and I said to
him, "Yes?" [laughter]. And he said, "Hello, how are you today?" I said,
"I'm fine, thank you." Then he rode right around to the front where I was
sitting. And he started a conversation, what a beautiful day it was and was
I alone, and I told him no, my sister was in the pharmacy. Right from then
was when we got friendly. He used to come to see me twice a week [laugh-
ter] on the weekends! Oh yes, on Saturday, child, we had to go to the show
on Frederick Street. Well, we would drive up. I lived at a place called
Prospect, which is Prospect Heights now. We would drive our buggy and
just put it in somebody's yard, our friend's yard. We would walk to the

show. The buggy was safe in the yard, tied to a post. The horse was tied, so he couldn't get into any trouble or get away. That's where we kept it until the movie was over.

I got married in 1923 from Mr. Baxter's house in Orange Grove. He was a millionaire who had a sisal place. And my brother was the timekeeper. He kept the records of who came to work and what time they got there.

Mr. Baxter was going away one time and he told my brother that he wanted him to live in his house while he was away. My mother had died. So it was my sister, myself and my daddy. The other two brothers, well, they was on their own. So he told him, "If you want your family, your two sisters to live with you in my house, you're quite welcome to that. When I'm ready to come back, I'll write and let you know. You can get the place ready for me." We lived there and that was where I got engaged. The house that Gail Saunders owns now was Baxter's place. Had a nice big dining room, a big dining room table, could sit about ten to that table, a big long table. Had a nice big piano in the house, nice living room, big yard. My brother had a car.

My husband used to come to see me, as I said, twice a week. Then afterwards, he used to come three times a week. He used to use a horse and buggy still. Then I could remember when he proposed to me. Still got my little engagement ring. He put it on this finger. I can wear it on this finger now. It's too small for this. And I still prize that. When I got engaged it was just the family. We sat around the table. We had supper.

My father was still alive when all my children was born. He knew all of my children. My mother didn't know that I got married. [She had passed away earlier.] She didn't know that I got engaged. She know that this young man used to come to the house, but she didn't know that he liked me. I didn't know at first that it was me [he liked]. I thought he only used to come because he was friendly with my brother [laughter]. They were great pals. They used to ride bicycles and ride horses. I didn't know for a long time. Then one day, he wrote this letter. He wrote my daddy. Oh, he was thorough, my dear. That man was well educated, too. He never went away. None of his brothers went away to school, but all of them was smart men. His father was a lighthouse keeper. They traveled from one island to another, one island to the other. So many years he put in at each island.

My husband was a printer. He had a little newspaper call *The Observer*. I never wrote for his newspaper. But I used to help him in his work.

The time I wrote was when I was about fourteen years old. I wrote a composition of my trip from here to Turks Island. That was the first time

I went back, just to visit my grandparents. I went with my uncle. And while I was up there, I sat down and I say, now let me write about my trip. I have it somewhere. I know that I wrote how my uncle came to Nassau and he asked me if I would like to go back with him for a little while to see my two grandmothers. I was delighted that he asked me to do that. I didn't know my grandparents. I was six when I came down [to Nassau]. So he asked my mother and father and they said, "Well, if she want to go." You know, that was the first time in my life that I left my mother without any fear or anything. I was so happy and safe with this uncle. He was a loving uncle. Mother said that she knew Uncle Bob would take care of me. His wife was my mother's sister. She knew I would be well taken care of. So I packed up my suitcase and off I went with him. I can remember stopping to Cat Island; we went ashore there. We stopped at Long Island. That was where I met the Turnquests, Hilda Turnquest. I got very friendly with her. I only spent a day there but I felt like I knew her for years. We went to Rum Cay and I had coconut water, sitting on the beach. That coconut water tasted so sweet. The people came right around us. You would think it was Christopher Columbus [laughter] for the way they treated us. We were on a boat, a big ship. It was a two-mast schooner. Then we met up with a storm. What a terrible storm! And I cuddled right up to my uncle [laughter]. I thought anytime we would drown. I said that I wasn't going to see my mother anymore. Yes, the sea was so rough and those heavy winds and claps of thunder and lightning and the waves were splashing from one side of the boat to the other. I was on deck all that time, you know, on deck with my uncle. They had nice berths, but I felt that if I went down there, I would suffocate. So I stayed up there. Had an umbrella over me. Holding that umbrella [laughter]. Then it cleared off and it was beautiful.

Next we got to a place called Mayaguana, little huts made out of straw, thatch straw. All the roofs had just little rods to hold those leaves together. It had rained a lot when we got there and all the place was flooded and rocky. I had never seen a place so rocky! I don't know yet how those people ever lived in those little huts. And this was 1915. They were still living in huts on this little island. They used to farm. They used to grow sweet potatoes, white beans. Oh, they used to grow a lot of stuff because they gave us things, sweet potatoes, pumpkins and white beans. They gave us quite a lot and my uncle, he was a merchant. He had a store on Turks Island and he bought a lot of white beans from those people.

The crew on the boat would catch fish as we would sail along, dolphins. Boy, that used to taste nice. It took us about a week to go into all these little places. We went to Inagua. Stopped at Inagua where a friend of my uncle's lived, Mr. Symonette. Oh, he was so glad to see us. We stayed there a couple of days and then we went on to Turks Island. I saw both grandmothers. Were they glad when they saw me! "Look at Sissie's child." You see, they called my mother Sissie because some of her smaller sisters couldn't say sister. And they would say, "Come, go to your sister," and they couldn't say sister so they would say, "Sissie." But her name was Cornelia. After a few weeks, my uncle brought me back to Nassau. I never forgot that trip. It was wonderful.

Eva Augusta McPherson Williams, born on November 12, 1912, Grant's Town, New Providence

Mrs. Williams is the daughter of Samuel C. McPherson, one of the few blacks to have served in the House of Assembly during the early years of the twentieth century. She is a slim, well-dressed lady who attends most of the "important" functions taking place in Nassau. I was impressed that she was so knowledgeable about such a variety of topics. The way she tells of her battle to resign as a teacher is hilarious. Knowing Mrs. Williams, it is easy to visualize her confidence as she told her aunt that she was "going out to take care of some business" and proceeded to travel around Manhattan to answer an ad for a seamstress. Needless to say, she secured the position. Mrs. Williams refused to allow me to photograph her, but a few weeks later, I received a charming photo in the mail.

Mrs. Williams lives in Grant's Town on New Providence. A number of Africans had created a settlement now known as Grant's Town over the hill in 1825. Grant's Town is an area where many African customs continue to survive.

When I was growing up in Nassau, I seem to remember from when I was five or six. I went to Government High. They brought in some young

teachers from England. After the first two years in '27 or '28, the Colonial
Secretary decided he would close the Government High School because
it was too expensive to supply the assistant teachers that this headmaster,
Mr. Woods, said he needed. They had given him two—Mr. Greene and Mr.
Jennings. One was supposed to teach mathematics and geography. The
other was supposed to teach scripture and Latin. When those two young
men came here, they were happy. They tried real hard in this backward
nation. They came for three-year contracts, but they sent their resigna-
tions to the headmaster. Since they had been living in Nassau, they
couldn't save a penny. They didn't know that the cost of living was so high
in the Bahamas. They might as well go home where they could work and
save some money. That's all this particular Colonial Secretary wanted to
know. He said, well, he would close the Government High School. My
father fought him tooth and nail. Poppa went to all the other members of
Parliament, asking them to give him support because a school that prepared children for higher learning was necessary. If they closed it, we
wouldn't have it open again for a half century. My father won the vote.

There was only three black ones in the House. Lawyer Toote, Alfred
Adderley and my father. There were only twenty-nine members then, who
received no salary. Before Poppa was in the House, one lawyer, an aristo-
crat of the Jewish ones, Mr. Solomon, was representing this district and
was going to resign. I don't know why, but he chose Poppa. He handpicked
my father. This is what you call Grant's Town. In those days, in the twenties, it used to be called the Southern District. When the House of Assembly went out that time, and then when they were assembled again, Poppa
was put in again. He got in a third time. When he was in, my mother cried
and said, "Sam, don't bother with that anymore. You can't afford it." He
was a tailor. Mr. Reuben Bethel and he were two tailors. But Mr. Bethel
was aggressive. You know, after the war, when the tourists began to come,
Mr. Bethel made so much money that he bought property on Market
Street. Well, Poppa, he wasn't that type. So he didn't run again. He got in
because of Mr. Solomon. He was in for ten years. Well, you might hear
about S. C. McPherson Secondary School. Because of what he did, they
named one of the schools after him. It hadn't been named until recently—
not in his lifetime. They were building schools in the early seventies and
Poppa died in 1973. They got around to naming his school in '75. A. F.
Adderley School was built first.

Just after I graduated from Government High, I guess Poppa arranged
it. I didn't realize it at the time. That's been many years, 1929. I took a job

as a teacher. In those days in the late twenties, there were only two things for girls to do. You teach or you nurse. My mother had been a nurse. She train in what we call the Bahama General Hospital. And then housewife, you don't go out to work.

After the first term or two, I went to the education department to Mr. Singleton, living up to the corner here then, on this same McPherson Street. This same white man had it named after my father. I gone and wrote my resignation and took it into what we call the Ministry of Education. So the gentleman in charge of education, one Mr. Albury, he said, "Miss Mac, your daddy know about this?" "No," was the answer. So he said, "You getting on with the head mistress? You and Miss Agnes getting along all right?" She was Agnes Lightbourn and she married Walter Archer. I say, "Yes, Mr. Albury. We friends." I say, "Her mother come down from the pond to visit my mother in the carriage and my mother and me used to go in the carriage and spend the afternoon with them." So whatever the case, when the term open again he took me from there and sent me over the hill to a school 'til the end of the year. Which would make three terms. You go in in January and you come out in July. At the end of the two terms, I went back again to the Ministry of Education. I told Mr. Albury that teaching was not for me. It wasn't that I couldn't do it. I didn't enjoy it. So he said, "You come here Monday morning and you work in our office and help Mrs. Maxie [the secretary for the education department]. Mr. Mac told me that he sent you to commercial school for typing and shorthand." I didn't fight him anymore. I said, "Mr. Albury, I didn't get a certificate in typing because I still got to look down. I only got a certificate in shorthand." He say, "Oh, so your memory is good." I say, "Well, I can bring my Pittman shorthand." This Mrs. Maxie Bowe, she had to do all the reports from the public schools. And those reports had to be done every month. That was more work than that poor young woman could do and he was glad to get me there with her. I did all the handwork and didn't have to type. She could do all the typing.

Most of the Out Island [Family Islands] commissioners were also schoolmasters. The poor girl was burdened down, her and Burrows, so with the three of us, we worked under Mr. Albury. I worked until I got married and then you didn't work anymore and you get pregnant right away [laughter].

Then I didn't go back to ask for a government job. I stopped teaching. I was doing sewing at home.

How I met my husband: We were going out to these matinee dances and Frank met me and got interested. Matinee dances were from 3 P.M. to 7 P.M. And anybody used to go to them. We would find the big men and the young teenagers there enjoying themselves. I was under eighteen. I was eighteen when I got married. Frank had girls who he used to escort and who wanted him. But we got married. Poppa said, "The boy had no advantages!" But women are different. Mother said, "Well, she's young and there's no use putting them off and something happen." So Mother used to encourage Frank. I got married at St. Agnes Anglican Church. We got married and lived with my parents. He was working for the Department of Customs and I was doing a little sewing at home.

Mother brought up my two children. My husband and me and the two children were still living with Mother and Poppa. And she had a great influence on McPherson and Carolyn [Mrs. Williams' two children].

It's now forty years since Frank, my husband, and I have been together. Well, he was with the glamour boys in the circle. He was from Marsh Harbour, Abaco. When his mother died, his daddy married again and he sent the children down here to Nassau to their aunt. His daddy was in charge of the timber. He was a coloured man married to an Abaco white. So these five children whom he had, they come up to Nassau and they had hard times. Their aunt had two children and no husband, so they had it hard. Anyway, with living on the hill, they were friendly with the Bosfields. And that's the circle they traveled in and they went to St. Francis Xavier [the Roman Catholic cathedral]. My husband wasn't a member, but the girls went to St. Francis and the Roman Catholic nuns help them. His sisters got married early and he was alone. He was living in a rooming house opposite Government House [residence of the Governor-General].

I didn't have the shop then. But Frank and I were able to buy a lot [a small piece of land] and build opposite Timmy Donaldson and those. So we lived there together. In the meantime, along with him working at the Customs, he had a little band. They used to call him Rudy Vallee because he had curly hair. Well, you know the girls were chasing him [laughter] and he was giving in, too [laughter]. A rich tourist who used to come here told my husband, "Rudy Williams, if you could bring your band to Massachusetts, I will give you three months' employment. You have a swinging band. Count Basie and those, they got about a dozen or more, and it's good music, but they're like symphony. You have a rhythm." At that time, he couldn't take the whole band. He took Freddie Munnings and Bruce Clark to Martha's Vineyard. And I lived in Brooklyn with his aunt—345 McDonald Street.

One day I got the *New York Journal* and I don't know what caused me to look in the want ads. They needed a seamstress. I knew that I could do it. I told Aunt Maude, "I going out to take care of some business." I went out and took the subway. I went downtown and they kept me that very day. That afternoon when I told her, she was angry. She say, "You come here to look for work and your husband working up in Massachusetts. You could keep up with these dressmakers?" I say, "Well, they took me on, didn't they? They told me they'll see me tomorrow morning." I was there until he finished his job and we came home together. We weren't getting on that well.

When I went to New York the next spring, they insisted that I stay for Thanksgiving. That Thanksgiving eve, I say, "Lord, what is this?" I never could make it in the cold weather. I had more coats! Born in November, but never like it when the weather change. So I came home, and staying away from him for the three months, we didn't make it. I just moved from the hill and came back to my parents. And left him in the house. When he came to put his argument, I said, "Frank, we've been seeing things differently for a couple of years. I'm not coming back. If I was coming back, I wasn't coming out." Understand now, he didn't drink liquor or smoke, but he had other bad traits. One day when he came to Mother to see the children, I say, "Frank, you never thought of going back to New York or Massachusetts? Why don't you try it over there? You still young. Get a position in some band or whatever." And I help him to go. I gave him what I could afford. He stayed. He didn't get in a band. I can't remember what he worked at. But that was the end of that.

Ivy Simms, born on February 24, 1913, Simms, Long Island

> *I very much wanted to interview Ms. Simms because she is famous throughout the Bahamas for her unique straw work. No other straw worker has been able to imitate the style of this exceptional artisan. She is a member of one of the first English families to settle on Long Island. Initially we sat in her living room, which is full of pictures and plaques showing her family's accomplishments. It was exciting to hear her trace her ancestry in the Bahamas back three hundred years. She is an articulate, highly creative seventy-eight-year-old. After I was*

served a wonderful lunch, we went outside and she educated me about the habits of soldier crabs.

Simms is one of the oldest settlements on Long Island, dating from the 18th century. The packing house, located here, is where farmers bring their produce to be purchased by the government. Once a week, the mailboat stops to pick up these goods.

I was born to the family of Lawrence and Susan Simms, but I was one of the youngest children. There were six that lived but she actually had thirteen. There was quite a gap between me and my brother before me, some ten years, because she lost children in between. I was not the baby. There was one after me, Joyce. They said that I was my father's favorite, but I don't know about that [laughter]. Joyce and I were just four years apart. The first children were near together, two years apart, but then it tapered off and it was like ten years. The ten-year period meant that children had died in between.

I should add that my mother lived to be ninety-three years old and I stayed with her and that, I guess, is one of the things [reasons] why I carried on with the straw work, so that I could be with her. Not being a mathematician, I was always asking her and counting my fingers while she tells me the answers. She did the maths for me and I felt it was good exercise for her brain. She had a cataract operation at eighty-nine. She was Dr. Steele Perkins' patient, and he was so proud of how well she could see. She lived for four years after and she could read. Well, reading was her life, but she also was a very hard worker, having all the children to look after. She actually had six children; the others died. My father died when she was reasonably young. She used to sew. She taught me how to sew. She used to sew dresses as well as men's coats. My father was reasonably well off at the time he died, so I don't think she really needed to work. But life changes so that you find the needs are more as the days go by.

My grandfather Simms lived just a few feet from me and my brother [lived] not far away. My grandfather Knowles was just a few blocks away from here. Mother said in her day, there were only Simmses around. The whole town was Simmses. The early settlers came, and you know, they named the place after them. They were the—what you call—the first settlers, the early settlers, the Eleutheran Adventurers from Bermuda. The Knowleses were the Loyalists who came from America after your Revolutionary War. But the Simmses were not. The Simmses were here from the 1700s, so we have been here over three hundred years. That's a long time. Why they chose Long Island, I don't know.

Do you see this [sea] shell moving? There's a soldier crab inside. He has a soft body, so he has to find an empty shell to crawl into. He can move quickly. If you frighten him, he pulls his legs into the shell and covers the opening with that big biter. See?

I guess we paid attention to things like that when I was growing up, because we had no means of recreation apart from going swimming or walking. And sometimes we would play parlor games. Life was very different. But we enjoyed ourselves.

Benjamin Saunders, born on December 25, 1914,
Staniard Creek, Andros

Talking to Mr. Saunders was a unique experience. At seventy-four, he is still healthy, involved and happy. His willingness to share both the positive and negative aspects of his life provided a fascinating interview. Mr. Saunders humorously described how he found out that the name he had grown up with (Watkins) was not really his surname. He explained to me that he had fathered forty-five children. To quote part of his explanation, "You go around fast and get children with different women." His description of making charcoal was fascinating.

I would not have had the opportunity to meet Mr. Saunders without the perseverance of the taxi driver who insisted we go to see him. Mr. Saunders did not invite me inside. Instead, I interviewed him in his backyard, sitting on a trunk from a fallen coconut tree, four feet from the ocean.

My father was a seaman. His parents used to tend farm. I was just like my father was. I would go around and get children. I was one of his sweetheart's children. So that was hard, because I didn't know who was my father until I get up to manhood to get married. My mother never told me and I didn't tell how many children I had with certain women, and that's how it was in those days. My mother was ashamed to acknowledge that. Because maybe it might have been an uncle or a first cousin, something like that, you go around and get the child with. You understand? For that reason, it look too shameful on all part. I mean, to acknowledge who's the child's daddy, because sometimes it's your near neighbour—live two houses—side and side. You feel like, I mean, to do that, your parents no doubt get down on you, tough. She tell me a different man is my daddy. She named someone who wasn't the daddy, though. Not until after I got married—I went to the minister, and them days you had to put up a sight [announce the marriage], as we call it here, before you get married. When I went to him, he sent me back. Because I went there as a Watkins, by my mother's appointment. She says I'm a Watkins. When I went to the minister he told me to my face, I'm not a Watkins, and that put a thrill on me. I was a young man then, twenty-one years old. I want to find out from him where he get this information, to tell me that I'm not a Watkins. He told me, "Well, Saunders nearby, ask him some questions." I say, "Well, it look impossible for me to go and ask him some questions when my mother told me who's my father. I'm a Watkins." He say he can't marry me except [until] I go and get my right surname. That's what the minister told me.

My mother was living in Nassau at that time. So I had to leave from here and went to Nassau. The minister took me to Nassau. They had a boat that used to sail to Bimini. See, that was in his district. And on his way to Nassau, he told me to get on the boat with him and go and see my mother. Get from her the information he need. I went to her and she told me she done told me who was my daddy, Watkins. I came back to the minister and I told him, "Well, I can't do no better than that because Momma didn't [laughter]. I can't tell her no way." I tell you how I find out. My daddy's wife was working with the minister. After the minister refuse to accept what my mother said, then she call me and she told me my daddy was Joel. That's her husband; he told her I am his child. She then revealed it to me. So I told her then, "Well, why you didn't tell it to me before? I woulda been able to tell it to my mother when she object to the question I ask her." She said, "Well no, I couldn't. Joel ought to tell you that. But he told me." He told it to his parents, but my mother wouldn't acknowledge it.

Finally, the time came when I said I was going on the voyage to go on the Contract to farm in the United States. And I went all the way to the labor board office to get sign up to go and when I go, they refuse to take me. He [the clerk] said because my surname wasn't clear. Now, I wanted to know how they get all that information. They told me that I got to go and try to straighten it out because I went there with the information I got from my daddy's wife and told them that I would like to go on the Contract. I'm a young man looking for something. I have a wife, and her and I intend to go on the Contract. I was married Benjamin Watkins, but I'm a Saunders. He said, "Well, you got to go to the office and get that straightened out." I went to the office and I looked the record up in the books and I searched them all over and then I come to it. In them days they even taking [recording] births and deaths; you're right in there. But I only had Benjamin, my mother's name, and no father. So then it give me the choice to make my decision, who I would own as my father. I leave there and I went to Cash, ex-Governor-General now, Sir Gerald, and he was the one who made up my papers. Swear me in right there to the office, wife and me. Then get our affidavits made out—Benjamin Saunders and Marcella Saunders. We went back to the labor office where they accepted that, and that's how I got on Contract. From that day, I claimed my title. But sure enough, I didn't have it while growing up.

My mother had other children. She was married to a different man. But she got me when she was just a young girl. I was her first child. And then there was the neighbours. She was afraid. My granddad, he was rough, and she was afraid that he might hang her up and finish away with her. So she didn't acknowledge it. She did before she died. She came to my grandmother and she called her and me together. I was already married then. She made all of her apology to us and the reason why she didn't acknowledge it. She said, "Ben is Joel Saunders' child, but I was afraid of my father. That was the reason I didn't acknowledge it."

My grandfather was Jamaican. I hardly could explain what brought him here. In those days, the people from different parts used to travel. Some from the Bahamas go all the way to Bluefields, Nicaragua and Cuba. Different parts of the world where you get [go] and you like that the best, well, no doubt, you leave the captain [get off the boat] and you stay to that quarter [in that settlement or island]. Maybe that could be his means of getting to be in the Bahamas. I met him here all my life and he lived a number of years after I was born, 'cause I was his first grandchild.

I tell you, I mean, those days I was a young one and do bad. I tell you, plenty outside children. My wife had seventeen children. And the sweetheart had seventeen. That's true. Besides, other women had three and four [laughter]. I didn't have to support them because you go around fast and get children with different women. Knowing that you done have your wife, they ain't coming out there to acknowledge it. Don't say, "That child is your child." I know the child is my child but they ain't want that to come out. That true. I being honest. I got about forty-five children. Some of them alive now but they don't live here now. Some live in Nassau and different places. Some die. I was fast!

I live with my grandparents when I got married. After my grandparents died, why, I live with my wife's mother for a few years. Like as I said, after I went on the Contract, that is where I started from. I got some money working on the farms in the States. [The year] 1946, that is when I began my house right here on this same spot. When I get my house completed, my wife was on the fifth child and living in my mother-in-law house! I had to get one house.

Well, I tell you now, I got married in 1935. Wife and I still live together, although now she's in Nassau. And when I first got married, after I done buy the little groceries to come home to my wife, I didn't have no money. I don't make ready for the wedding. No money, only had sufficient to buy groceries to come home for it to last about four weeks. I gotta go and struggle to get me something else. You see, providing when this get out, she'll have something to go on. Well, I had the opportunity to get a little job down—you might hear about it—Cat Cay. [Cat Cay is an island where Louis Wasey had founded a private vacation community for his friends.] I went down there for about three months. It was tough for me to leave and go. My wife didn't have nothing for me to leave behind with her to eat. I'm a Methodist, so I gone to the minister and ask him if he would loan me £1 [$4.80 U.S.]. Then I be able to give my wife to get some groceries while I'm gone. Sure enough, he give me the £1 in a check. Yeah, £1 was plenty money then. The value in the money today was about three hundred dollars to me. She had to catch the boat and go to Nassau, to the Royal Bank of Canada.

You didn't have to pay to go to Nassau. We sail on the sailing boat. It wasn't no motor boat around the islands at them times. You get on the beach and you go on the boat by dinghy. Those days, passage was free, because everybody was poor and you didn't have nothing to pay your passage with. So the captain take you to Nassau. We all was seaman and farmers.

When things were hard, if you couldn't go fishing during the season, why then we used to go in the pine yard and cut pine and burn coal [make charcoal]. Burning coal is something to explain, all right, but maybe you wouldn't be able to understand. It's the pine. We cut them with the axe. And we cut those pines and we put them in a pile. You get weed and put on it. Cover it down with dirt. Catch the fire underneath it. Let it burn and after it's beat down, it comes to charcoal, you see? Then you got to take that and put it into bags and carry it into Nassau. We sold it. Wasn't much you got out of it, but we had to be satisfied. That's all we was getting. Sometimes the highest you could get—in those days it was pounds, shillings and pence—was one shilling and sixpence. Thirty cents could buy... If I tell you the truth for the cost of living, it was far better than it is right now. When I say that, I mean, the things were much cheaper. So I know then, I coulda take a shilling, that's twenty-four cents, and buy me five quarts of rice in the 1920s. Eight quarts of white grits for one shilling. For clothing, you coulda buy readymade material as well. But then, most of the Out Island people, you go and you buy your cloth and you have someone make your trousers. Ladies, I mean, get their dressmaker some cloth. You could go and get—we call it gingham. I coulda buy me a nice blue trousers for one and sixpence, because three yard coulda make me a trousers and then it only cost me twelve cents a yard. Well, take what I said from the beginning, things was better. In any case, now, if you want a nice blue trousers, it might cost you twenty dollars or twenty-five dollars.

I never had a second wife. You call them sweetheart. You only have one wife you married. My wife is alive. She's in Nassau, sick now. That's the woman I carried to the minister. The old folks say, "I married off." But all the other, they was just girlfriends. I was a charming boy in them days [laughter]. The Reverend don't know nothing about that. What he gonna know about that? I ain't gonna tell him. Other people not gonna tell him. Now, I'm the lay preacher in the church. That's why I telling you the truth so glad. Ain't no good to hide it, you see?

John Newman, born on March 31, 1917, Clarence Town, Long Island

Mr. Newman's appearance belied his seventy-four years. He continues to be active and involved as a taxi driver and postman. My tape recorder did not work when I went to his home for the interview. He promised to visit me the next day to re-record. When he arrived at Mr. Carroll's Guest House in Deadman's Cay, I remarked that I didn't think he'd really travel the distance so early in the morning. He answered that if he made a promise he kept it, no matter what. Mr. Newman's father died when he was eight years old. I found his description of his and his brother's efforts to survive quite poignant.

My daddy died when I was eight years old. I had five brothers and two sisters. There's only me and the brother who is sick now left. We were the two smallest. The rest was away. So we had to work hard to take care of ourselves. When my daddy died, he had a couple of sheep. That wasn't much to feed us. We go to school. The old lady had us take off and work. You go and cut sisal in the evening. Come back in the morning and cut it open. Then come back in the evening and carry it to the sea and wash it. Continue with that. Well, we had some sheep and goats. We had to go to school every day. We really had it tough, 'cause sometime we didn't have our lunch to take to school. The old lady was lucky enough; she always had food for us to eat when we got back. It was very tough for us. It was just me and my brother and one sister there.

But several years later, my older brothers got to find out how things were so tough here. The brothers were living in the United States. They used to help take care of us. Sisal went down, that's what happened. You couldn't get money to buy clothes and shoes. Sisal was the only way you could make money. So our brothers had to take care of us through that until we was able to take care of ourselves.

When I was sixteen years old, I started farming. I was the last one and I was softer than my brother, so he used to do all the heaviest work and let me do the lighter. We went on like that until we could go for ourselves.

Alfred Nathaniel Love, born on January 9, 1919, Nassau, New Providence

For years I have seen Mr. Love and his friends sitting next to the wall of the cemetery playing checkers. When he was approached about the possibility of being interviewed, he instantly agreed. At the designated time, he and a friend arrived at Dillet's Guest House immaculately dressed and eager to tell his stories. It was especially interesting to hear how his family's value of honesty and the after-school jobs held by his brother and himself carried them through the Depression. Mr. Love is a trim, attractive man with a ready smile. He shared his knowledge of traditional practices and his experiences growing up in the city of Nassau, the capital of the Bahamas.

Nassau is located on the island of New Providence. Although this island is only twenty-one miles long and seven miles wide, it has the largest population in the Bahamas, more than 172,000 residents.

I born right in Nassau in Nassau Street. My parents had eight children, but the eldest one died at about sixteen months. But Momma have seven children living today, five girls and two boys. I was the fourth. Like all other children, when I growing up, we played different games, such as shooting marbles, hide and seek, and ring plays. I went to dances.

One of the interesting parts of life, I would say, as a small boy, we more or less had to get out and hustle to make ends meet. [There was] a farmer who used to raise vegetables named Mr. McCartney. He used to hire boys to water his vegetable gardens. Me and my brother was living very near. So every day we used to be hired to water. What he did was, he dug two trenches 'til he hit water. So the water spring. Then they had what you call hand pumps. And you take a bucket. That's how we got the water. We use what you call watering pots—something like a bucket with a nozzle put into it. It has a head with fine holes. We made a little money; they used to call it sixpence in those days. It was pounds, shillings and pence and we used to make sixpence watering from three o'clock until around six or seven. It coulda buy lots of things in those days.

When we got our sixpence in the evening, we carry it and give it to Momma. She put it up for us and when Easter come, she buy clothes and things for us. In those days, everything was cheap. The cost of living wasn't high. Wages was small. What you could have buy in those days for what was ten dollars then would probably cost one hundred dollars now. So we did well, because you find that married men at that time only made a shilling a day. And we, as boys, from three o'clock to seven, we made half what they made for the whole day. Yet they have to pay rent, buy food for the family and take care of their children. But the amount of fish, what you could get for a sixpence, today you paying maybe fifteen dollars for it. Blue overalls with the straps on it—in those days it was only four shillings, which was about a dollar.

What I really consider the hardest time was up until the forties. It was the Depression until then. I was a boy when we used to farm. We farm and sell farm produce to help. They used to take the corn blade [leaves] and sell them to the coachmen. There were horse and carriage then. The horses ate it. We got a penny a bundle. That's less than two cents now. When the blade was over, me and my brother—for us to have money to buy candy—we used to go and cut some grass called guinea grass. Bundle them up and we sell 'em.

I decided I'd go into carpentry. In school we used to do a certain amount of carpentry. Therefore, I had a good start. I did a small amount of buildings.

In those days there was very little work for women. My mother used to be a laundress and took in laundry. Like when the British Colonial Hotel burned down in March of 1921, foreigners came in from Jamaica and whatnot, to build it back. They used to bring their laundry for her to do and she would get money like that. After the hotel opened again, she used to be a cleaner in the hotel.

My father was a house painter. But in the days when you hear me tell you about painting, you coulda count the stone houses that were built in one year, in the whole of New Providence, on one hand. So painters used to only paint in the winter season. They would paint the outside and the inside of the stone houses. I know. My daddy was considered one of the best painters in the island. He could have mixed any colour you wanted. Not like how today, you go look at a chart and they mix it for you. You had to mix your own paint in those days. Very few painters could do it and he was very good at that. But it wasn't no work as such. He was employed about six months of the year. He farmed the rest of the year. He was a land lover like myself. So that's how we survived.

Those were the days when you had to be honest. Pay your bills and if you be a honest man, you got credit. Then the storekeeper would trust you during the time when you wasn't making money. My mother used to only work after the hotel was built. Then she got a job in the hotel. In those days, the tourists used to only come in here about three months a year. So after the winter months, she don't have any work. But she was very honest and she taught us that. And if you be honest, you will make it through life. There was a white merchant on Bay Street named Mr. William Sands. She could have gone to him from the day the hotel closed until the day that it opened again and he would trust her. Sometime she would go in for one item and he would say, "Mrs. Love, get some nice hats and some nice cloth." He would show her the whole shop. She would say, "But I don't have no money, Mr. Sands." He'd say, "That's all right. I know when the hotel opens, you gonna pay." He would credit her until the hotel opened. My daddy, he was the same way. Honest. And he would get credit from the grocery man. So it meant that through being honest, without money, he coulda keep us going.

That was how we made it in those days. The economy wasn't nowhere. Our money wasn't on par with American money. In those days you get an American dollar, you rich. Today, not bragging about it, each one of us seven children, wherever we work right to today, people trust us. My brother take care of millionaires' houses, painting in Lyford Cay. They go away and leave their keys in his care. Everybody trust the Loves.

Harcourt Stevens, born on August 19, 1919, Cove, Cat Island

When I arrived, Mr. Stevens' wife and grandchildren were sitting on a large piece of cloth on the ground, sorting corn. Only once during the hours he and I talked did she interrupt. That occurred when she felt he was telling me more than I wanted to know. I can still hear Mr. Stevens' laughter. He continued unabashed and supplied me with history, politi-

*cal commentary and folklore
that was priceless.*

*Of the islands I visited, Cat
Island is the most extraordinary in respect to natural
beauty, with its peninsulas,
large cliffs and hills. Comer
Hill, also called Mount Alvernia, is located here. At 210
feet, it is the highest point in
the Bahamas. Mr. Stevens'
settlement of about 100 people
is located in the middle of Cat
Island. The island is forty-five
miles in length and ranges
from one to four miles in
width.*

Me and my parents were born right here on Cat Island. They was farmers.
Yeah. Some of the fellows went out sponge fishing. There were certain
times when you could get some. The men knew where to go and find a few.
They were not really sponges because they don't have a sponge garden
here.

When I was little, things were very tough. We had no roads. The road—
what was here—was only about four feet wide. We didn't have no cars, no
trucks. We used to use horses. A horse could get anyplace. Some people
used to walk the sea rock to get to the next town. And what happened from
there, from time to time, the government would try to get roads. Beat rock
with a hammer and your hand, that's what we used to do. Sit down in the
road. Beat the rocks with hammer. Sometimes, you mash your hand and
you get blood from it. We didn't have no steam roller. Nassau had light
bulbs burning in the street lamps. They never come on with that here until
after the twenties. Then they start getting electricity, power here.

We in this island here, in 1933, people were so hungry that they start to
use the cook oil to boil the papaw [papaya]. Boil it green and try to use it.
The things that grow on the bark. They boil it and had it to eat. There was

a certain kind of drought. You hear them talking about seven years plentiful and seven years famine? Well, that's how it was. It come to the time
that there wasn't no seasons. And people run out of crops. Some people,
they have to live off cocoa plums and sea grapes. Wasn't much to live on.

There wasn't that much animals to eat at that time. After we get out
from there, we had plenty potatoes and plenty cassava. Now to make a
tale, I could tell you most things. If I go to tell you, I'll cry. Things were so
tough. I myself worked for one shilling a day. We make all this road. That's
what the government pay. And after that, we had a chance to plant some
sisal. Then I got a dollar a day cutting bush. We had to take the cutlass and
cut the bush and lay them down on the ground.

And when I look, I see I been all around them places today and fellows
come behind me and never had a boss man and could afford to build a
castle. I been all about when I was under Contract and this house all I
coulda build. That's true, true, true.

Let me tell you the joke. In the twenties, we had one plane come
around. First time I ever gone see a plane. The plane ain't built like the
planes are built nowadays. They zing on two wings and the people underneath. And this thing coming up, *wong, wong, wong, wong.* We was out in
the sea washing a horse the first time we hear something like that. I had
on nothing but just a robin [underpants]. It wasn't no go and buy in the
shop. I run back until it split. That's the first time I ever see something like
that [the plane] in my life. You see that thing coming, *wong, wong, wong,
wong.* Then, the horse what was in the sea, washing his skin, come in the
house. We gone and went right under the bed. Now, we won't come from
underneath the bed. The horse run behind me. The horse couldn't catch
us. This house was only just one bedroom. It was small. But we ain't had
time to shut the door. The horse come inside and we gone under the bed
and we won't come out and the horse standing up there in the house. The
horse start trembling, he scared so.

I always tell people that, how I was scared. So after I get used to it, that
was before the Contract, one day I see it flying overhead and I say, "I
wonder if one day I'll be traveling in that!" And I did. I did that! I traveling
to the States. When I first gone up, I almost pulled down the man sitting
next to me. I know right there lately, since I come from the States, Mr.
Barber take me and carry me across to Eleuthera. What he did, he
bounced the plane right up and then he turn it loose. I almost grabbed the
roof down. I tell that plane to stop!

Mildred Bethel Campbell, born March 22, 1920, Nassau, New Providence

Mrs. Campbell is an attractive lady who is well-spoken and thoughtful. I was most impressed with her creative abilities and her deep commitment to others. In addition to her involvement with her children, grandchildren, church, volunteer work and sewing, she finds time to write delightful poetry. Although her adult life has been difficult, Mrs. Campbell has retained her religious faith and her cheerful disposition.

Reuben Bethel, Mrs. Campbell's father, was a very successful tailor. He was one of the few blacks who had a shop located on Market Street in downtown Nassau during the early part of the century. Her brother Marcus later became a member of the House of Assembly and a leading undertaker.

To start off with, my husband wasn't a provider. This is why my children caught so much hell. I had to fight for them. If my husband had been a provider, we wouldn't have gone through all that, the children not having this or that, you know? So I had to be the man and the woman in my house. There was very little I could do with seven children, so this is why my children had it so hard. I caught eternal hell. I was always going to sleep crying, 'cause I wasn't used to it.

My father took care of us when I was growing up. We were really a middle-class family when I was growing up. Because, in those days, you didn't have to be really rich to be middle class. But my dad was okay, on top of the hill. Me, Sybil, Carl, Neville, Marcus—we never wanted for anything. He took good care of us. And then when I got married, the whole world turned. There I was at the bottom [laughter].

The good thing about me was, I didn't believe in asking my family for anything. I said, "I put myself in this situation, so I gotta get out. I'm not going to ask my family for nothing. I'm just going to battle with it." I would not ask Marcus; I would not ask for anything. In fact, Marcus told me that I made my bed hard, so I had to lie on it. When Marcus told me that, I knew exactly when and where I was staying. Mom used to always encourage me, though. She said, "Millie, see all those children you are struggling with, one of these days they're going to take care of you."

And here it is today, I don't have to worry about anything; my kids take care of me. Sometimes I'm scared to tell them what I want because I know they'll try to get it for me. I've had my car now for about eleven years and it's dropping to pieces [laughter]. I need a car, but I told my friend the other day, I said, "You know something? I only need a car to carry you all around. 'Cause I always carry all of you around [laughter]. I asked the Lord to send me one car this year." And she said, "You know something? You're going to get that car soon." I don't ask my children. I don't know, I feel like if they want to give me something, they'll give it to me. I wouldn't go to my children like one woman I know. She told me, "Who, they owe me that." I tell her, "Those kids don't owe you nothing. They're not responsible for being here. I don't ask my kids for anything. They will give me whatever they want to give." They give me money and I put it in the bank. So okay, I told them, you know what I'm going to do to get my car? I'm going to start saving up my money. As soon as I get two thousand dollars, I'll put it into fixed accounts. When I get another two thousand dollars, I'll do the same. And you know something? The Lord going to help me get that money. If my children know I want a car, they will help me now. For my birthday and Christmas, I'll tell them that I have a project and want money. Just give me money [laughter]. If they give me money, I'll put it in the bank and I'll soon have enough to buy a car. I don't believe in asking, asking. I never did it.

A lot of people don't mind going to people and telling them what they don't have. I couldn't do that. But with all my problems with my kids, I never did that.

One time Val and those went over to Aunt Olga and Val said, "Mommy, we didn't have anything to eat that day and you were over here wondering what you was going to cook for us." So she went over to Aunt Olga and Aunt Olga had this peas and rice, and fried Jacks [fish] and fried plantain. She said, "Mommy, I was so hungry and I wanted some of Aunt Olga's dinner so bad. And you know, when Aunt Olga asked me if I wanted some dinner, I told her no thank you." Val came back home and said that she wanted some of the dinner. Aunt Olga came over here and did she fuss at me! Why did Val tell her no thank you when she knew Val wanted that? I told my kids, I said, "Now look, we don't have, so we don't have. Let's stay right here until we can have. But don't go around people's place looking at what they have and wanting it." They knew I never begged for anything. I brought up the kids not to ever ask for anything. They could be dropping down dead and they'll tell you, "No thank you."

So here it is now, they're all grown and they're working. They have no one to thank. They don't have to go to anyone and say, "Well, you brought me up or you helped me when I didn't have anything." I didn't want my children to be in that situation. Marcus and Carl's children had, but my children didn't have. I used to go to bed at night crying; wake up in the morning crying. But I wouldn't go to my family. Especially after Marcus said I made my bed. He was one brother I wouldn't ask for anything. If I really got in a tight scoop, I would ask Neville [her youngest brother] for four shillings [96 cents U.S.].

My husband couldn't care less whether the children—I don't know, I must have married a Gypsy. You know how Gypsies live? I just call my husband a Gypsy. They can live in any situation and just don't care. He was a nice person and all that, but he didn't believe in taking care of the children. And to top it all off, he was an alcoholic. His father was a white man from Scotland. His father had a family, left them in Belize, and came here with the maid, which was an Indian, my husband's mother. His father left his wife with eight white children. Came here to live with this maid. So when he came here, he worked for the government for a couple of years and when that fell through, he just rented houses and drug up [raised] these children. He died and the Indian mother kept, like, a little petty shop. And she just drug up these children. So my husband didn't have any parental guidance. He didn't know how to take care of anybody else's children. When I got married to him he was working at the hotel, waitering and driving the bus. But after we got married, Arlington Granger took him down to the Water Works Department and taught him how to be a plumber. So then he was a plumber and he worked for the government until his death. Every week, that man had a paycheck on Friday. I didn't see him. He was a man that went in the bar with a lot of friends, drinking and carousing, having a good time. Kids right home here hungry.

You know what I realized, just last week? I was telling my kids, "You know what I just realized about Kermie and Vincie? The teacher would always say that they were not dumb children. But they're so slow." The teacher would always ask me why the kids were so slow. When everyone else was through with their work, these kids were just coming up with their work and it's too late. So they never had a chance to excel in school. I was telling someone just last week and they said, "Mrs. Campbell, it took you fifty years to realize that?" It took me fifty years to realize that maybe my kids were hungry—[that's] why they couldn't study. They were hungry! Mornings when I send them to school, if I didn't have lunch, I would tell them to stop at Momma's and get lunch. Now the kids might have had this attitude just like me. "We're not going to Mom Bethel for our lunch. We'll just go to school without lunch."

You know when I thought about that? Just last week. And all these years gone by and I just realized, you know something, really, why they didn't learn in school—because those kids were hungry half the time. Those kids would have been smart in school, because they are smart and intelligent. They would have been high-school graduates if they had had the opportunity—not the opportunity, the food. They had what it took them to grow. The basic things in life, my mommy saw that my children had. It wasn't that bad that they got malnutrition. Momma wouldn't have let that happen. They had enough food and I even took care of my sister's little boy, Baldwin. Nobody else in the family didn't want him. And I had this small little house, struggling with my kids. My family is a family that I never understood and this is why I think I'm a loner now. 'Cause someone said to me the other day, "Mrs. Campbell, you Marcus' sister? Regardless of who you married and how worthless they were, you were still his sister. Why didn't they come to your help?" My daddy put my sister out because she was having a baby. My daddy would have killed her if she didn't move out. He was so mad with her! You see, Sybil was a smart, intelligent girl. And my daddy loved Sybil so much. He really loved Sybil now. Sybil was lighter; I was dark. He used to call me his little black beauty [laughter]. I guess I grew up with that, so it didn't bother me. But my daddy treated me well. Anything he gave Sybil, he would give to me.

The Lord is a wonderful Lord. He gives justice where justice is due. Like I tell you, it's always nice to be nice to people. You don't know. I've seen too many people what had [who used to have], who don't have [now] and those that didn't have, have. I've seen so many. And now you know that I'm over that and that's water under the bridge. You know what I think? Everybody keeps saying, "Millie, this was what had to be. For you to marry this man and you go through this situation." I say, "You know, maybe it's true, because maybe I'd have been a black, proud woman." I would have been up on top of the hill. You know what I mean? That's really true, you know [laughter]. But it's made me a better woman, a stronger woman—even spiritually. I would have been a black fool [laughter]. And I could thank God for the problems He gave me when I could have stand them. I thank God for my problems, you know. I say, "Lord, you must know why." I must not say I should not have done this or I should not have done that. Because God, He must know why. It made me a better person. I can face any situation now, I think. I can go on Government Hill to tea and lay off and be Millie. One of my friends came down and said, "Oh, you got to change now. You can't be just plain old Millie now." I said, "Let me tell you something right now. I was always little plain Millie. And I will continue to be little plain Millie." No changing for me. You don't know what it would take to change me. I've been through too much.

I go on Government Hill every first Monday in the month for the tea of the Queen Mary Needlework Guild. You go up there and you have tea. They have all the nice silver with the Queen's initials on it. Aunt Olga is the one who took me up there first. Because I used to sew for Aunt Olga. I used to sew all of Aunt Olga's work to go up there. So she said, "Now look, Millie, you're doing all of my work, so go up here with me." So I went and I've been up there twenty-five years. They wanted me to be president the other day, but I told them that I didn't think I wanted the responsibility. It's a guild that was formed by the expatriates. You had all these British people in government, so the wives needed something to do. Naturally they formed this needlework guild. The Queen's mother is our patron. She sends us invitations to come to England every year, anybody who could afford it. We have two seats every year. So it was formed then for the expatriates' wives to have something to do. During that time they had the Royal Air Forces [R.A.F.] here. They were training to go to war and all that stuff. Then the guild started sewing things for the R.A.F., helping to make them feel at home. We would sew and make things and send them to England. We would sew and knit and send them back to the Queen Mother in England and she would give them to the poor people in England. They were all under the same umbrella, I would call it.

But when all the expatriates went back, it was like Aunt Olga, Mrs. Elder, Mrs. Adderley, Mrs. Toots, Mrs. Sweetings. There were a lot of that type of people. After the expatriates left, they were trying to fill the vacancies in the guild with Bahamians. I wouldn't say black people, because white people came in, too. We sent our work back to England up until four or five years ago. Why we stopped was because it was difficult getting boxes and stuff back to England. So then the Queen Mother's secretary wrote. She always communicated with us, not the Queen Mother. She wrote and said that since it was difficult getting the work back to her, just make a contribution. So what we do now, we just send the money. We sew now for the Bahamian people. Every year we give things to some charitable organization. We go down to the Salvation Army. They have a senior citizens' center and we donate hundreds of garments. I'm one of the cutters. I don't sew. We get our monies to buy these materials from donations from the members. Like, I will cut and take my work back up there, what I cut. I have ten people under me—associates. I'm a vice president. The associates take the work and sew it and bring it back the following month. When they bring in a piece, they take out a piece.

To top it all off, I went to Freeport and worked for the Queen Mary's Guild. I went there to take care of my grandchildren after my daughter, Dee, died. I knew what it was not to have. I felt like I would help. I didn't want them to go through that situation that my kids went through. Now they are okay.

Enid Sawyer, born on December 24, 1920, Knowles, Cat Island

> *Mrs. Sawyer is an unusual woman who has been a skillful parent and nurse. She has a lively sense of humor and projects contentment and serenity. Mrs. Sawyer has spent most of her adult life in Nassau. Her description of how she and her husband of fifty years met shows the value of Bahamian bird peppers in promoting romance!*
>
> *Knowles, where she was born, is located in central Cat Island and is the site of the only elementary school for children living in the middle region of the island.*

I grew up at Knowles, Cat Island. I was ten years old when my mother died. She had a ruptured appendix. In those days, there were no planes to bring you to Nassau to hospital. She was about thirty-one years old. There were no doctors or nurses on Cat Island. Nobody knew what was wrong, but they couldn't do anything anyway. It had ruptured. Now I know what it was, because she was vomiting all this green stuff. Everybody wondered what happened. She didn't last very long. She died in a couple of days.

The others were behind me, so I was like a surrogate mother. My brother, Felix, was six months. I raised my mother's five children, two boys and three girls. My father was in Nassau, so we lived with our grandparents. They were very good to us. My grandfather was a farmer. My grandmother used to help in the farm, too. They had a lot of land in Knowles and they used to have people come and help them in the farm. My grandfather had a couple of farms. He used to raise corn, peas, potatoes and all kinds of vegetables. Then he had a farm on the white land, where he raised the other kind of corn, cow peas and things like that. He had horses. They ate corn and fodder. Fodder is what you get when you cut down the cornstalk. Before I came along, they used to have cows. We had sheep and goats. After a while, we got rid of all the horses. Down to one; its name was Jill. He was the one who did most of the work on the farm. The boys used to take the goats and sheep out in the morning and bring them back at night to the pen in the back of the yard.

My aunt kinda introduced me to nursing and I decided I wanted to be a nurse. She used to go and come to Nassau and she told me about the nurses. At the age of eighteen, I came to Nassau. I lived with one of my aunts, Mrs. Johnson. Then I went to the hospital. I did general nursing and then I went into the maternity. I did the whole of maternity. The matron wanted me to go back to Cat Island because they were short of nurses on the Out Islands. But I told her I couldn't do that. I couldn't go back to the Out Islands. I told her I couldn't see myself going back at that time, because I had no means of support there. I didn't see myself making a living there. They didn't want to pay me a salary. They wanted me to go there and work and let the people pay me. The people didn't have any money. They would have given me some farm produce and things like that. So I didn't go. I left the hospital at that time. I stayed out of nursing for a while.

I got married while I was out of nursing. I met my husband, Herman, when I went to visit my cousins on Cat Cay. They were working down there. I saw this young man. I knew Gladys, his sister-in-law. I said, "Who's the young man in the car?" She said, "That's my husband's younger brother, Herman." They used to come into the restaurant to have lunch, but he never came in. He used to send to tell me hello. So, one day, I didn't even know he was around. I was doing some conch salad, mashing the red pepper to put in the conch salad. And you know how the little bird pepper squirts up? It went in my eye. When I shout out, Herman was there. I didn't even know he was there. He came and got the water and washed my eye and face. He went to the store, because he was the storekeeper, got some witch hazel lotion, and sent it back for me. That's when we became friends [laughter]. I only stayed there about three weeks. It was just a vacation. Then we corresponded, and after he came back to Nassau, we kept on seeing each other. That's how the relationship grew.

I was married for five years and didn't have any children. So I decided I'd go back and finish nursing, 'cause I wasn't finished. I wrote the matron and she accepted me to come back. Within a year, I got pregnant [laughter]. I was pregnant in the first five years, but I didn't save [she had miscarriages]. Finally it was almost time to deliver my first baby. The matron said, "Now go and have your baby and come back and finish your nursing." That's what I intended to do. But the problem was, who's going to take care of the baby? I kept staying home and in four months, I was pregnant again [laughter]. So now you know I didn't go back. Now I had two babies. That made it very difficult. So I continued to stay home. I stayed with them until they were big enough to leave them with somebody. Then I start nursing again. I was nursing ever since. I had three more children, but they didn't stop me from nursing [laughter]. I worked right up to the time I had them and I just stayed out long enough until I was strong enough to work.

We've been married fifty years come November second [laughter]. Raising my children and working was rough going. You have to look for somebody to look after them. I picked doing nights. I did the eight-to-twelve shift. That was more convenient for me. In the daytime I was at home with them. I sleep when I could [laughter]! It was kinda difficult. But I made it. I used to hire people to help out with the housework. Altogether, I had seven little boys. At that time we was washing in a big tin tub. You hang out your clothes, all these little underpants [laughter]. The little clothes are so much harder to get clean than the big ones. So I used to have to hire someone to come in and help me out. Herman used to help before he went to work in the morning, too. Like Sunday mornings, he would help get them ready for church, get breakfast and things like that. We used to live in East Street, right next to Our Lady's Catholic Church, so it was convenient [laughter].

Herman Sawyer, born on February 12, 1921,
Dixon Hill Lighthouse at San Salvador

> *Mr. Sawyer is a warm, friendly man. His intelligence and verbal abilities shine through in spite of the fact that he says getting an education while traveling from one lighthouse to another every two years was virtually*

impossible. I was anxious to interview him because he had grown up at various lighthouse stations. His perceptions of lighthouse procedures is fascinating.

The Dixon Hill lighthouse, where he was born, stands seventy-two feet from ground level and about one hundred and sixty feet from water level. This lighthouse is one of the few still operated manually [it uses hand-operated lights].

San Salvador was, until the late twenties, known as Watling's Island. The island is twelve miles long and about six miles wide. It is presently named as the site where Columbus first landed in the New World.

My father, Mervin, was a light keeper. I was born at five o'clock in the evening. Around that time, they go to put on the lights, which lit up the whole of San Salvador. So I always tell people I was born on the light [laughter]. I stayed there, they told me, for six weeks. I start traveling from there. From there we went down to Castle Island in Acklins. Then Momma, after a year and ten months, came to Nassau. She gave birth to my last sister, Agatha. The baby only lived about three months. My mother died when I was twenty-two months. She died three days after she had my last sister. We said she died in childbirth. When my mother had babies at the lighthouses, we had those old women we used to call the grannies. So, in my day, my granny brought me [laughter].

My mother had six children. There was Fred, Ellen, Eric, Muriel, Herman—which am I—and Agatha, the baby. My sister, Ellen, was the oldest sister, so I looked up to her. After Mother died, Poppa used to have a woman come in to take care of things.

My father usually stayed at a lighthouse station for two years. But sometimes, you're moved within that two years. Then you go to another station. You may only spend six weeks, so it was hard to go to school. When we went to Inagua, Fred, Eric and those that were old enough went to school. After that, we went down to the Berry Islands, which was Stirrup Cay. It was school over to the main land at Bullet's Harbour. We were able to go there for a period. You had to take a boat to go. Then we went back to San Salvador when I was twelve. We left when I was fourteen. There were eleven light stations. Every two years, my father transfer from one to the other. Every two years, we had three to four months' break in Nassau. Then we would go to the next station. Whatever we picked up in the way of education was whatever the assistant keeper or the older brother knew and mother wit [common sense]. [Laughter.]

People don't understand that the Colonial Governor was the governor that was the head of state on the land and the Imperial Governor [Imperial Lighthouse Service] took care of marine matters. He was the commander in chief of marine matters. Both were appointed by the Queen. So the two of them were co-equal. You applied for a job as lighthouse keeper just like you applied to be a teacher. Then you would be elected by the Board of Trade, which was part of the Imperial Government. He send you out as a lighthouse keeper. The colonial government sent people out as commissioners, teachers, policemen or telephone operators. Every island had a little telegraph station. That's the way it went.

Sometimes, like the two years I was in San Salvador, I went to school. The other children thought I was special because my father was a lighthouse keeper [laughter]. They looked at me as Herman, Mr. Sawyer's son. The lightkeeper and the commissioner were more or less elevated by the other people on an island. I was at Bird Rock in Crooked Island, Castle Island at Acklins. Acklins is two miles away from Crooked Island. There was a lighthouse on Acklins. About four to five miles from there was Bird Rock, Crooked Island. I lived on the lighthouse at Bird Rock from the time I was five to [the time I was] eight. Landrail Point was the first settlement about two miles away.

Poppa always had a woman come in to take care of us. One time he had his sister come, but they couldn't get along. He sent her away. He haven't talk to her from then [laughter]. He used to call her "the hellcat." Then we had a woman called Mrs. Sargent. She used to take care of us in Inagua. When we went to Bird Rock, he had her come in periodically from Inagua. Poppa say wherever he be, he want his children to be. He want to bring us up together. If Momma had lived, we all would have been able to come to Nassau and have a good education like the majority of the people. But we just had to catch it. Good thing we had mothers' wit [laughter].

We were under the Imperial Government. If anybody get real sick, we had what you call signal flags. We hoist flags. Any ship traveling, if they have a doctor, they must stop. That was the system. Only two lighthouses have keepers now. All of them are run under the Bahamas government. They altogether different. We were run under Britain. All those stations have gone right down to nothing. When we were at the light stations, we had to keep those stations like palaces. You had a tall tower in the center and the principal keeper's house and the assistant keeper's house. You had a place that you call the storeroom, where they send you up your provisions and your groceries. We always had that stocked. Every month the principal keeper would go and he would issue the assistant keeper his monthly allowance. Everybody was equal in the amount of provisions received. The principal keeper may get a couple of shillings more [laughter]. And then your wife, give her a certain amount of groceries. By the time the children become fourteen or sixteen, they have to leave anyhow, because they didn't have too many children at a station at a time. Say you a keeper and you just start having children every two years. By the time the oldest one become fourteen, the more fortunate people will send their children into Nassau. What caused me to be on the station for as long as I stayed, was because of Momma's death. Most of those keepers used to send their wives into Nassau. They'd be hermits on those islands [laughter].

We came down here because Poppa got married to my second mother, Beedee Dean. When Poppa got married to Beedee, that was the wife and we were the stepchildren. We didn't have such a pleasant life, but it was bearable. She didn't have any children herself. You know that feeling. "I taking care of Aggie's children; I don't have none."

When I left the lighthouse at sixteen, I came to Nassau and went to the water and sewer department, where I took up the trade of plumbing. I went there as an apprentice. After about three years, you become a plumber. It take three years being an apprentice to become a plumber. But I didn't stay. I pull out from there and I went on my own.

After I left there, I went to Cat Cay and spent about a year and a half in storekeeping. Eric, my older brother, was a big game fisher. That's where Cat Cay comes in. We was in Gun Cay before Cat Cay started this tourist business. They had a manager there, which was a woman. So Fred and Eric, we had a boat and we had to go to Bimini just to get telegrams and food and stuff, because the boat would only come from Miami once in a while. So when they came and start construction and start building Cat Cay, Eric and Fred were key. They were two of the first people to work at Cat Cay. When the big game fishing start, Eric was the head of that. Fred was the second manager. When he came back to Nassau, he was an engineer. He took care of all the mailboats and everything.

Since my older brother was in charge of the island, I went as his assistant. That was a private island just like a private home and we were responsible for everything. The owner had everything come in there. He had the stores, the little wine cellars. It was a fishing haven, Cat Cay. It was a private place and tourists came for big game fishing. They started in '32 or '33. Poppa Weiss was the American who owned the island. At that time he was fairly young.

When I came back from Cat Cay, I went back into plumbing. My father had sent me away because he didn't like the crowd I was keeping. He didn't want me to be a bad boy [laughter]. So he had sent me along to live with Granville Rogers. That's where I become a Rogers by people believing [laughter]. They [the Rogers] were my guardians. I stayed with them from [age] sixteen until I got married at twenty-two. If we see November 2, we'll have been married for fifty years. I'm looking for gold [laughter].

After I start working to Standard Plumbing, the most outstanding plumbing firm in the Bahamas, I became the traveling plumber to all the islands. I worked for them for twenty-one years. Then I went on my own. Even during the time I was working with them, I started working on my own, subcontracting from them. I subcontracted from them for about four or five years. But now I'm retired because I couldn't do the work no more [laughter]. For a while I had assistants. But things went to such a stage, to get people working for you, you had to be a harsh boss. I turned out quite a few young plumbers. If I have something to do, when I tell them to do that, they want to tell me what to do. They make a mistake, I still have to go over it.

I met my wife, Enid, on Cat Cay [laughter]. In Cat Cay you used to have people come down to work. So she just came down as a vacation. At first sight we fell in love. She left and came back to Nassau. She was in the hospital doing nursing. We knew I had to come back in Nassau. So after

I came in Nassau, things were very slow. Money wasn't making. So we didn't get married until 1943. Then we said, "It's time to do the thing [laughter]."

Lawrence Zachariah Smith, born on May 24, 1924,
Kemp's Bay, Andros

> *Mr. Smith is employed as a caretaker of one of the vacation homes in the village of Adelaide. His employer asked him to talk to me and he readily agreed. We sat on the beach at sundown and Mr. Smith described his very difficult life. He was separated from his family and the island where he was born when he was five years old. Contrary to the stories that Mr. Smith told concerning his behavior, he seemed to be a gentle man.*
>
> *Adelaide is a small settlement on the southwest bay of New Providence. The village is sixteen miles from Nassau. In 1831, Governor James Carmichael Smith created Adelaide as a home for about 150 Africans who had been liberated from a Portuguese slave ship. The original thatched huts have disappeared. Many of the villagers' homes now have electricity and telephones. Some Nassauvians have second homes on Adelaide beachfront property, where they escape to tranquil seas and glorious sunsets.*

I been living here in the village of Adelaide from when I was five years old. My mother bring me here and give me to my cousin. 'Cause I was so bad when I was growing up, you see? So Ma take me away from Andros after my daddy die in 1929. They say I almost drown myself after I hear my daddy drown. So I going swimming in the sea and my mother done come, and got one of my uncle's sons done catch me from drowning. After that, my uncle, Uncle Harvey McKinney, that's my Ma's brother, bring me over here. Mommy bring me here to Adelaide and give me to Miss George and she what raise me.

I get in plenty trouble growing up. I get in trouble after they keep teasing me and bothering me. Well, I used to like fight. I used to fight plenty. Might as well tell you the truth.

Rita Edwards Wood, born on October 23, 1927,
Nassau, New Providence

> *Rita Wood is a bright, articulate woman with a wonderful sense of humor. Even though Rita's parents were Jamaican, she has spent most of*

*her life in Nassau. The
cause of her estrangement
from her father provides insight about how strictly
young people's behavior was
circumscribed by some parents. Although she never
took psychology courses, she
has a great understanding of
other people. I tried, but
was unable, to determine
when and how she devel-
oped her exceptionally positive self image.*

I remember one day before I went to Jamaica, I had a sister who was
unruly. And she said, "Let's go for a ride." We went for a ride on the bicycle.
I was on the handle bar and my twin brother was on the fender. You know,
I have a twin brother and we did everything together. We're still the best
of friends to this day. He doesn't live in Nassau, though. I had my twin
brother and my brother had me. We were about eight or nine. The three
of us on one lady's bicycle. She [her sister] took us up Market Street hill.
We had to cross streets to get up the hill. And we came down Blue Hill
Road. We were making about thirty miles an hour. Dr. Bethel's mother saw
us and called to my mother, "Lillian, Lillian, there are your children."

Mother was looking for us. She saw us coming down Blue Hill Road at
thirty miles an hour. We took the corner by St. Andrew's Church. The skin
on my hand scraped off. When we got home, I always remember, we had
salmon fritters for supper. No supper! We were put in the tub and she saw
this black stuff. She thought it was dirt and I dare not say ouch. She
scrubbed it. She liked to spank. She would beat me and I would cry. She
would beat my sister and my sister would not cry. And then I would get
another beating because I wouldn't stop crying and my sister would get
another beating because she wouldn't cry [laughter].

When I was growing up, we left and went to school in Jamaica. I was
in Jamaica from the time I was ten to [the time I was] seventeen. Our
mother went with us. In Jamaica, my brother and I liked to go to scary
movies. And before we got home, we knew it was time to jump off the tram,

the electric car, because we wanted to go in the house while the lights from the tram were still on [laughter]. I was a tomboy. Football, cricket, marbles, pushing car tires. I always wanted to be like my brother.

When I came back to Nassau from Jamaica, I still went to an evening school to catch up with the people here in Nassau. During the war years [World War II], things were difficult, so I had to leave school before I finished. And then, I went to work with Pearl Cox. She had a dress shop.

After that I went and worked with the Armoury Company, business machines. I did everything because I grew with the business. I could tell you the model and capacity of any machine you wanted to buy. I went to work for them because I had a friend who was leaving to go to England to become a nurse. I wrote and applied for the job. I enjoyed the people I worked with. And whenever new staff came in, young people, teenagers, I enjoyed them. I trained each and every one of them. Once when I was on vacation, I had some new staff that came in and the older staff must have told them about me; they said, "Well, we won't be staying." In the end, I became administrative supervisor and accountant. So the boss said to me one day, "You're not doing a good job of—" I said, "Don't even try to tell me what I am not doing." As far as I was concerned, I was always a supervisor. So I said, "Don't even think about it." This man was from the States because by then, NCR [National Cash Register] took over. He was a man from Puerto Rico. I stayed with them until I went to Washington, D.C.

When I was leaving they gave me a nice, big card of the Butlin Building. Butlin Building is a building you build out of aluminum, steel. You have to put lots of nuts and bolts in. So they took out this nut and bolt from the top of this and the thing collapsed. But it was all signed by every staff member. They even sent it to Freeport for the staff there to sign. They all said their own thing and sent it back. And when they gave me the card, it could say, "Well, at last the nut is leaving," 'cause they called me every name in the book. Or, it could say, "The business will collapse when the nut leaves." They said, "Oh, Mother, you hit it on the head." They had a party for me and everything. Gave me a gift.

And then, after I went to Washington, I came back after several months. We had a man there who stammered. He said, "Ms. . . . Ms. . . . Ms. . . . They replaced you with three people." And none of those people stayed. They collapsed in the end. I think just some copying people are doing the repairs on the computer. They wanted everything for nothing.

I met my husband several years before we got married. Setella Dillet and I were walking up George Street one day and she introduced me. But we never became friends. He said that his name was Reginald L. Wood. I asked him what the L was for. He said Longfellow and I believed him [laughter]. I still call my son Longfellow.

I had a terrible experience with Dada [her father]. He was fussy and he was also a strange man. He spoiled everything when he beat me that time, and after that I had nothing to do with him. That was when I was twenty-four years old. Didn't even have a boyfriend yet. I met Reggie before, but we were not boyfriend and girlfriend. But Reggie met me on the street and he said, "I heard you got beaten." I said, "Yeah, everyone knew I got beaten." The whole of Nassau knew I had gotten beaten. I got beaten because I went out with the Dillets—people I lived with. Sometimes I wonder if that was really the reason. Something must have bothered Dada and Mommy Dillet told him that I went out. That just set him off. He gave me a beating. The doctor was called. I didn't give Dada a chance to apologize, because I had nothing to do with him after that. Years later, before he died, we talked about it. He didn't apologize and he didn't say why. But he did say Vernice's father, Cyprianna's father and another friend of his came to the gardens to find out what was going on. And then my sister was going to beat my brother for not beating Dada. My brother lived with my father, but he was not the type to fight. He was at work when the beating happened. He just spoke to Dada and told him about it.

How the beating happened was . . . When I lived with Mommy Dillet, I used to go and clean out Dada's apartment every Friday. And he met me head on. 'Cause the woman was there mopping up when I got there. After the beating, I was so stupid, I still went ahead and cleaned his room. I was still afraid of him. I was afraid of Dada, but as the years went along, we became friends again. I was not afraid of him anymore. If he had ever done that again, I would have hit him. At that time, I couldn't run. The door was closed and all. But for all of this, I still loved him. It was amazing. My sister asked me, after Dada died, "How could you put up with him?" They had nothing for each other. She was jealous of me and Dada, you see? She was just jealous of us. It wasn't my fault that I was Dada's favorite.

I never had favorites with my children. Although they say Nina is my favorite, I say, "How could Nina be my favorite? Fifteen months later, Reginald was here. She didn't have a chance to be a favorite. Natalie, you tell me about Nina was a favorite? You were six years without a child behind you." And then when Indira came, I heard them [Natalie and Indira] quarreling one day and she [Natalie] said, "Don't forget, you're not supposed to be here." So I just waited for the reply. "I'm here now. What you going to do about it?" They still quarrel! Nina, the oldest, has her squabbles, too—her funny ways. We have a picture we took in the new house. Nina was sitting in the center and I was on the end and Reginald on the other end, but it happened that Reginald was hugging Natalie and I was hugging Reggie, because they were sitting in front. So she [Nina] was left alone. She didn't like that picture. A couple things she didn't like. Sorry about it, but it was unintentional.

I worked the whole time I was raising my children. I had a housekeeper to take care of them. I could write a book on housekeepers. A housekeeper came to work for us when Indira, my last child, was four or five months old, and she stayed with us for nineteen years. She went to Washington with us and she's still in Washington. She was dependable; she was loyal. But she had her days. Sometimes when the food was like the ocean [salty], you know she had a problem. One time I said to her in Washington, "You know, Beatrice, the Ambassador went to the doctor today (this wasn't true), and he has high blood pressure and you give him too much salt. Cut down on the salt. I don't want anything to happen to the Ambassador. Cut down on the salt." She did.

Beatrice stayed in Washington and went to her daughter's graduation. She brought her daughter with her when we moved to Washington. Her daughter was seven years old. She said she could not go if she didn't take her. She left the boys here with her brother. I went to her daughter's graduation, because she was not supposed to graduate from high school. She had a learning disability. I had to go to attend her graduation!

When my husband finished his tour, we went to Florida to live. But I missed home, Nassau, and my children and friends. So here I am [laughter].

𝒞

Beliefs, Values, and Customs

Bush Medicine

Practitioners of bush medicine are frequently known as herbalists. For the most part, they use traditional, natural remedies to prevent sickness and to promote healing. A variety of indigenous herbs, bushes and barks are utilized as healing medicines. A few of these are supposed to increase sexual potency or to assure or prevent pregnancies. Today, bush medicine continues to be practiced in the Bahamas. Many people refer to it as "common knowledge" rather than bush medicine. "It's just what you do for certain illness. It's always been done." Some Bahamians regard bush medicine as traditional medicine.

Fred Ramsey, born on September 2, 1909, Smith Bay, Cat Island

> *Edmund Johnson took me to Mr. Ramsey, whom he described as "the best bush doctor around." I was taken aback when Mr. Ramsey immediately offered a small glass and a bottle of tonic for me to pour a drink. Because I very much wanted to interview him, I quickly poured a drink, turned on the tape recorder, asked a question and gulped the tonic down. There were no ill effects. In a very calm, confident voice, he informed me that if I had been pregnant, the tonic "will kill the baby, but it won't do the woman nothing." I was impressed with his willingness to share his tonic and his knowledge.*

According to what you need, there's two parts to bush medicine. Now see, the tonic what I just give you is good for all pain in your back. If a woman carrying a baby, you don't drink it 'cause it will kill the baby, but it won't do the woman nothing. If you ain't breeding [aren't pregnant] and you drink it, you'll breed right away. But it help a man always. If you taking pills, the medicine ain't gonna do you no good. I got all of those samples here. I'll get another sample for you.

That's a tonic. It got seven different roots. You boil the roots. That's straight. I don't pour anybody any. You got to help yourself. That's the medicine right there. It's just the roots. If you use it with a little cream [evaporated milk], it's all right. You can use that with cream. We generally use pumpkin and breadfruit leaf for high blood pressure. Get breadfruit leaf from Arthur's Town. Stomachache is a small item. You could use the bitter sage. You boil that and drink it and that will take it away. You have this one bush for headaches—three finger. You inhale it or you rub it up or put it in your hat. We generally use alcohol for a cut, you know. Wash it clean and you get a little thing [scab], then it heal right up. We generally use the butter and a sour [Seville orange] for coughs. A sour looks like an orange and it's sour like a lime. Just warm that butter and squeeze that sour in it to cut the mucus.

I learned about bush medicine from my old auntie. She was a midwife. I took it from her and that's where I get it.

Alfred Love, New Providence

I was surprised that Mr. Love had so many remedies, since he had grown up in Nassau with access to doctors and hospitals. But, as he said, since money was scarce, "you either use bush medicine or you die." I was especially interested in his cure for cancer.

When it come to bush medicine, in old times, you either use bush medicine or you die. You didn't have no money. For a stomachache they used to boil catnip and they used to beat that and soak it in water and then drink it—bitter, bitter. It used to ease your pain in the stomach. They used bay rum bush for pain in the stomach too. They had some bush here called turpentine and bay geraneum—that was good for stomach pain.

If you had a cut, they had some bush you used to call horse bush. They boil that and wash the sore in carbolic soap. Then you take and you parch some of the leaves. When you parch the leaves, you beat it up and then you take and you dust the sore with that. And heal it.

For a headache, you had to go to the drugstore to get something worthwhile. But they also had guinea hen bush. I get some in my yard. You dig the root of the guinea hen bush and you beat it. And that's very good. Some people used to take it and put it behind their ears. It has a stinging kind of smell because it's strong. Match me if you can was good for that.

If you got mucus from flu or got cancer, cerasee make you better. You pull up the vine and boil it, leaves and all. Put some honey in it and drink it hot as you can.

They use castor bean when you're in the sun and want to cool off. You take the leaves and put it in your hat. If your head is hot, you can use almond leaves in your hat and whatnot, like that.

They had bush for sores, too, pound cake bush. You boil that and then you beat it and parch it and put it on sores.

Gumelemi bush was good. You take the bark of that and you make tea. They used to use pear leaf [avocado] tea and sour orange tea. They had some stuff called briarroot. It tear up your flesh if you walk through. That's what they throw Bro' Rabbit into [laughter]. Take the root of that and dry it. It make lovely tea. People don't use them anymore. They get too sophisticated. All that could have save them money, but they don't go for it anymore.

Bob Dean, born on March 28, 1920, Love Hill, Andros

Mr. Dean took me on a two-hour walking tour of the bush at Fresh Creek. He pointed out twenty bushes and patiently explained how each was used medicinally. Many of them were described as "sex bush!" He also knew how love vine can tell you if "that girl love you." He seemed to know the properties of every bush and tree at Small Hope Bay Lodge. Mr. Dean even explained why a crab has a soft shell in the spring.

Let me show you about this bush. This is what you call rice bush. Now, that is good for a woman. This is for a particular woman. You broke it, about twelve heart of these. You break it up and you boil it. You get the root from this and you break that up and put in the pot and you boil it. And when you done boil it, you strain it off and you drink it. That's for women overrun their time. They supposed to go five and they go six. You take two drinks a that and you go right back. Well, this here is jumbay. You dig the root of that, but it got to be a bigger tree—this is young. You dig the root of that and you get the root of this. This is sinecord. You put them together and you boil it. After you done boil it, you strain it off, either get a little bit of sweet milk or cream, just how you choose it, and you drink that. You'll have a bunch of children! You can eat the fruit, you know. The fruit, when it green, it got a lotta colour like the leaf. When it full, it black. Then you burst it open and you eat the meat from the seed and it's very good.

This is jackmada. That good if you get a pain in your tummy and you can't get around. You see any of them bush, you just pull off five or six leaves and you chew it. Chew it and swallow the water. A little while after that, you hear your belly growl. Taste it. You taste the bitter? This here mint. You know those?

My daddy taught me about the bush. My mother was a bush doctor. None of my children are interested. This is a poinciana tree. And that's a wild cotton tree. This is a garden. We grow all of this. When we run short, we used to come up here and get vegetables. And we used to get plenty bananas, papaw. We got some trees now. There's pear [avocado] and mango and orange and those big lemons.

That's poisonwood. You gotta dust up underneath those barks. Now, you see that black there? That can't do you nothin,' but it's one brown dust up inside there and if it get on your skin, it start to go through like acid. But now, it don't go right down [inside], just follow the skin. But what you gotta do, you turn over a rock. You get the dirt from underneath there and you rub it all over that. That kills it dead.

And, what you could do again, you could get a gallon can about that high. You punch two holes in it. You get a wire and you put it around the tree. You take a pocketknife and you stick it into the tree and you let it drip until you think you have enough. Then you take it down and you get some white lime and you make a paste. Make it and lay it out in the sun. Leave it there for three days. And after three days, you pop off piece if you got a bad teeth and jock it [push] down in there and you even won't know when that gone. The pain stop and the teeth come out. Teeth come right out.

When you could get no soap to wash things in, they use this greasy bush. So, what the old ladies and them used to do, get off a good handful like that. And they work with every grain of that grease. After they done work with all that grease, they dip that in hot water. Come clean.

And this here, this is soldier vine. Now, this good for sores—sores on your skin. You boil this, bathe the sores. So, when you done bathe the sores, you get the leaf from this and you parch it. Then you beat it in strong piece of cloth. Then you dust all over the sores and when you get through, you can always tell when the sores getting better, 'cause that black stuff which you sprinkle on that, they gonna turn up until that drop right off. That will be finished.

You get a good handful of this love vine. You boil it up like that and get a piece of wood and you beat that fine. Get a gumelemi and put it together and you boil it. When you done boil it, you strain it. When you done strain it, you put some sweet milk. That's the third thing—not the cream, the sweet milk. And that goes in there like lumps in your throat. That's the thing what makes the babies. After the love vine ripe, it kill some of the trees it on, some part, sure. The onliest way you can get rid of it is, you have to break it off. You see, they has no root to the ground. They winds around any tree. They got to come from a bird, 'cause no one don't plant it.

What we do when we used to go to school, we go to a half-and-half tree—half ripe. And we go to the tree and we spread love vine all over the tree, and if we see a girl in school that we like, we call her name three times. In three days' time, if that girl love you, the vine'll catch [attach itself to the tree and grow], and if she ain't love you, the vine'll die.

See that buzzard [a kind of hawk] there? Buzzards like to go on madeira tree. They never go on the ground. That's mistletoe right in there. That's what's for the pain. You can dry it, smoke it, drink it, anything. It reduces pain.

What you know about crabs? They got an upstairs and a downstairs. You ain't never know that, hay? Yeah, well, in the night, they leave the water and come upstairs in there. Yes, and when the day comes, he comes back down. When they growing, they shells right up. You ever see them? All the top shell gets soft. Underneath be soft, soft, soft. He drop right out and the same length what this [the shell] got, the inside got. Then when the wind hit it, he turn hard. I'd say older fishermen, they like to eat the soft ones, but most [people] don't.

This a macre bush. It good for pregnant women. And if your back is weak and you mess up [miscarry] two children, boil this. Drink it without sugar. And this make the baby big and fat. And you have a quick delivery.

This called five finger, and this called old man. But now, the right thing for this, these two bush is sex bush. These your sex bush. You boil the two of them together and you don't bother with no milk. Just drink it right so. Just about three mornings. You'll chase your husband out the bed [laughter].

Obeah bush good for pain all over your body. You boil it and bathe in it. But you could drink it too. You know, it's bitter. Ain't too good to drink too much of bitter things. It break your system down. This good for—you could take this and you and me going fishing. I don't know you got it. Put it in your back pocket, you'll catch all the fish. I'll catch a couple and the rest will drop back in the sea.

This is the bohog bush. Now this is a good sex bush again. The bushes we gonna get now is sex bush. You boil this until the water gonna look like oranges when they start to ripe. You drink this for at least about four mornings. It'll keep your old man crazy [laughter].

White tile, yeah, this one of your sexy again. When you boil this, it looks like something you make, Kool-Aid. It's red, just like when you see fire. That's one of them dangerous one.

This is rock bush. If you got a cold, heavy, you beat this up. Take off all the leaf. You beat it up and take a piece of cloth. When you done, you get a glass and you squeeze it out. And this can't hold enough water. Drop a little water into the cloth. Squeeze again. You get through, you cut a sour in half. And cut one half in half again. Squeeze that into the glass. You get a tiny grain of salt. You drink it and that keep the cold afloat [prevents constriction of the lungs].

Olive Ramsey, born in 1934, Cove, Cat Island

Mrs. Ramsey works as a housekeeper at Fernandez Bay Village. Physically, she is a tall, graceful, dignified woman. Mentally, she was extremely knowledgable and thoroughly responsive to questions I asked. Among other things, she shared what an expectant mother should drink during pregnancy to assure that "everything working."

We use some bush medicine. We use aloe. I'm a diabetic. I'm going for my checkup tomorrow. I suppose to be in Nassau on the eighteenth of Febru-

Olive Ramsey (left) and Mr. and Mrs Rufus Hepburn

ary. The doctor told me that my sugar is down. I have to go and take a test. I drink aloe every day. I have a big tree right there. You mix it with—some people call it periwinkle, but we call it sailor's choice. Sometimes I put another bush with it. We call it bitter sage. Boil all three together. Sometimes I drink the aloes alone. I only hot [boil] the water and throw it on the aloes. From November eighteenth, when I come from Nassau, I drank that every day. I was weighing 250 pounds. That's how big I was. But now the doctor says I have to take off all that weight. I'll feel much better. The doctor say that will give me a chance to be back a certain way [to be healthy].

When I had my children, the only thing I used to drink was what we call bohog bush and bay vine. That's a bitter vine. It run on the ground. You hardly have that vine in the yard, but it's on the beach, north beach. We call it North Side. Bay vine don't have any flower. I could have brought a piece and show you. When you go to it, it smell good—smell almost like thyme. I drink that a few mornings during my pregnancies. Didn't put no salt. A midwife delivered my babies. Everything was okay.

Edmund Johnson, born on February 2, 1942, Bimini

I met Mr. Johnson because he was the gardener and handyman for Ms. Bain of the commissioner's office, at New Bight, Cat Island. He was fascinating—although younger than most of the people I interviewed, he still had their values. He had been raised on Bimini, so the culture of Cat Island was not his original frame of reference. I was impressed with his quietness and willingness to "fade into the woodwork" when he was at an interview with me. Not once did he ask a question or contribute a comment. After each interview he asked if I had gotten what I wanted. Later, when I asked him some questions, he became completely verbal and had marvelous information.

I believe in bush medicine. I am knowing how to cook up bush and give it to you, it'll kill you. You see how good you sleep since you been staying at Ms. Bain's? [Laughter.] That because of the tea I make every night. Now, I ain't gonna tell you what vines and leaves I use, but it's got three things in it. They grow in Ms. Bain's yard. You only boil it for five minutes. More [boiling] make the tea bitter. It work, don't it? You get a good sleep, don't you? [Laughter.]

Obeah

West Africans who arrived in the Bahamas most likely brought their religious beliefs with them. These African practices formed the basis for Bahamian Obeah, a form of religious belief involving witchcraft and/or sorcery. Believers contend that the techniques of Obeah have the power to harm individuals, to cause physical and mental illnesses and even death. Obeah is also used to furnish answers to the questions and problems of everyday life. Practitioners of Obeah use medicinal herbs, manmade charms and incantations to achieve results. One of those interviewed described the technique of utilizing the Bible to determine who has stolen from you. Some practitioners refer to this as white magic and say that it is used to counteract evil or for good purposes.

Alfred Love, New Providence

I doesn't practice Obeah. But when it come right down to it, I personally know people what fix you. They can get what you want done. If you go into a person farm and steal their corn, they can fix the field in a way. I can't tell you how, but I know it happens. You go and eat the corn; it swell your stomach up. If you don't admit to the person that you stole the corn, eventually it kill you. It happened when I was in Cat Island. This fella went and cut the man's corn. He fed his horse with the blade from the corn plant, and the horse ate it and the horse died. The fella start to swell. The farmer came and said, "Now, if you tell me that you stole the corn, I could save you." But he wouldn't admit it. When you look, his stomach keep swelling. They had to send him on the boat from Cat Island to the hospital here in Nassau and he died. I was there when that happened.

The lady who I lived with, she wouldn't allow me to take field produce from certain people. She would tell me, "Don't take nothing from Ranny, because he steal from people." Some of the loveliest ears of corn, he brought for me. The house wasn't no further than fifteen feet from the sea. When I looked, those ears of corn were floating, going down the sea. She threw them away.

They had people who used to fix their farm. You go in that farm, touch anything in that farm, you can't come out of that farm. If they don't go there for days, you stay right there and can't come out. Just walking around the boundary of the farm, right round the boundary of the farm. The owner of that farm, he'll come there and he'll see you and he wouldn't speak to you. He'll stay right there and if he mean, he'll go back home and stay days more. You just be walking round and round the farm. Can't find your way out. Mind, it's nothing you can see with your naked eye to see why you can't come out.

They had people who could work Obeah. But mostly, people use it if you did something to them. They just don't jump right up and kill you. I know certain ways that people used to find out if you steal from them. I'm a professor on that! If you steal something from me, I try what they call the key and the Bible. Now you have a key. Call this the ears of the key, right? So you'll put your finger under there and I'll put my finger under the other ear. You put this key in the center of the Bible. And you strap it with cord or cloth. Strap it tight so the key can't slip. You continue to touch the ears of the key above the Bible. Open the Bible to the center. The center of the Bible is in the Psalms. You take your finger and put it under the key like that. I'll call any amount of people's names that they stole my stuff. That Bible will stay right there and won't move. Once you say, "By St. Peter, by St. Paul, whoever stole my whatever." Then the person holding the other side say, "By St. Peter, by St. Paul, that person didn't steal your whatever." And you can try any amount of people. As long as you don't call the right person's name, that Bible will stay right there. As soon as you say, "By St. Peter, by St. Paul, so and so stole my stuff," [and] the person holding the other side say, "By St. Peter, by St. Paul, that person didn't steal your stuff," the Bible start spinning, spinning, spinning. The key and your fingers stay in the same position. It ain't say like you pushing it around. It's just on the tip of your fingers. You'll see that Bible spin. If you don't catch it, it'll fall right on the ground. I could do that.

Once my daddy had a Lodge brother [a member of a local branch of a certain society or club], and they were good friends. He trusted that man when he go into his farm. He always look after my daddy farm when he wasn't there. Being Lodge brothers, he had the greatest confidence in him. So we used to grow bananas in bunches. This day, Poppa gone and somebody cut the bananas and the gum was still dripping from it. He came home brokenhearted. He told my momma—she be named Drusilla, but he call her Dru for short. So he say, "Dru, somebody went and steal my bananas." That was in the height of the Depression. They had some Conchy Joes, these Bahamian whites, just move out in the area where our farm was. You couldn't tell my daddy it wasn't them who stole those bananas, because they had just moved out there and when I tell you things was tough, it was tough. So Poppa say, "It got to be them. They come out here stealing my banana." My momma say to him—he was Joseph—"Joseph, don't be accusing people. The one you are accusing may not be the person." So he say, "Oh, don't tell me, got to be them. But wait a minute. I know when I was a boy, my grandmother, anyone steal anything from her, she would know by using the key and the Bible."

So he had a long brass key. I got it home right to today. This happened from in the thirties, fifty-three years ago, something like that. He said, "I gonna try the key and the Bible." He got this key and he strap it up in the Bible and he call all those Conchy Joe fellas' names, all of them. And the Bible ain't move. Momma say, "Well, the Bible ain't move. You better try somebody else." He mention everybody he know. The Bible ain't move. Momma say, "You better try your brother in the Lodge name." He say, "I ain't goin' to try him, because I know he wouldn't do that to me." Momma say, "No, you gonna try him." He reluctantly decided to try him. So when they say his name, the Bible start to spinning. He say, "Oh, my God, I couldn't believe my brother in the Lodge would have done me that." And that is true, true, true.

I know just here the other day, a friend of my own sister went and stole all of her sister's rent money, electricity bill money, and whatnot. She swear she didn't do it. And I don't know her. I told her sister, "You know, I could find out who stole your money. But I don't want you to go to the police, because this won't hold up in court." She call everybody's name. She had about five other sisters. The Bible stood still. As soon as we say this sister, that Bible start to move.

I try it with quite a few people. I know a Haitian stole this fella's dog. And a lady told him, "No, he wouldn't do that." And my brother went and told this fellow who lost the dog, "Go tell my brother. He know how to work the key and the Bible. He'll find out who steal your dog." He come to me and I say, "Now, you name any of the people in Grant's Town who you know." As soon as he call the Haitian name, doggone, the Bible spin.

You see this thing, there's nothing art into it. It is strictly a spiritual happening. So you could do it. Take the instruction like I telling you now. It's nothing like no Obeah or nothing. God is moving in this manner. I know a young man in Grant's Town, he had those good old-time gold rings. They were his mother's. You know, those old people prized those. One of her sons went and stole them. His brother come to me and tell me how his mother was so worried. I tried her sister, some of her sons, quite a few people. Even people who used to be around them and whatnot. When I call his brother name, the Bible flew.

Another spiritual thing is if you have a long strand of hair and you get the same gold ring. You tie that onto the gold ring. Put it in a glass of water. As soon as you call the person name who stole your things, you hear that ring hitting against the glass. All those things, I saw people did in life. But it don't hurt.

You also get people who can kill you with that same Bible. It's certain Psalms. They will read a certain section in the Book of Psalms and turn the Bible face down. Maybe you might even ask them if they did it. They wouldn't admit it. But you'll get sick and die. I really don't know which Psalm it is. Personally, I wouldn't do it.

Harcourt Stevens, Long Island

I had the distinct impression that Mr. Stevens was much more knowl-edgable about Obeah than he admitted. He was the first person to de-scribe how to prevent a thief from escaping before the police arrived.

Some people say you can use Obeah if someone stealing your corn. You could drunk them. You could drunk them with liquor. You fix your liquor and dig a hole in the ground and bury it. Bury it with the wind. But you have to move it with the wind [when the wind changes direction] and keep the whole field drunk. Okay? And when they go in there to broke your corn or your cane or whatever, they get drunk. They can't come out. So you go get the police and hold them right there. When you go, you meet them in the field. You hold them right there and the police come and grab them.

Then you talk about Lily and things. I see them caught some Lily stuff [fetishes, charms] in bottles and hang them up in trees. I couldn't do that, you know?

Edmund Johnson, Cat Island

Although Mr. Johnson said that he didn't believe in Obeah, he shared some colourful stories, including how to kill someone by "taking his track." He seemed to feel that Obeah worked in the "olden days," but was no longer effective.

I knew a man who had a book of his ancestors. He had this book and anyone who went in there, he was telling you these things about Obeah. But as far as performing, when people came, he'd tie a black cloth around his head and mark on his face and all.

Many years ago, people say they going to take your track. They'd go around and pick up the dirt off the road where you walked. Put that in the fire. When the fire dry up, you dry up, too. All those things, if you believed it, it happened. It worked. I don't believe in that kind of thing.

I heard of a man, it was before my time, who could do a lot of things with books. He had books like the *Black Heart* book, the *Seventh Book of Moses, Bow-Wow,* and he could do all kinds of different things with these books. These books were teaching to tell you exactly what to do about this and that. The man that had all these books, at that time, he was very talented. But he didn't have no clothes. My mother used to say, "He's trying to help me? Oh, come on. He just jiving me. Then he telling you what gonna happen and he don't even have clothes."

Okay, you remember a man in Nassau they used to call Pape? One man from my settlement heard of Pape and he decided to go see if Pape could help him. So, his friend took him to Pape house. He saw this man on the roof patching some shingles, so he went in the house and said that he wanted to see Pape. The man in there said that he wasn't home. But he should come at any time now. He said Pape was gonna fly back home. So, he said, he waited. It ain't been long. A man come right there and bam. He said, "Yeah, I just arrived." So the customer said, "You just arrive? I just saw you patching shingles." [Laughter.]

I could tell you things I've heard about a coconut palm. These boys went fishing and come back hungry. They were passing through the coconut farm or grove or whatever it is, and the coconuts were on the ground, so they stop and eat them. And when they get home, their stomachs start going on [making noises] in an hour or so. One of them called his mother, Old Granny and a lot of people around. They get hot water and ashes. Put it on his stomach to get his stomach full. Old Granny said that maybe the children et [ate] something. So they went in to the child and said, "What you eat?" He said, "Only one thing. We stopped in a grove and had a coconut in this particular farm." So the mother and father went over to the farm. I mean, to the home to see this fella and say, "My son stole a coconut from you." He said, "He didn't eat it, though." They said, "Yes." He said, "Oh well, he gonna die. Just fill you up all empty. By then you pop up, and by that time you die." And the boy died. That was many years ago. But today, they pick the coconut, eat the coconut and offer you some of the coconut. Today, the kids go steal the corn and then sell it back to you.

Religion

Church affiliation is an important component of Bahamian life. A majority of Bahamians are affiliated with some denomination. The major religions are Baptist (32%), Anglican (20%), and Roman Catholic (19%). Most other Bahamians (29%) are affiliated with Church of God of Prophecy, Greek Orthodox, Jewish, Lutheran, Methodist, Plymouth Brethren, Presbyterian, Seventh-Day Adventist, or Jehovah's Witnesses. On Sunday morning, most members of a settlement attend a religious service that may start sometime in the morning between six and eleven o'clock. Seniors are invariably dressed in their "Sunday best," which includes their finest clothing, fancy hats and gloves. Some of the younger people, however, have begun to question the teachings of the churches.

In 1994, the Anglican diocese, including the Bahamas and Turks and Caicos, was divided over the question of the ordination of women into the priesthood. Bishop Rt. Reverend Michael Eldon and his assistant bishop, Drexel Gomez, were in favor of inclusiveness. They pointed out that there existed an extreme shortage of priests in the Bahamas and that the Bible does not restrict the ordination of women. A resolution was passed at the West Indian meeting of priests, stating that when at least two-thirds of the dioceses agreed, ordination of women might begin. In 1994, only one more diocese needed to cast an affirmative vote for the resolution to be passed.

Some of the people with whom I spoke agreed with the Reverend Canon McSweeney, who was opposed to the ordination of women. They reminded me that Jesus never had any women apostles. They also cited the Roman Catholic tradition, which they seemed to admire, of having no women priests. One priest mentioned Bishop Barbara Harris in the United States. He assured me, "If she ever comes here, I won't take communion from her. And if the Bahamian church ordains any women, I'll leave and become Roman Catholic." He felt that the controversy began as a result of the women's liberation movement and should be ignored.

By 1996, Antigua, Barbados and Jamaica had women deacons. And, in March of 1999, Archbishop Drexel W. Gomez announced that Mrs. Angela Palacious, wife of Father James Palacious, rector of St. Matthew Church, would be ordained the first Bahamian woman priest.

Quite a few Cat Islanders mentioned Father Jerome (John Hawes), who began his work in the Bahamas as an Anglican priest and architect

from Britain. During that time, he supervised the construction
of St. Paul's Anglican Church. Later, he became a Roman Catholic
priest and built St. Peter's Roman Catholic Church. St. Augustine's
Monastery and College in Nassau were designed by Father Jerome
and completed in 1947. Although Hawes built many other beautiful
churches and other structures, he is most famous for the miniature her-
mitage built on Cat Island, which he modeled after traditional Fran-
ciscan hermitages. His carved stone interpretations of the stations of
the cross are positioned along the path leading to the hermitage. Father
Jerome spent his final years on Cat Island at this hermitage on Comer
Hill, which he renamed Mount Alvernia. He died in 1956.

Clementina Adderley, Long Island

Mrs. Adderley's commitment to her church was most unusual. Although
she had a farm, she was willing to "let it go" in order to make her contri-
butions, including "knead[ing] 100 bags of flour."

When I was young, they used to have plenty parties. But I never used to
bother. I never liked no parties. I went to church every Sunday of my life.
St. Athanasius, that's my church. Before she was built, I was a member
of St. John's to Buckley's. After Mr. Richard Carroll gave us this lot for
the church, we went and got that clean out. People were so generous in
them days. Then, Father Pyfrom, that dear precious soul, he [was] put in
charge of it. He went off. When he come back, a man by the name of
Ignatius say that his wife will always pay for the lunch for the people
workin' [to build the church]. Child, Father Pyfrom sent the catechist
down here and ask me to come. Well, the building was just gonna start
then. They were getting all the things ready.

He sent for me to come and I went. He asked me if he plant, will I grow.
I told him I didn't think I would grow anywhere [laughter]. So he said, now
he want me to assist. Mrs. Ignatius' husband promised that his wife would
furnish all the lunches. But she didn't want to. So I said, "Father, what do
you want done?" He said, "Here's what I want you to do. Make bread and
tea every twelve o'clock." So I said, "Well, Father, I got a farm I gotta grow."
He said that I didn't have to do it all the time, just when I could. And my
dear, when that boat come, Father Pyfrom sent all the flour. Sent the corn.
Sent the tea. And said that when lunch done, he'll send a man to come and
get it. Every evening, me and my two boys had to go look for wood.

Everything was baked on the fire and use wood. There was no stoves in them days. There was no cars in them days. Worked hard in them days. Not like now. I knead as much as a hundred bags of flour from time to time until our church was done. I parch and beat that coffee in the mortar. I couldn't go to my farm. When they worked here, I just had to continue to do that. Let the farm go 'til I get a special time to go to the farm. Then, twelve o'clock, Father Pyfrom sent the men to come and get the bread and the bucket with the tea. Sometimes, two buckets of tea and some time, three buckets of coffee and nine loaves of bread. And I'd take the butcher knife and I'd go out there and cut it up. Everybody would get their lunch.

The school was over here in one house I got over here—prep school. The children used to go out to Jerry Wells and pick up lumber and bring it. I used to feed them lunch and they go back to school. And I did that until that church was completed.

They started to build lime kilns. The horses had to tote every bit of the lime and sand from all over in back of the woods. Had a kiln right over back where the airport is. Boats used to have to bring it from Hog Cay, and then the horses tote it to here. After the church was finished, I move my membership. And that church today is sixty-six years old. From [the time] she been finished, I been going there. I can't get there now. The priest comes and gives me my communion every week. If he gone this Wednesday, he'll come next Wednesday.

The church was worked on the other day. Father Pyfrom's son [Roscow Pyfrom] and his wife take up Father Pyfrom's bones and they bury him right here inside [the church]. His wife, she give the flower garden right round the church. And he took money of Father Pyfrom and repair the church from the tower right down, inside and outside. See, Father left that for it to be done like that after she [the church] was completed.

The only thing the members had to do was to put the new pews in. Still, plenty of the members didn't want to spend that amount of money. Every one of them pews cost $500. One man, who used to be at Hog Cay, he give two pews. And I only used to get from the government $100. Every time I get it, I give so much until I got a pew myself. I bought it and paid the freight for it. The man ready-made my mahogany pew in Nassau. Then they got the shelves for you to kneel on. Put your book and everything right there. But I haven't been to church now for one year. When I get to church, I can't get up the steps. But was a time I used to go every Sunday when I was well and hardy and coulda go. When the preachers used to be there, I used to cook for them. I used to cook for the bishop, all the bishops who used to come here. Well, the last priest I do for was Father Cooper. 'Cause you know, Father Cooper fell in church in Nassau. Just like he fell, they took his picture and sent it to me and I got it right here in the house. I don't see why people running from church to church, 'cause it's only one God, only one God and one Bible.

Joanna Bethel, Grand Bahama

Mrs. Bethel's experience of having only one church in the settlement and the use of an itinerant priest was unique.

There was only one church at West End in the thirties, one Anglican church. Everyone went there. The activities at church were primarily on Sunday. We had a visiting priest. We had a catechist. He conducted the service when the priest wasn't there. The priest seldom come, because he had to come by sailing boat and the priests were few in those days. He served between Bimini and Grand Bahama.

I think the schoolteacher used to take births and deaths. If I had a baby, I would tell someone to tell the teacher. He would come. Before the teacher was there, I had a cousin who used to do it. She got paid very little for doing it. Most things done cheaply or freely.

Rafaleta "Goddie" Williams, Andros

Mrs. Williams explained the socioeconomic status of blacks and whites in the Bahamas using the story of Cain and Abel. I was flabbergasted!

I so appreciate, I can't done thanking God for being here during you all days [being alive now] to enjoy some of you all joy. And you all have joy.

Young people want too much that God ain't put them in the world for. If He did want you to be rich right away, He would have sent you with that. They have two pattern in the Bible: black and white. When God tell we [blacks] to choose ours, then what we done? What we done in the Bible as Cain and Abel do? We gone and pick up ax and cutlass. But the white, what they do? They pick up pen and ink. So that surely mean we gone work. We coloured gone work. But some still got the intelligence to be more than the next one. See, He give we [us] a pattern for all the things in our life.

You white and hire me? And if I gonna work for you today, I gotta say, "Miss, my boss lady, oh Miss thus and so." But you could call me right straight out, "Rafaleta, come here." But I can't do it to you, 'cause you hired me. See the fingers, the toes? God give you a pattern. And that's what these people ain't looking at. Look at the young. Some of the young people get education. They could be high. But they want higher than they ready. They want to do it before their time. They want to grab it one time and go right up in the world. Oh no, no, no. You can't get it so. You got to take your time and see what God got for you.

I can't go to church now days. My priest come to me every Sunday. I [am] a Catholic. If he don't come, he send the deacon. If he have to go somewhere else, he send the deacon. You see, when I coulda go, I don't neglect my church. That's why they tend me so faithful. Night or day, soon as that bell ring, I'm going. And if I can't get there, raining, sister and them, they come for me. Thank you, Jesus, 'cause for me one now, the way I is, when father meet me kinda feeling bad, when he get in church, he explain that and some of the members will come. He asking the members, "Go there and help that sister. She alone." And they have to come. That's what our church sign for [describes as] charity. Charity we must have. When he come, he done give me communion and he hold my hand like I hold yours. That feel something good!

For every time members come, they does bring a box. If they don't bring the groceries, if they know I can't spend, they'll buy. Then he come, and bring. The members, sometime they come in between. They drop one loaf of bread or two, or they bring a pack of rice. They bring this or they bring that. Sometimes, I overflow in here with groceries. People, they come and help me.

Some people, they don't notice you. Everybody can't give. Everybody can't give one person, because what I gonna do with it? Other people need just the same as me. Although other people ain't blind, although they ain't cripple, they need. Plenty people need; I could get around. But still, if you have it to spare rather than you throw it away, you give it. That's what God say, "Let's feed one another. Give freely, give freely, give." Bless you, daughter. God bless your family, too.

Carrie Lunn, New Providence

As Mrs. Lunn described how her family became members of Christ Church, the Cathedral, I wondered if the Bishop treated all newcomers so graciously. Although I had been told that the church was segregated in the early years of the twentieth century, her version was very different.

I attended Christ Church, the Cathedral. My parents were always Anglicans, and when they came here, they knew the Bishop, because he used to come around to the confirmations at Turks and Caicos Islands. When we came down here, my mother wrote him a letter. She and my father wrote him a letter that we was here, and he invited us up on Bishop Hill [where the Bishop's residence used to be]. He had dinner for us that night. And he introduced us to his housekeeper. Her name was Miss Tappis. She was an Englishwoman, very nice person. He also introduced us to Nettie Turnquest. And both of them was very nice, so they were our friends. Then the Bishop introduced us to the Cathedral. He asked if we would like to be members of Cathedral and my mother said yes right away. From a little girl, I used to go to Christ Church Cathedral, right up until this present time.

As far as I know, I've heard some of them saying that some of the churches were segregated, but where I was concerned, in Christ Church Cathedral there was no segregation there. So I cannot say anything about that. Because right up until today, there are a few of the old members who went to Cathedral when I was a child and they are still friendly and nice with me.

Ivy Simms, Long Island

Ms. Simms is the only person who put her involvement in church in the past tense. Since reading the Bible is very important to her, I tried to find out why she had not joined a church where she could have actively participated. She changed the subject.

I was involved in church, but I did not actively participate, you know. Because in our church, Church of God, they believe that women should be silent in the church [laughter].

Joseph Carroll, born on July 13, 1918, Deadman's Cay, Long Island

Mr. Carroll was the most outstanding businessman I met in the Bahamas. It is not because he is a genial, gracious person who operates the local grocery store, a furniture store and a guest house at Deadman's Cay. Nor is it because he has a car rental service and sells gasoline. Rather, it stems from his understanding of himself, his vision and his steadfastness. His love for his wife and his pride in his family were a delight to observe.

After fifty years of marriage, he repeatedly referred to his wife as a "wonderful girl." I was impressed when he changed the conversation to a discussion of Saddam Hussein and the "fulfillment of scripture."

The Depression coming again, you know. What we are seeing in the Gulf today is prophesy fulfilling before our eyes. And, in my opinion, according to the word of God, we can focus our attention on the Far East from now on in. That's right, my dear. It's fulfillment of Scripture. It takes a man like Saddam Hussein to fulfill it, you know?

Kathleen Dawkins Thurston, born on March 28, 1923, New Bight, Cat Island

During the last few years of Father Jerome's life, Mrs. Thurston, a devout Roman Catholic, washed his clothes and generally cared for him. Her description of how she found him after his stroke is powerful. As she describes their last few days together, her love and respect for him are deeply moving. Father Jerome built eleven churches and chapels in the Bahamas. I saw two of his twin-spired churches on Long Island. The view from St. Peter's tower is spectacular. He lived the last seventeen years of his life at his Hermitage on Mt. Alvernia on Cat Island.

I always been active in my church. Did you hear about the old priest, Father Jerome? Is me what attended him when he fall. I just wash for him, bake his bread and do everything. Climbed up there every evening. When the boat come with he [his] things, I had to climb up there, carry the boxes on my head.

You see the church down there in front? Well, he built one old white one just as big as that, and all about there was others. He would walk to all of them. Walk! Tell you, that was a strong old man. I walked all the way up there with box on my head. Man, I must do that six years before he fall and gone and die. Sometimes when I'm tired and don't want to go that way, he had one road round and I go round. And I just walk around the road carrying that one box. Put it in the house and come back, get the other one and carry that.

He wasn't sick long. He had Mass that morning, Saturday morning. He say he come out after he had Mass at the church right up on the hill there. That's the first little church. And after Mass, he say he gone to test the pump to see how much water he have. 'Cause, you know, sometimes it rain and sometimes it don't rain. And he does have to use the pump for water, you know? 'Cause, man, I couldn't haul water up there. He fell right there in that sun, heat.

See, I tell you, I gone deal with my Jesus. I don't go to him [Father Jerome] until the sun like right there [afternoon]. From that morning, [he was] in the sun. And I gone when I done baked the bread around one o'clock. Me husband named Lewis. I say, "Lewis, my mind run on Father. My mind run on him. I'm going up there." So he say, "Yeah, go on then, so you wouldn't have to go later." And when I go up there, I meet that man laying right off on his back. He head and all, he cut up when he fall. I had gone and set on water, warm the water, and wash he head, you know? Then, when I done, he had the medicine. When I first found him, I gone and see him laying down there. When he looked on me and he opened his eyes, he laughed. He say, "Oh, I fall and I can't get up." I couldn't raise him up. He had gone and had some new rope. I had to tie the rope around me waist and put it around him and tell him to pull on the rope 'til I could get him to sit down. Then I gone and I wrap the rope around, and he say, "Miss Thurston, you expect I could get up?" I say, "No, Father." I gone round and I say, "Hold on to the rope and get up." I put the rope short. And I hold under he arms and he get up. Man, when I get him to the house, he looked on me, he laughed. He say, "Oh, God bring you here." When I done clean him off, I had to go back and cook for him. He say he want a cup of tea. I had to make the tea first. 'Cause he ain't ate that morning. And I gone and

I do that. When it done, I say, "Father, you want me to sleep with you?" He said, "No. You could come in the morning and see how I is. The guardian angel will take care of me." That time, your hair rise when he say that.

When I went the next morning, I meet him sitting down. He say he just read and make a cup of tea. I say, "You want me to cook some soft grits for you? Father, I have some sardines. You want me to cut up some onion, thyme, and with the sour and thing to put over it?" He say, "I just want it cooked the way you said." When I went and do that, from then, he say he want me to do that all the time. "Lord," he tell me, "oh, that taste nice." Man, that old priest was a good old soul. Oh, he was good, good, good.

He been here long time before he get me to wash, you know. He does do his clothes hisself on a hand and thing. And, you know, he don't clean he long robe, and he does come to church. I say, "Oh, Lord. Father, he does wash clothes and they ain't clean and they ain't iron. I didn't tell he nothing. So, when I come out of the field, my gal say he been here and he left a letter here for me. When I read the letter, it say I must do bake the bread and wash for him. I been want Father to tell me that a long time. Man, and I just wash the clothes clean and iron it. And when he seen them, he didn't want to put them on. He wanted to put on the old patched-up ones. I tell him, "Father, just as you dirty it, I could wash it."

Oh, Lord, that was a nice old priest. He was nice to me and my husband. He was nice to everybody. The people go up the hill and ask some favor. I never ask no favor, but he does give me. He don't give me nothing like he give people, 'bout ten or twenty dollars, you know? He does pay me good. Man, I miss him. Every time I talk on him, my heart flies [flutters]. That was a nice man. But meet me with that good smile. And every time I go, sometimes he have his spy glasses and he spy on me coming up the hill. He say, when I get up there, "Oh, my poor Kathleen. My poor little Kathleen, you're tired." He open me boxes. He give me a drink of juice. Father, he was a nice priest.

Hazel Winifred Newman, born on March 4, 1926,
Deadman's Cay, Long Island

> *I interviewed Mrs. Newman at her office in Clarence Town. Although I arrived without an appointment, she graciously invited me in and obligingly answered my questions. At sixty-five, she was considering retiring from government service and getting involved in future activities to*

benefit her community and church. Mrs. Newman's philosophy of "anything I put my hand to, I did it as good as I could," is illustrated again and again throughout her entire narrative.

My father was a seaman. My father didn't belong to Long Island. He was from Nassau. He only made stops here. He was the captain of a mailboat. Actually, he didn't belong with this island at all. I saw him when he'd stop. He did his best to take care of us. Maybe he used to come every two weeks like that. My mother had four children. She didn't do very much farming, because she used to do sewing. She used to sew a little bit. And then she would cook for the Catholic priest. So I had to help her. Farm and work. I didn't like it, but anything I put my hand to, I did it as good as I could. You have no other choice. You have to do it to live. Not to say that I enjoyed it [laughter].

The pastors appeal to people to become involved in church affairs. So we have in my church, the young people doing what you call the commentary. When I was growing up, it was just the altar boys. I'm a Catholic. I was very involved in the church from I knew myself [as a young child]. I taught in Sunday school, and I did the altar linens and so on like that, and cleaning the church. Right up to this day, I'm still doing. I'm not teaching in Sunday school; last year was my last.

"Colour" and Class

Most Bahamians have a dual cultural heritage—part African and part European. By 1901, the census report found that only 6% of the residents had been born in Africa. Each of them was over seventy-five years old.

Because of European racism, Bahamians came to see themselves according to their degree of pigmentation. The jargon that was used divided Bahamians into categories based on the visible degree of white mixture. This terminology included "Conchy Joe" as a description for locals who looked white but may have had a bit of a mixed heritage. Bahamians who had a little more pigmentation were called "near-white," "bright," or "high yellow." "Coloured" or "light brown" are terms that many older Bahamians continue to use when describing brown-skinned people. "Dark brown" and "black" were the terms used for Bahamians whose colour closely resembled that of Africans. White Bahamians valued the perceived higher status that accompanied their skin colour and sought to maintain it through marital selection. On the Family Islands, certain settlements were completely white, others had whites and blacks with the whites in control, and some were integrated. Conchy Joe families on the Family Islands produced Roland Symonette, Stafford Sands and Harold Christie, all of whom were extremely dominant in Bahamian politics and economics for many years. The Bay Street Boys, who were white Bahamians, were politically and economically powerful merchants in Nassau. Even after 1973, when political power in the Bahamas had begun to shift to the black majority, the wealth of the nation continued to be controlled by these white Bahamians.

During the 1900s, some settlements in the Bahamas continued to be almost completely white. Spanish Wells (north of Eleuthera) and Hopetown, Abaco, are two examples. Craton (A History of the Bahamas, 256) has described the situation in Spanish Wells in 1903:

> *. . . a survey team from the Geographical Society of Baltimore visited these islands. Living in hopeless depression, these poor folk, descendants of proud Loyalists, maintained their racial identity with the tenacity reserved for the retention of the last family heirloom. The results were pathetic. Persistent inter-marriage at Spanish Wells, where Negroes were not allowed to build or even spend a night, had produced a population in which dwarfs, and afflictions such as locomotor ataxia and cataract, were common. "We noticed also," wrote C. A. Penrose, M.D., laconically, "that the mental acumen of many of the inhabitants of the place was rather low."*

My conversations with white and black Bahamians in the 1980s and 1990s revealed strong disagreements as to the extent to which these practices continue today. Some white Bahamians with whom I spoke said that their children had married whites because they went to segregated colleges in the United States and married students they met there. On Long Island, some blacks insisted that race was no longer an issue.

Class distinctions were as important as skin tone in determining the divisions within Bahamian society. Some people who were interviewed talked about "first-class" and "second-class" citizens. Dr. Saunders has stated that World War I acted as a catalyst, bringing many blacks and coloureds together who would normally have been separated by class. Historically, most whites were engaged in commerce. Affluent whites lived in segregated areas and did not socialize with people of colour or with immigrants. The majority of blacks were employed in production, agriculture or both. They tended to socialize with family members, neighbours and fellow workers.

The shift in the government power structure from white to black profoundly affected many Bahamians' attitudes concerning colour and class. With this change, blacks began to receive a greater amount of respect. In addition, because the new government officials included rank-and-file Bahamians, class differences became less important.

One sixty-year-old Bahamian, who did not want to be interviewed formally, told me how she, as a black woman, first came to feel pride and dignity because of having Sir Lynden O. Pindling and the Progressive Liberal Party in political control of the Bahamas. She said that in her youth, she had been unable to attend a certain secondary school because of her colour. She also talked about family members and peers who used to call her "chocolate," or who did not invite her to parties when their light-skinned friends were present. It was obvious that she still felt uncomfortable when she discussed, over forty years later, the hostility and ostracism a family of a light-skinned suitor had heaped on her to end their relationship.

Carrie Lunn, New Providence

Aunt Carrie's marriage to a "Lunn" further assured her place in the "coloured elite." Her comment, "The light-skinned people socialized mostly with the dark people," seems to indicate that class was more important than colour for this group. The "dark" men seemed to marry women who were lighter than they.

The elite when I was young were George Roberts and his family and the Kellys. White folks. And they were businesspeople, you know. They were moneyed people, had plenty of money. And the Solomons, all of those, they were the elite of the town. Big society. They had their own homes in certain sections. No coloured people lived where they lived. All those white people had their own friends living near them. Plenty of them lived by the water. The Bethels, you know Charlie Bethel, big liquor people? All of those were the elite of the town.

Then you had the second class. Well, they used to pal, too, with these other people in certain things. Plenty of them were in the House of Assembly together. There was A. F. Adderley. I guess you've heard of him. He was considered a wealthy man. Thaddeus Toote and some of the Knowles family. They were coloured. Adderley was dark; Toote was dark. The Knowles had fair skin, but they palled with these other men. They would socialize in certain things.

In my day, you would hardly find a white woman marrying a coloured man. No, you'd hardly find that. Maybe somebody from away. A dark man might come here with a white wife, but not the Bahamians. Now today, they marry, white marry black.

The light-skinned people socialized mostly with the dark people, like the Adderleys and the Tootes. Now, Mrs. Toote was a very nice-looking person with pretty brown skin. Mr. Toote was a dark man. But they were styled [classified] like the upper class of coloured people. And like us, we used to pal with them. Do you remember Ethel Adderley? Ethel was my husband's sister. She was a Lunn. She married Adderley. And those, you see, used to pal with the Tootes and Carl Knowles and that bunch.

Eva Williams, Grant's Town

In my opinion, Mrs. Williams was completely honest and accurate in her description of the class and race situation in Nassau during the early years of the twentieth century.

When I was growing up, white and coloured people didn't socialize. Only the whites used to go to some churches like Trinity Methodist Church. Then there were the dark-skinned people like Lawyer Adderley, who married a Lunn. The ordinary black boy could never have done that. When Sir Etienne, in 1956, broke that colour line in the House of Assembly [through his Anti-discrimination Resolution], he had to hide to get home that night. We black Bahamians took pride. You go to the banks fifty or sixty years ago and you would only see white girls. I could remember after it change,

Mother Donaldson saying to me, "Our banks getting the blacks, wonder where the white girls gonna find work. We're chasing them out." I don't think the white girls work anymore—not the type who used to be the tellers in the banks.

George Leopold Roberts, born on January 8, 1917,
Dunmore Town, Harbour Island

Mr. Roberts was born on Harbour Island, grew up in Nassau, and served in the United States Army. He is retired and spends much of his time visiting his great-grandchild in Nassau and his daughters and grandchildren in New York. When Mr. Roberts talks about his early experiences, his sense of humor enhances each event. For my visit, he prepared a gourmet meal of Bahamian foods. At one point, I asked him whether a family to whom he was referring was black or white. His green eyes twinkled as he gave me a lecture on families in the Bahamas and the mixing of the races. One of his conclusions was, "When they try to explain this white and black business, they can't."

The Bay Street Boys what owned the stores were Conchy Joes, except for Reuben Bethel. They from Abaco, Harbour Island and Spanish Wells. Lots of Conchy Joes made money through the lumber mills in Wilson City in Abaco. See, that's where Reuben Bethel used to work. He was a tailor. He was a young man. That's where he met his wife. And from then, he got together with them people. He was a good talker. So he talk himself up on Market Street for his tailor shop. He was the only black one who got a building in that part of town.

The Symonettes and Pyfroms got black children. Conchy Joes are mixed. They went out and they mixed themselves. They didn't think anything about it. That's why I tell you I don't remember being segregated like that. Maybe I was segregated, but I didn't know no difference.

In Harbour Island, the whites had to rent the seats in church. They pay sixpence [about 6 cents U.S.] a week, I guess. If they don't come to church, you can't sit in those seats. But they can give you permission. Maxie Roberts from Abaco, now he carried a lot of weight, 'cause he was the only man around there that could use dynamite. So they were frightened of him [laughter]. Maxie's wife used to sit in the white woman's seat. But they gave her permission to use a seat.

Maxie used to fish and farm, get drunk three months a year [laughter]. Mrs. Roberts was the only woman allowed to sell liquor without a license, you know. 'Cause she was in with the Kellys and all those people through her husband. He was respected, because he was dangerous with his dynamite business. He had a license for that. He used to dynamite shipwrecks. Plenty of shipwrecking, him and the Sawyers. They was big in shipping. Maxie was a mariner also. He used to go to sea. If a ship get wrecked on a reef, the ship was no more good. So he dynamited it to get it off the reef. They stripped it. They get the parts, brass. They would take all what they could take. Big wooden barrels of liquor. Take whatever parts they could use. Had plenty parts.

To me, I didn't know the difference between white and black. We ain't had that. It probably was so, but it wasn't talked about. When we went to a party, anybody would be there who was invited.

Only Bay Street was white, you know. All the way, going east. You ain't have that many what you call whites. I don't know if a coloured person could buy a house there in those days, but the Isaacs lived there. Whites lived on Shirley Street, too. And that's it. Then, when they opened Mount Royal Avenue, what we used to call Conchy Joe town, they migrated from Abaco and stuff. Then they didn't like it [living there] because, I guess, hurricane damages and stuff. It used to flood.

I remember when the first Jew came to Nassau. They had long beards and stuff. They were [named] Jacks and Rubens. They went right down to the Pine Barrens [a native forest near the western end of New Providence], down Blue Hill Road where we were living. They were migrating into the United States, and some went to the West Indies. But I remember these, because they were attractive. Black outfits and hats. The story was that they bought themselves a donkey and a cart. And they carried their luggage and whatever they had down into the Pine Barrens. They were farming. Nassau was free. See, that's what I say, if the blacks could have see ahead, blacks owned all that property west of Gambier on the water. Delaporte belonged to the Huylers. They owned all of that.

You see, when you say white, if I look at them and they got one black child, I call them, actually they were black, too. You take the Fountains, all right? You take the Blacks. The Aranhas. They had black children. Just like Iris Collins. The DeGregorys. I figured the DeGregorys was black. Those were the people in the House. They were part of the government. They got a black Christie. You got Buster Christie. He was black. He hang with us. But Christie was big man on Bay Street. So that's what I mean. When I say the whites, I just talking about the father, but their children didn't live out east. Their children lived with us. Just like the Grangers. Katherine was a white woman. Dean was a black man. The Grangers came out all different colours. They got white Grangers. They're the ones in Inagua manipulating the salt ponds. But see, that's how, when they try to explain this white and black business, they can't.

Some blacks were rich enough to be white. Basil Smith went to Queens College and he was black. But his family had money. Some black people went to the Savoy Theater. Arthur Hanna went there. He had the hair [straight], but he didn't have the colour. And Arthur's brother went there and they sent him back. He had the colour, but not the hair. It's not that you couldn't go into the Savoy Theater. They were a club. And the Hannas were not members. You could only be invited by a member to that theater. You couldn't go in the Colonial, the Royal Victoria restaurants, because you didn't have the money. Mr. Adderley could have gone. He had the respect. They paid him homage. The way I feel, they said those were clubs. They had the Bahamian Club and other clubs that you couldn't go in unless you were a member or were invited by a member. Either you had the money to go or . . . First, I don't believe the Bahamian black people wanted to go. They wasn't interested. But the foreigners [blacks from other countries] were the ones that felt it.

The Greeks brought their discrimination here. Now, they owned the restaurants, the Greeks. They let a black girl in there, but she had to be very, very light. You had to be light, light, light. That's the way I see it.

Certain women were salesladies in G.R. Sweeting and Black's. They were recognized. They were the same class. They could go where they wanted to go. Class is mostly what it is. If I got ten dollars more than you, I'm better than you. You see, with money, you could do anything. They will recognize you like that. And if you dress nicely, decent, you were recognized. They had classes. My aunt had class, because her husband work for Kelly. Her husband was a builder in Nassau. He built a lot of Bay Street.

His family had some Conchy Joes in there, too. Just like the Blacks, I don't know whether they were Jewish, Greek or what, but they were light skinned with kinky hair.

Alfred Love, New Providence

I appreciated Mr. Love's explanation of what the term Conchy Joe meant to him.

A Conchy Joe is a Bahamian white. I guess you know your history. During your War of Independence, the Loyalists came. That's how the white people got in here. They came in through slavery. They were the slave masters and whatnot. Conchy Joe was in the dictionary some years ago. 'Cause I remember when I was going to school, this girl named Hilda Black, she asked our schoolteacher, he was a Conchy Joe, say, "Mr. Thompson, what the meaning of Conchy Joe?" He went and got the dictionary and he say, "A name given to Bahamian whites." But it don't mean that they aren't white. They are white. I believe the Americans didn't term them as real whites. Americans use the term. In my time, the coloured use it. But the Bahamian whites ain't gonna say nothing like that. They got a mixture now. Coloured married into white and white married into coloured.

Rita Wood, New Providence

Mrs. Wood is brown skinned. As I listened to her, I realized that darker Bahamians whom I interviewed were talking about colour, and most light-skinned Bahamians were emphasizing class. Her statement, "The light-skinned people thought they were white," is quite revealing.

When I was young, blacks couldn't go to the hotels, certain theaters, the Savoy Theater. I've never been in the Savoy Theater, even later, when we were allowed to go. You wouldn't go, because you knew you hadn't been allowed. Black tourists didn't go, either. They couldn't stay in the hotels, so they were staying at a guest house run by Flo Major. She had all of the big entertainers, the judges, the lawyers from New York who would come down and stay at her guest house. If you were an entertainer at the hotel, you would stay at Flo Major's.

When I was growing up, there were divisions between blacks and whites. You still have some divisions. A lot of it has to do with some people still don't want to change. A lot of things have to do with how you were brought up. We had black schools and white schools. Years ago, when we were children, even Lawyer Adderley's children could not attend Queens College. They were sent to private schools. Each church had its own school. The churches owned the private schools. The Catholic school, which is Xavier's, out there. You had Queens College, which was Methodist. The nuns from New York were big. They taught them how to discriminate [laughter]. Government High was mixed. It was a very elite school. Now, you can go to any school. Two of my grandchildren go to Lyford Cay, and one goes to St. Andrew's [nondenominational].

When my children grew up about thirty-eight years ago, there was St. Anne's [Anglican School]. But they went to private school. My brother and sister and I all went to private school. We went to a private school owned by Ms. Cassie Kinnear. My father never liked public schools. And the funniest thing, she decided to close the school, and that was the end of us. My father had nowhere to send us. So, then we went to government schools. And that was an experience! We were not accustomed to the mixtures. One day I was working diligently at my schoolwork and I heard a commotion. A fight! Among themselves, the children were rowdy. But they never bothered me. I think they more or less looked at us in awe, you know? When the children were allowed to play out in the streets at Christmastime with fire crackers, we had to stay behind the gate.

The blacks had their own dances. The light-skinned people thought they were white. I tell you one thing. We went to a Presbyterian church, and it was divided in three sections. The blacks sat to the west. White in the middle. And those that were not sure [because they were mixed] sat to the east [laughter]. It went on until the forties, and now you have black people preaching at that church. Blacks in the choir. The changes came about because of Sir Etienne Dupuch, the editor and owner of the *Nassau Daily Tribune*, the evening paper. He brought it up in the House of Assembly. I remember it happened when I was having my first child. Because I was too heavy with child, I was not able to go out to Bay Street for this event. And this was in 1956. He was brown skinned and his wife was white. He had been bringing it up for quite some years and nothing really happened. Because of his actions, everything opened up. I don't think the hotels were much into who came or who didn't come, because the hotels were mostly owned by the foreigners at that time, you know?

Asues and Friendly Societies

*Bahamian Asues appear to be identical to the credit institutions and co-
operative savings and loan groups in parts of West Africa and the West
Indies. Since each member is known to the others and is considered
trustworthy, no collateral or interest is required. Some working-class
Bahamians continue to prefer using an Asue rather than a bank.*

*Bahamian Friendly Societies performed functions similar to those ac-
complished by the associations of the Igbo communities of West Africa.*

*Although their structure in the Bahamas was derived from the English
model, they retained African cultural values similar to the Igbo title
associations. Ex-slaves established Friendly Societies as a method of
dealing with new responsibilities. By 1910, it was estimated that one in
seven Bahamians belonged to a Friendly Society. The chief objectives
of Friendly Societies were to aid the sick and elderly, and to furnish
financial and psychological support to families of deceased members.
Even today, when a member dies, the entire society marches, with ac-
companying musicians, to the funeral, usually dressed in white and displaying some form of identification. Friendly Societies also provide fel-
lowship and a sense of belonging. In addition, they came to perform a
political role and to foster Pan-African awareness. Burial Societies are
a modified form of the Friendly Society concept. Burial Societies were
formed so that members could contribute enough money to provide an
adequate funeral for themselves when they died.*

Ivy Simms, Long Island

Let's go over to the burial hall. We work at the Simms No. 1 Burial Society
Hall. There are two burial halls in this district. We don't have undertaking
parlors like they do in Nassau, so when people die, we use a burial hall.
This one was started by my father and the other by my grandfather, Uriah.
Because of Papa starting it, they let me use the building to do my straw
work. It's my factory.

George Leopold Roberts, Harbour Island

*It was interesting how Mr. Roberts, as a youngster, participated in the
Asue, even though his salary was less than the weekly contribution.*

Asue is a club. And everybody put so much a week in it. If you got twenty people, everybody put a dollar, so that twenty dollars. The first week you get twenty dollars. The next week I get twenty dollars. Until you come to the last one. They had these, because you could set a date when you want to do something. Say, like if you want to go away. I want to go away in August. I got the draw then, right?

The club will get together and say how much the club will pay. 'Cause you see, it have to run out in a certain time. Ms. Russell, she had one price. If you want to join this Asue, you pay ten shillings a week. It was a hell of a lot of money, 'cause I was making six shillings [$1.44 U.S.] a week. Okay, so there would be five of us. Each one put two shillings. Who ran the Asue got tips. She may have two or three shares in there herself. Like if she get tips, she will turn that into a share. The five of us, we get our draw. It's good for us on Christmas. 'Cause ten shillings [$2.40 U.S.] a lot of money! When you get your draw, you could go to the Penny Savings Bank [started by a group of black Bahamians for the black community] and deposit it.

An Asue was much handier than a bank. Asue was in your neighbour-hood. You couldn't go to no bank. You had to catch this Post Office Bank [Government Savings Bank] when you could catch it. So, before I could get to the Post Office Savings Bank, I gotta pass Black's Candy Kitchen and I'd stop to buy popcorn. But, for the Asue, I could give it to my aunt right quick. She made us do it, though. Oh yeah, me and Mae and Jack, she make us save that money, although she gave it to us. She always teaching us to save.

Enid Sawyer, New Providence

I was impressed that Friendly Societies and Lodges continued throughout the twentieth century to provide these important functions.

Friendly Societies started long before I was born, so that the poor people of a settlement would get some financial support during periods of sickness, old age and for respectable funerals. Then they were changed to Lodges and Burial Societies, and quite a few people who weren't poor joined. I belong to a Lodge. I pay dues and am active. Friendly Societies provide members with funerals, plan various social activities and work to protect the interests of the people they serve. When a member dies, we have a memorial service and we give money to the family. If a Lodge member is in trouble, we help out.

Herman Sawyer, New Providence

Mr. Sawyer's discussion of how the group handled people who got an early draw [received one of the first payoffs in the Asue] to insure their continued participation left me wondering how you "keep on checking" on them.

When we used to make four shillings [96¢ U.S.] a day, £1 [$4.80 U.S.] a week, we used to join a thing called Asue. A group get-together, we pay four shillings a piece. This week is my draw; next week is your draw. Say it's a £5 [$24 U.S.] draw. Every week, a different person get the draw. When everybody get £5, then you join again. Let's say it was ten persons. Everybody put in ten dollars. This week I get a hundred dollars. Next week you get a hundred. Next week the next person. Sometime you have problems, because people drop out. If somebody got an early draw and drop out, you couldn't carry it to the court, because Asue was not legal [laughter]. But you didn't have much problem. Like if you working on the job, we used to say a job "come." That mean a job finished. Now, if I'm in the middle of an Asue, I got a chance of dropping out. But you gonna have to keep on checking on me until I finish [paying my share]. You always pick one person to be the runner [the person in charge]. You'll say you'll run the Asue and every week when I give my ten dollars, I'll probably give you a dollar for running it. It was like what we pay in interest now [laughter]. Sometime you don't have to pay it, but it was more or less routine. This goes on up to today. But in those days, instead of going to the bank and borrowing five or six thousand dollars and paying all that interest, we would cooperate. Instead of building an eighty thousand dollar home, we would build a thirty pound home [$144 U.S.].

Rudolph Moss, Nassau, New Providence

"Mr. Moss" (a fictitious name) is a highly educated, verbal gentleman whose adult credentials prevent him from qualifying as an "ordinary" Bahamian. However, the fact that he grew up with working-class parents in a working-class neighbourhood gave him some valuable insights into the lives of average Nassauvians. His description of the function of Burial Societies, Friendly Societies and Lodges helped me to realize the importance of these support systems.

People used to form, like, a club for a Burial Society and Friendly Society. I think they were an African thing. They were organizations that black people were allowed to have. Generally, the Lodges took the place of the Friendly Society. After Emancipation, that's when the Lodges began to emerge. The members may be neighbours; they may be all from the same island. Like the Elks and the Free Masons in the United States. Here, you would have the Good Samaritan. You have all kinds of Lodges. Men and women belong to the same Lodge. The Lodge has secret orders and all that, where they have their ceremonies behind closed doors. They try to espouse some philosophy. Members turn out to do volunteer activities. My father was a member of several Lodges. Even today, you still have a separation of the Free and Accepted Masons. You have a white Masons, the Scottish Masons, and they have now accepted some black Masons. But the Black Accepted Masons is a very strong body by itself. They didn't integrate.

You can have all kinds of Lodges, because the ACL Lodge has members from Acklins, Crooked Island and Long Cay. You have a Long Island Burial Society and a Cat Island Burial Society and a San Salvador Burial Society. Basically, from each island you have one of these Burial or Friendly Societies. The Friendly Society went further in that it provided assistance to its members when they were in difficulty. They would take up a collection among themselves when a member was sick, or collect food if it was needed. These groups keep their dues down very low. They have uniforms and they attend the funerals of their members.

Funerals are very important in Bahamian culture. They provide an opportunity to pay your last respects and to support the bereaved. Funerals are also social events. If you belonged to a Lodge, then your Lodge members attend your funeral in a group. Have you ever seen a funeral procession? There's music and everyone walks behind the hearse to the cemetery. It's quite a sight.

Old Stories

My most pleasant memory of the 1994 Festival of American Folklife at the Smithsonian Institution in Washington, D.C., was listening to Dr. Cleveland Eneas tell stories. For two afternoons, this fine storyteller captivated his audiences with descriptions of growing up in Bain Town [New Providence], using old stories and riddles. Dr. Eneas states that he is a descendant of the Yoruba peoples of West Africa for whom story-telling is an advanced art form.

Many Bahamian folktales include animals that are not indigenous to the Bahamas but are found in Africa, such as lions and elephants. This fact would seem to substantiate Dr. Eneas' claim that most of the stories were handed down from generation to generation, going back to the original Africans who were brought to the Bahamas. Courlander (Courlander, 112) also suggests that these folktales have West African antecedents.

My parents and uncle were excellent storytellers. My father's stories usually contained a moral, although, according to Courlander, this is not typical of most Bahamian tales. Uncle Austin's tales dealt with the cleverness or gullibility of his characters. He also loved riddles. Even though he normally spoke using the King's English, one of his favorite riddles was: Can you construct a sentence using the words "defense," defeat" and "detail"? (At least, that's the way my sister and I heard the question.) His answer to the riddle was "De cat jump over de fence, de feet 'fore de tail."

Old stories in the Bahamas begin with:

> *Once upon a time was a merry good time*
> *de monkey chew tabacca an' 'e spit white lime.*
> *Bull frog jump from bank ter bank.*
> *an 'ain touch water till I say eh!*
> *Stories end with:*
> *E-bo-ben'*
> *my ole story en'*
> *I'll never tell a big lie*
> *like dat again!*

> *(Tertullien 4)*

I was amazed to discover stories similar to some of my parents' favorite tales in collections of Bahamian old stories. I have included two versions.

My father's version was:

When my cousin Bruce was growing up in Palmetto Point [Eleuthera], there was a man who knew witchcraft. He could put his head by the side of the road and cut down a tree. Bruce was a little boy, still wearing short pants, and he saw him doing it. When Bruce asked him what he was doing working without his head, the man became very angry and asked if Bruce couldn't see what he was doing. Bruce was frightened and ran away.

Right past the schoolhouse, Bruce saw an old woman who had leprosy. She was going to the colony in Nassau. She asked him to come and wash her feet. Bruce told her, "Not on your life!" And he walked that whole day, in all that heat, until it was dark. He couldn't get anything to eat. Nobody would give him anything—not even a piece of Johnny Cake. So Bruce starved and died. Those old people had put bad-mouth [a curse] on him for being rude and not having respect for his elders. And that was the end of Bruce.

Elsie Parsons, during the first decade of the twentieth century, recorded folktales on Andros. Her version (Parsons, 18) is:

Dere's an ol' man once, seemed to be a witchcraf,' cutting down de trees wi' no head. Den came a leetle boy up near de tree where de ol' man was. Den he said, "My leetle boy, do you see what I was doin'? You come ax me what I was doin' cuttin' down tree wi' no head on." Den again he went on, he saw an ol' lady all so'—leprosy. An' she ax him, "Do, my leetle boy, can't you come here an' bathe my feet?" Den he said, "I looks well come bathin' your feet!—Good befo' you, bad behin' you." An' he went on de whole of dat day until night. An' he died on de way, he couldn't get a morsel of bread to eat. De en' of him. Dose ol' people put mout' on him, an' I was dere to de en'. De las' of him. Says, good for ev'ry chillun to have manners for ol' an' young. Ditto, my big toe.

Brother Boukee and Brother Rabbit are main characters in many Bahamian folktales. I grew up hearing my parents refer to situations that were difficult and hard to get out of, as "a real tar baby." They explained this term by saying, "You think you want to get into it. But once you're there, it's complicated and sticky and you wish you hadn't gotten involved." They also called a tricky, clever person "a bro' rabbit."

Tar Baby as recorded on Andros by Parsons (14):

B'o' Boukee an' b'o' Rabby goin' along. B'o' Boukee was foolish, an' b'o' Rabby was wery wise, wery wise. Dis day dere was a man put a tar baby in his fiel' to ketch t'eves. B'o' Boukee was passin' dis man fiel'. An' dere was plenty papaw in de tree ripe, Now, b'o' Boukee wanted dese papaw. But seen dis tar baby man in de fiel' consider dis man coulda talk. He gone up to de man, he slap him wi' de right han'. "What you doin' here?" Dat han' hol' fas'. He slap him wi' de nex'. Dat one hol' fas'. He tu'n roun'. He take his foot. He kick de tar baby. Dat foot hol'. Den he say, "You wouldn' le' me go?" He say, "You wouldn' le' me go?" He say, "What you mean?" Say, "I betcher I bite you." He take his tee'. He sink in de tar baby. Dat hol'. So de man dat evenin' he come by his fiel,' he half kill him wi' a lickin'.

In standard English, an approximation of this story reads:

> *Bro' Boukee and bro' Rabby were going along. Bro' Boukee was foolish, and bro' Rabby was very, very wise. This day, there was a man who put a tar baby in his field to catch thieves. Bro' Boukee was passing this man's field. And there were many ripe papayas in the tree. Now, bro' Boukee wanted these papaya. But he saw this tar baby man in the field and thought the man could talk. He went up to the man; he slapped him with the right hand. "What are you doing here?" That hand stuck. He slapped him with his left hand. That one stuck. He turned around. He took his foot and kicked the tar baby. That foot stuck. Then he said, "You won't let me go?" He said, "You won't let me go?" He said, "What do you mean?" He said, "I bet you I'll bite you." He took his teeth and sank them into the tar baby. They stuck. So in the evening, the man came by his field. The man half-killed bro' Boukee with a whipping.*

Celebrations

JUNKANOO

Junkanoo is the premier cultural celebration in the Bahamas, and an important public symbol of the African heritage of most Bahamians. Junkanoo is celebrated on New Providence, Grand Bahama, Abaco, Bimini and Eleuthera. Unlike the pre-Lenten carnivals most associated with Brazil, Trinidad and New Orleans, Junkanoo has its basic origins in West Africa, probably among the Ashanti and Fanti peoples of what is now Ghana.

Junkanoo includes a colourful parade, with impassioned dancing, live music, elaborate costumes and main sculptures called lead pieces. Goombay drums, used to create the beat, consist of a wooden barrel covered at the top with stretched goat or sheepskin. The drummer plays his instrument with his bare hands after heating the drum to obtain maximum sound. Other musicians use various combinations of guitars, cowbells, whistles and additional drums.

Junkanoo celebrations were historically held on Christmas Day and New Year's Day. In the early 1900s, however, religious leaders, the media and others objected to having the festival on Christmas Day. Consequently, in 1938, Boxing Day—the day after Christmas—was declared a holiday and replaced Christmas Day for the first parade. Traditionally, Boxing Day was the day on which employers permitted household servants in England a day of rest and provided them with bundles of food.

During the first half of this century, most of the celebrants of Junkanoo were working-class people who used burlap, crepe paper and decorated street clothes as costumes. Now, the revelers "dress up" in elaborate costumes as they dance [rush] down the street to the music of drums and cowbells. Presently, all categories of citizens can be observed taking part in the festivities. Even Sir Lynden has rushed with a group referred to as the PIGS (Progress through Integrity, Guts and Strength).

As it became obvious that Junkanoo was a major tourist attraction, regulations were placed on the participants. Starting in 1960, in order to rush in Junkanoo, participants were required to wear disguises. Consequently, the importance of performances by individual dancers was lessened, and groups that had themes, elaborate costumes and lead pieces became the main attractions. Groups such as the Saxon Superstars, Valley Boys, Vikings, Music Makers and Fancy Dancers are now main attractions. The rivalry is heated. Great secrecy surrounds the theme of each group. They usually receive sponsorships from various businesses to help cover the cost of creating their lead pieces and costumes. In addition, thousands of dollars in prize money are awarded to the winners.

For observers as well as participants, this is a very exciting night. The beat of the drums, the excitement of the crowd and the enthusiasm of the competing groups transport one to a level of excitement that is quite extraordinary.

George Roberts, New Providence

Mr. Roberts' depiction of Junkanoo during the 1930s sounded downright dangerous—firecrackers, fights and fear of getting crushed. But, from the twinkle in his eyes, I presume he enjoyed every moment of Junkanoo.

When I was growing up, Junkanoo was just cowbells and drums, no saxophones and stuff, not the modern stuff. They used homemade costumes made out of tissue paper. Crepe paper in different colours. Some were dressed up richly like angels. They were rushing up and down [dancing along] Bay Street. All the people would be on the sidewalk, watching the people rushing up and down. Spectators weren't allowed in the street just like you have it now. It start around three or four o'clock in the morning. It used to be Christmas Day. You go out there after church. After church you go to Bay Street and you hang around Black's Candy Kitchen.

I wasn't allowed in the bars, so we just stay out there with firecrackers. Lot of firecrackers. They don't use firecrackers now; they're too dangerous. But everyone had firecrackers. They throw them at you, everything, but most nobody got hurt [laughter]. We had one guy out there who get hurt all the time. A guy named Josh Symonette. He had paralysis or something, limpy. And so he was famous for going to Bay Street and getting hurt [laughter]. Every morning after Junkanoo, he'll come on Blue Hill Road where I was brought up, 'cause he lived down the street there, you know. So, you see him come down with his cowbells and things. But he done got beaten up and everything. Every Christmas he expected it. Get him a nice pretty girl, fix up her face with a lot of rouge. Women didn't take part in Junkanoo. It was all men.

There were some fights. You know, you got a group come from the east, group come from the west. Blue Hill Road divided the east district from the west. Blue Hill Road, straight across. So them groups would come down to Bay Street. You'd get a little fight, but nothing to talk about. Some get hurt, but they asked for it.

I never rushed. I was too small. They would have to hold me by my hand so I didn't get crush [laughter]. After that, everybody go home and have their parties and everything.

When the Duke of Windsor came, Junkanoo stopped being on Christmas Day. Then they started having it on Boxing Day. All the priests and stuff, they say Christmas Day suppose to be religious. So since Boxing Day was the next day, they move it. You see, they still have it on New Year's Day.

Rita Wood, New Providence

It was exciting to see how Mrs. Wood's daughter's dissertation relates to the music of Junkanoo.

We never participated in Junkanoo in my time, because we were afraid of the Junkanoo. To a child they were scary. The way they acted, you were afraid of them. They were not well put together. There was just anything.

Just the "natives" participated. Still, I don't think up to this day, white people take part in Junkanoo. The shack business [base camps where costumes are made] has only happened in the last ten years or so. They used to make the costumes at home. They used crepe paper. Now, the whole of the Bahamas and people from the United States of America come to watch Junkanoo. One year, you had all of the Kennedy clan. It's a beautiful performance. It takes place twice in less than a week. It's hard on them to prepare two sets of outfits. They have started already [in March] to prepare for next year. And they have to think what their theme will be. There are about four big groups.

My daughter, Nina Wood Charles, is studying music at Indiana University. And she is doing Junkanoo in her dissertation. For the past three months, she has been interviewing different older people about how they make cowbells, drums and everything.

You know, sometime when they are having Junkanoo, they have candles inside the goatskin drums. Otherwise, the drum goes dead and they have to fire it. That's heating it to regain the proper sound.

Nina is concentrating on the music of Junkanoo. She has everything on video camera. The first time she participated was December 1994. She enjoyed it. She said it was tiring, but she was able to see what made it tick. She made her costume. She was the tallest in the crowd. She's six feet, four inches. Her husband came to town. He used the video camera for her. She will receive her degree in June of 1995. So, I'll get a copy of her dissertation for you. She still goes as Wood, so you'll have to look for her books under that name [laughter].

Rudolph Moss, New Providence

Mr. Moss provided a fascinating description of the history of Junkanoo from the early thirties to its present form.

Junkanoo has gone through several stages of change. When I was a boy and we had Junkanoo, there weren't even fringed costumes. From the thirties to the fifties, they used newspapers for costumes and cowbells and goatskin drums and a bugle. They didn't have a brass section the way they have it now. In those days, they were all basically scrap gangs [informal groups]. You had one from out here in Virginia Street. You had groups who come from out east. Come from Bain Town; come from East Street. We were all scrap gang groups. Some may have a half-dozen people and some may have sixty or seventy. But they didn't have these monstrous groups like you have now. You had the fringe costume and you rush. Bay Street was two way then [it had two-way traffic]. So you would have these great clashes. They wouldn't have knives and bottles and stuff, but you had shows of strength. You may wind up with a cowbell across your head [laughter].

The change came about when they started to introduce prizes for best costume and so on. The Saxons and those, they are over twenty years old. New people just go and ask if they can join, so the groups continue to grow. The sponsors pay for the costumes.

Only recently, some of the Family Islands have Junkanoo. You have it in Freeport, Exuma, and I would suspect they have one in Abaco. You see, it's a recent thing. As the Nassauvians moved to other islands, they took the Junkanoo culture with them.

GUY FAWKES DAY

King James I of England, on assuming the throne, continued the anti-Catholic policies of Elizabeth I. Catholic priests were persecuted and Catholics were forbidden to receive their sacraments. Many Catholics had expected that he would moderate this oppression.

In retaliation, a group of Catholics led by Robert Catesby plotted to blow up King James I and his dignitaries, who would be present at the opening of Parliament on November 5, 1605. However, their "Gunpowder Plot" was revealed and Guy Fawkes was discovered in the cellar of the House of Parliament with casks of powder. Catesby was killed while resisting arrest, and Fawkes and the other co-conspirators were hanged in 1606.

The fact that black Bahamians did not identify with the Catholic minority, but rather celebrated their defeat, emphasizes the extent to which many Bahamians viewed themselves as loyal British subjects.

George Roberts, Nassau

Now, how I understood it to be, this guy [Guy Fawkes] was an Englishman. And something in the House of Parliament. And what I understand, they was going to assassinate the King or something. This Guy Fawkes was involved in it. So, instead of him killing the King, they burned Guy Fawkes [actually, he was hanged].

We made effigies of him and came out on the beach or up to Fort Montagu and burned him. I only know what I said. Everything [celebrations] England do, we had to do.

Rita Wood, New Providence

Mrs. Wood also erroneously refers to the burning of Guy Fawkes. The facts of the Gunpowder Plot seem to have been unimportant. She aptly sums up the celebration by noting that "blacks had to create their own entertainment."

Guy Fawkes Day is November fifth. It's a British holiday. You celebrate the burning of Guy Fawkes. He was burned alive in Britain. I don't remember, at this moment, what he had done. So we would make monuments to Guy Fawkes and burn them, too. We would make it and stuff it and put a suit or whatever on it. We would take him to Fort Charlotte and we burned him up there. As usual, you have your cowbells and you have your Guy Fawkes with you. You parade through the streets with Guy Fawkes. People from a certain area carried theirs. I think most of these things were done by the blacks. I think—perhaps I'm wrong—that the whites had more to do. So the blacks had to create their own entertainment.

Rudolph Moss, New Providence

Mr. Moss accurately described the dynamics of this activity. His explanation of why black Bahamians are not hostile to whites was particularly informative.

Guy Fawkes Day is not a holiday. The burnings take place in the evening. Guy Fawkes was a gentleman who attempted to blow up the English Parliament. And so we all commemorate Guy Fawkes Day with the burning of the effigies, principally up here on Fort Charlotte. And again you have Junkanoo music and so on. But basically, what you do is you make a doll of some varying size and you take it someplace and you light it afire.

You may wonder why we celebrated it. In colonial settings, I don't know that black people were particularly polarized as to class, power or race. We tend, even today to some extent, to celebrate these English holidays as historical occurrences. We don't attach any social class or racial tone to it.

There is very little hostility of black Bahamians to whites. When you're in the majority, you don't have to be. Black Bahamians around here want to kill up all the illegal Haitian immigrants [laughter].

EMANCIPATION DAY

Emancipation Day, August 1, 1834, was the day on which slaves were freed throughout the British Empire. On the anniversary of Emancipation Day, it was the custom, prior to the sixties, for representatives from various settlements to walk to Government Hill and present the British governor with petitions concerning matters of major concern to the black community. These processions were often organized by the combined Friendly Societies of Nassau and were led by the Grant's Town Friendly Society Band.

Later, Emancipation Day developed into a day for social activity. Because Fox Hill held the biggest celebrations of Emancipation, the day is frequently referred to as Fox Hill Day. Fox Hill, named after a free black man, Samuel Fox, is part of what was the Sandilands estate in eastern New Providence prior to Emancipation. In 1838, the village of Fox Hill was allocated to ex-slaves. The celebration is not as widely attended today as it was in past years.

Rafaleta "Goddie" Williams, Andros

Mrs. Williams discussed the only two recreational choices that existed when she was growing up on Andros.

Every holiday, like August Monday [Emancipation Day], the school open. That school what they have up there now, that was a big hall. That wasn't cut off, like you all got it cut up into rooms. One big, big, big place. That's where the dance hall used to be. That's where all the programs used to be. I used to enjoy that. When I ain't dance, it's church. That's all. We, in the olden days, that's all we used to do anyhow.

Rita Wood, New Providence

Mrs. Wood, in addition to explaining the festivities, alluded to the class structure and shared an interesting fact about the "native" beer.

Emancipation Day is the first Monday in August. It has to do with the freeing of the slaves. This [celebration] takes place in Fox Hill. That's in the eastern section of the city. They attend church first thing in the morning. Then they have ceremonies and then they have games and whatnot. It's an all day thing. The people of Fox Hill supply the food. It's Bahamian food, the usual—conch fritters, conch salad, peas and rice, fried fish and Johnny Cake. They have some Bahamian drinks and they have sodas. And, of course, later on you have the Bacardi [rum] and the Kalik [beer]. Do you know why it was named Kalik? Because of the cowbells. They make the sound of *kalik, kalik, kalik*. Kalik beer is made in the Bahamas. The brewery is in the Bahamas. The brewery's at the western end of the island [New Providence] past Lyford Cay, nearby the Bahamas Electrical Corporation.

Almost everyone attends the celebration. But we never were involved in Emancipation Day activities when I was growing up. Our father used to say, "No, you're not going to be mixing up with those people." And even to this day, we still don't mix up with those people [laughter]. When we were children, our mother took us up once or twice. We had a car, so Dada would send it for us. Most people still look forward to Emancipation Day.

Rudolph Moss, New Providence

Mr. Moss's question gave me something to contemplate.

Emancipation Day, Fox Hill Day, is the first Monday in August. It's when the slaves were freed. Don't you celebrate your emancipation day in the United States? It's basically a day for social activity in Fox Hill in particular. I presume that in the other ex-slave villages—Gambier, Adelaide and so on—something went on. But Fox Hill was the one village that had the biggest celebration of Emancipation. It was a black thing. Hardly any whites attended. I suppose they would have had church services to commemorate the historical aspects. They would have Junkanoo music and so on.

INDEPENDENCE DAY CELEBRATIONS

On July 10, 1973, the Bahamas became an independent member of the Commonwealth of Nations. Lynden O. Pindling was appointed the first prime minister. The festivities continued for a week, culminating on July 10. I attended most of the celebrations in Nassau.

On July 5, 6, and 7, 1973, there was an Independence Regatta at Fort Montagu Bay. On the sixth, Prince Charles arrived on the HMS Minerva to serve as the Queen's representative. A folklore show was staged that evening. July 8 was designated as a national day of prayer. Prince Charles attended the ecumenical service at Clifford Park in the morning, and a community choir presented a concert at the Botanical Garden in the evening.

Crowds began to gather at Fort Charlotte long before sunset on July 9, 1973, to assure that they had good seats to see the Bahamas attain independence. The program started at 9:30 P.M. with a prayer, followed at 10:30 P.M. by a musical and cultural presentation. The flag raising ceremony was at midnight. Children had been taught the new national anthem in school and exploded into song at the appropriate time. The festivities concluded with a magnificent display of fireworks.

On the morning of July 10, Prince Charles read the Queen's message, and Prime Minister Pindling gave the Bahamian reply. The celebrations concluded at 4 A.M. on July 11, with an Independence Junkanoo Parade.

Independence Day celebrations have been held every year since 1973. From July 3 to 5, a Commonwealth Fair takes place on the grounds of Government House and at two school locations. Booths are staffed by organizations selling all kinds of food, from pigeon peas and rice to various conch dishes—salad, fritters, scorched and steamed. People who are experts in the areas of woodwork, needlepoint and smocking [fancy stitching of clothing] have handicraft booths. Live entertainment is provided by the Royal Bahamas Police Band, school choirs and marching bands. Every year, church services and regattas also take place. But I doubt that any celebration will ever compare to July 10, 1973.

Rita Wood, New Providence

The first Independence Day celebration in 1973 was glorious. Before independence happened, there was a whole week of celebrations. And because of my husband's position—he was then the Financial Secretary of the Bahamas—we were invited to everything. I had three functions for each day. So I had to get myself organized, and I would have three different outfits and things all planned each day. It was beautiful. We enjoyed every minute of it, almost like when I was in Washington. The most outstanding event was that Prince Charles came to the Bahamas to represent the Queen. And at the end, the tenth of July came around.

On the tenth of July, we were going to have the big celebration. We were invited to Government House for dinner. Prince Charles was there with all the hifalutin dignitaries. It was a dinner for twenty-four people. It was a black-tie affair. So we left Government House all dressed up for this event and went to Clifford Park for the extravaganza. Our names were on our seats so we did not lose our positions, even though we arrived late. We were taken to our seats when we got to the celebration. By then, you had thousands and thousands; there were more than ten thousand people. There were more than twenty thousand people there. Because you had the tourists come in; the people from the islands come in. You had dances by the schoolchildren, everything. It was an entertainment like they can never have again.

And then, just before midnight, the then prime minister of the Bahamas, Lynden O. Pindling, took down the Union Jack and put up the Bahamian flag. You know, I can still hear the cheers. Cheering, cheering. I have a book with that, you know. We had fireworks at the end. We didn't leave until after one o'clock in the morning. We sang the national anthem for the first time, "Lift Up Your Heads to the Rising Sun." All the schoolchildren had been taught the song. Any child who was a schoolchild, even the white children, took part. There had been a faction of whites in Abaco and other places who had opposed the independence movement. Some white Bahamians had gone to London and had their talks and they didn't want Independence.

The night of Independence, they had ten balls. Prince Charles was taken to every one. I have a picture of him with Lady Pindling, dancing the night away. They had a party! The balls were at the hotels. He went from the balls to his ship. I think he had stayed at Government House while he was here. There is a celebration every year, but nothing to compare to what we had the first year. That was out of this world.

Rudolph Moss, New Providence

Mr. Moss cogently described the annual activities that take place in Nassau to celebrate Independence.

The celebration of Independence Day is marked by formal events. The Bahamas Christian Council, an inter-denominational organization, initiates a religious service on Fort Charlotte. At that service, a lot of officials attend—the governor-general, the prime minister, his cabinet, members of parliament, members of the diplomatic corps and the public, all and sundry. It's an occasion that is really a culmination of a week of events. There are quite a few events that lead up to it.

After the church service, you have an inspection of the guard, if you want to call it that, but the guard is more than just the military and the paramilitary. It extends to all the regular touring bodies, their representative elements, from the police, the defence force, from customs, from immigration. Then you have the police dogs, they do a thing. The police motorcyclists, they do a routine. The police in cars do a routine in formation. It's quite a colourful thing. The night before, they may have a special function again on Clifford Park. Clifford Park is the parade grounds at Fort Charlotte. Then they have functions at several other places. They may have a particular formal opening of some building or some school or something. Then, too, the Bahamian marine elements arrange special sailing regattas. In many of the islands, they celebrate with a regatta. The government plans it in conjunction with civic groups. The children also participate in the parade. They will have kids on parade on Independence night. They will have some things down at Fort Charlotte again. The police put on a special performance the night before Independence. They take several hours. They demonstrate fire drills and other routines of theirs. On some occasions, they end up with fireworks on Arawak Cay. The governor-general is always present. He is the official representative of the Queen, but we have had, on occasion, members of the royal family here to participate in the celebrations.

Cuisine

Many Bahamian dishes are unique to these islands. Conch is an important staple. At Potter's Cay, in Nassau, vendors have wooden stalls where they sell various conch dishes. Each stall has its own following of Nassauvians, who insist that the best "vittles" are made there. Recently, a festival village has been created at Arawak Cay, which is now the center of the prepared conch trade.

At these stalls, conch salad is prepared before your eyes to your specifications (somewhat). Typically, the first steps are to wash the cutting board with salt water and to sharpen a large butcher knife. Then a conch, which has been stored in a bucket of salt water, is retrieved. After it is skinned, the conch is scored [cut into small pieces, one-quarter to one-half inch]. The size of the pieces varies from stall to stall.

Next, vegetables are cut with a swiftness that is unbelievable, consider-
ing the sharpness of the knife and its proximity to the man's fingers. Half
a green pepper, a stalk of celery, an onion and a green or ripe tomato are
then added. At this point, the purchaser is usually allowed to determine
the amount of bird pepper to be included. Salt is sprinkled and, using
the knife, the man mixes everything together and flips it into a plastic
dish. The last ingredients are half of a sour orange and a lime, which are
squeezed over the mixture. There is an art to making conch salad, and
most of these vendors have an abundance of talent.

Although rice is not grown in these islands, it is an essential part of
the diet. Rice was first introduced in the Bahamas when the British were
in control, and it continues to be imported from other former colonies.
Pigeon peas are usually cooked in the rice but can also be served in a
soup with dumplings. Fatback [salted fat from pork] is an ingredient in
almost all rice dishes. Chopped onions, sweet peppers, hot peppers and
celery are important seasonings.

The waters of the Bahamas hold a huge assortment of fish. And, for
most Bahamians, fish is an important staple. It is prepared in a variety of
ways and served at breakfast, lunch and/or dinner.

Coconut cakes, lemon meringue pies, pineapple tarts, soursop ice
cream or the typically Bahamian guava duff with rum sauce usually
finish a dinner.

A number of Colonial Reports, during the early decades of this cen-
tury, expressed concern over the fact that large numbers of children were
suffering from malnutrition. The problem continues to exist. Since most
foods in the markets (with the exception of chicken, tropical fruit, and
tomatoes) are imported and expensive, one wonders how poor families in
Freeport and Nassau can provide nutritious meals for their children. At
least on the Family Islands, many residents have a household garden and
some livestock.

Clementina Adderley, Long Island

I cherish Mrs. Adderley's recipe for conch chowder. With at least
seventy-five years of experience, I'm sure that she has perfected the
procedure.

When the wind blowing and it cold and I put on a sweater and still cold,
I makes some chowder. I get out about enough oil to cover the bottom of

the pot and cut up half cup each of onion, celery, sweet pepper [green], carrots and potato. Dice 'em 'bout this size [the size of a sugar cube]. I get two nice-size conchs and cut 'em up. I cook some pork in oil 'til it browns up, put in everything. Put in a bay leaf and sprinkle in a good amount of thyme. Let that simmer for a few minutes. As it cooking, I chop two tomatoes and put them in the pot to cook for about ten minutes. If it don't look like I want [colour], I add 'bout a third a can of tomato paste. Then I put in a quart of water and some hot peppers and let it simmer for an hour and a half. While it cooking, I get out my iron frying pan and make some Johnny Cake. I keep tastin' it [the chowder]. If it taste fresh and need more seasoning, I add. If it greasy, I skim off the grease. Then I sit down with my meal and get warm all over [laughter].

> *My mother had quite a reputation for her pound cake. Many years ago, she patiently wrote the recipe down for me. I have never been able to replicate the flavor and texture that I remember. The recipe includes:*
>
> 4½ cups of flour at room temperature
> 1½ teaspoons of salt—sift with the flour
> 1 lb. butter—stir butter until creamy. Add sugar.
> 2 cups of sugar
> 10 eggs—slightly mixed
> 2 teaspoons of vanilla
> Bake at 325 degrees for 20 minutes. Increase heat to 350 degrees
>   for 40 minutes.

George Roberts, New Providence

> *Mr. Roberts is an excellent cook who thoroughly enjoys serving gourmet meals to his guests.*

I got some peas and rice right there. You want to learn how to make them? [Laughter.] Well, you saute onions, celery, tomatoes, sweet pepper or bell pepper, hot pepper, salt, thyme. Put the salt and the pepper to your taste. Use a half teaspoon of thyme. You have to blend the flavors in the saute. I never measure the amounts, you know. You fry pork first or bacon. They fry bacon now but in those days, we fried fatback. Then you add the tomato paste to taste. I use half of a tomato-paste can. I don't like it too yellow. Then you saute that. But you got to boil the pigeon peas first. I buy peas in the can. They got 'em in the can. They got the green and the dried ones in the can. If you're using the can, you put one cup of rice to one can of peas. Just enough water to cover the rice. You leave the pot open. 'Cause the water got to evaporate out. If you want it gummy, you put the cover on. I prefer dry rice. Cook it on a medium flame. I'd say about three hundred at the beginning. Then you keep lowering the fire. Cook it 'til it done. I does taste it [laughter]. Let it simmer for a half hour. Then you check it. But you got to stir the peas and rice up together. One woman tell me nobody don't stir it, but I can't get 'em to mix unless I turn it over. And then you leave it open and you check it every fifteen minutes. Then you got to taste it to see if it's done.

I'm gonna make some conch fritters right now. I don't cut up the conch, I put it through the machine and grind it up. You grind the conch. I can do [explain] this one, I think [laughter]. Then you cut up celery, Jamaica peppers, green and red sweet peppers, thyme, salt to taste. You mix them up. Then you take a cup of flour. They didn't have no self-rising flour. You had to use a teaspoon of baking powder. You put water 'til it get like a batter. Then you whip it up good, 'til it get like if you making brownies or cookies, that consistency. Then you get your wooden spoon. You heat the oil first. Don't make it too hot! If you make it too hot, it gonna burn too quick. You set the stove to a certain temperature. Let the fire stay to that temperature. I prefer three hundred degrees. So you let the oil heat to that temperature. Say five minutes. I drop some water off my fingers into the oil to tell if it's the right temperature. Then you ready. Keep it at that temperature. You got to watch it. You have to have a sense of time that you got to cook it. The old way is that—we used coal fire then, smooth, widen up your coals, and put your pot with the oil on and fry them [laughter]. It had to be professional with my family. They used to make them to sell. That was a big deal, sell them with the donkey cart [laughter].

In the beginning when you drop them [the fritters] in the pot, they gonna sink. But then when they rise, they gonna float on the top. But you got to keep turning them over. These the round kind. You can make the flat kind, too. Them, you don't deep fry. You just put a little bit of lard or whatever you put in the pot. And they come flat like pancakes. Modern people make little fritters that you got to pick up with a toothpick and dip in sauce. You can use a hot salsa. You can make it with ketchup, bird peppers and mayonnaise, too. It's up to your choice.

Rudolph Moss, New Providence

The Nassau grouper is a large striped fish that can usually be found near coral reefs. Boiled fish, using grouper, is a popular Sunday morning breakfast dish.

Grouper is a favorite Bahamian fish. One method of preparation is to make boiled fish. You need a heavy pot with a cover. Wash about a pound and a half of the fish and season it with salt, black and hot pepper. Cut the piece of grouper into smaller pieces, about two inches by four inches. Use two medium-sized potatoes cut into one-inch cubes and a large onion sliced thin. Add about four tablespoons of butter and the juice from two limes. Pour in enough water to cover everything and cover the pot. Let it simmer over a low flame for half an hour. Taste it to see if additional seasoning is needed. Boiled fish can be served with Johnny Cake or grits. You didn't know I could cook, did you?

Calypso Lyrics

Any effort to describe the Bahamas must include Goombay music. Although Calypso is considered to have its roots in Trinidad, the Bahamas have a unique form of this genre, referred to as Goombay. Reading Goombay folk songs as text is not totally effective, because three important elements are missing—the intricate harmonies, the Bahamian accents and the beat of the music. In spite of these omissions, the words give us an important glimpse into Bahamian culture. The songs are witty, humorous and/or full of double entendre. Their themes usually relate to special occasions, Bahamian women's enticements or advice about conducting successful relationships. Those appearing here convey popular attitudes on social, economic or political situations.

Various performers use different words to sing these songs. These lyrics represent typical Goombay folk songs as sung in the Bahama Islands.

Ugly Woman

If you ever want to be happy and live a king's life,
Never make a pretty woman your wife.
If you ever want to be happy and live a king's life,
Never make a pretty woman your wife.
All you got to do is just as I say,
If you want to be happy and merry and gay.

REFRAIN

Therefore from a logical point of view,
Always marry a woman uglier than you.

A pretty woman makes her husband look small.
And very often causes him his downfall.
Soon as you married, in the day she starts
To do the things that will ache his heart;
In the night when you think she's belonging to you
She calling on somebody else to do.
REFRAIN

When you make an ugly woman your wife,
You can be sure to be happy for all of your life.
She wouldn't do things in a funny way,
To give the neighbours something to say.
She wouldn't disregard her husband at all
By running around with Peter and Paul.
REFRAIN

An ugly woman gives you your meal on time;
Try to make you comfortable in mind.
In the night when you lay on your cozy bed,
She's coax, caress you and scratch your head.
That's not the time that she'll leave you alone—
That she wouldn't melt the fat from your bone.
REFRAIN

Matter not that your friends say you have no taste;
Marry an ugly woman without disgrace.
One who is cute looking, robust and rough.
With skin like alligator; bumpy and tough
Beak for the mouth, olives for eyes,
Around the mouth like confirmation bow ties.
REFRAIN

Love Alone

Come a reeling, come a rolling upon my mind
But I just can't leave Ms. Simpson behind.

REFRAIN

It was love, love, love alone caused King Edward to leave the throne,
It was love, love, love alone caused King Edward to leave the throne,
It was love, love, love alone caused King Edward to leave the throne.

If a ship or a plane will carry me free
I will walk with Ms. Simpson across the sea.
REFRAIN

Now I know my mother, she's going to grieve
But I just can't help it, I'm bound to leave.
REFRAIN

Now she got some money and she got a talk
And a fancy walk just to suit New York.
REFRAIN

I didn't know Ms. Simpson was a woman like that
She wear tight dresses to make King Edward fret.
REFRAIN

Let the organ play, let the church bell ring
Let the nation sing, "God Save the King."
REFRAIN

Island Woman

The fishing's good near your island
That's why I came back for more
I saw you swim near my boat
And I followed you back to shore

REFRAIN
Island woman, Island woman, making me forget who I am
Island woman, Island woman, making me forget who I am.

Forgot to sail back to market
To bring the fish and get paid
Forgot my wife and the children
Forgot we soon will have eight.
REFRAIN

You dance for me in the moonlight
We drink some rum and have fun

When I wake up in the daylight
You take me money and run.
REFRAIN

My pocket is full of empty
I'm back with my family
But some day when I have money
I'm coming back, you will see.
REFRAIN

The next song refers to the loss of three small boats that started out from New Providence, headed for Andros in 1929. They were caught in one of the worse hurricanes of this century. According to legend, all of the passengers drowned, and each of the ships sank.

As with many of the Bahamian calypsos, a background choral group beautifully sang the same refrain in three-part harmony after each verse: "Run, come, see, Run, come, see Jerusalem."

Run, Come, See Jerusalem

1. *Twas nineteen hundred and twenty-nine,*
I remember that day pretty well.
Nineteen hundred and twenty-nine.
2. *Right then, they was talkin' about a storm in the island*
My God, what a beautiful morning
They was talkin' about a storm in the island.
3. *Right then it was three sail leaving out the harbour,*
With mothers and children on board
Was three sail leaving out the harbour,
4. *Those sail was the Ethel, and the Myrtle and the Pretoria*
My God, they were bound for Andros
The Ethel and the Myrtle and the Pretoria.
5. *Right then, the Ethel was bound for Staniard Creek*
With mothers and children on board
Then the Ethel was bound for Staniard Creek.
6. *My God, then the Myrtle was bound for Fresh Creek*
My God, what a beautiful morning
Then the Myrtle was bound for French Creek.
7. *My God, Pretoria was out on the ocean*

Dashing from side to side from waves
The Pretoria was out on the ocean.
8. Right then when a big sea build up in the northwest
Then children come holding on to mothers
When a big sea build up in the northwest.
9. My God, when the first sea hit the Pretoria
Then mothers come holding on to children
When the first sea hit the Pretoria.
10. My God, then it send her head down to the bottom
Then the captain come grabbin' for the tiller
When it send her head down to the bottom.
11. My God, it was thirty-three souls on the water
Swimmin' and prayin' to the Daniel God
Thirty-three souls on the water.
12. My God, then George Brown, he was the captain
He shout, "My children, come pray."
Now George Brown, he was the captain.
13. My God, he say, "Come now, witness your judgment."
He shout, "My children, come pray."
Come now, witness your judgment
'Cause I've seen Jerusalem.

("Run, Come, See Jerusalem," words and music by Blind Blake, TRO, copyright 1952 [renewed] Hollis Music, Inc., New York, N.Y.; used by permission)

Bahama Brown Baby

REFRAIN
Ah baby, ah baby, ah baby from Savannah Sound
Ah baby, ah baby, don't upset me with your cool Bahamian brown.
1. I turn my head and look at you
With such fine shape there is so few
And even they share not your view
So rosy and so round.
REFRAIN
2. I look at you and wonder where
You get that shape beyond compare
I look again and then I swear
You've got undeveloped land.

REFRAIN

3. I dream all night and hope all day
That sometime soon, you'll come my way
And that day babe I hope you'll say
I love you, that's my man.

REFRAIN

Nassau Blues

REFRAIN

Why oh, why oh, why oh, why oh, why 'a
Why oh, why oh, why oh, why oh why 'a.
1. Sitting by the ocean, me heart she feels so down
Ain't got no money to take me back to Nassau town.
Find calypso woman, she cook me fish and rice
Find calypso woman, she cook me fish and rice.

REFRAIN

2. Those Yankee hot dogs don't treat me stomach very nice.
In Nassau town, one dollar buy papaya juice, banana pie
Six coconuts, one female goat, and plenty fish to fill the boat
*One bushel of bran, one barrel of wine, and all the time, she comes to
dine.*

REFRAIN

3. But here in States one dollar buy one cup of coffee, ham on rye.
Me throat she hurts from necktie, me foot she hurts from shoes
Me pocket full of empty, I got calypso blues.
Why oh, why oh, why oh, why oh, why 'a
Why oh, why oh, why oh, why oh why 'a.

REFRAIN

A New Day Dawning

*This song was introduced when the Bahamas were gaining their
independence. It was immensely popular during the seventies.*

People moving up, a new day is dawning
Let's put our heads together and face reality
Oh yes, together, we gonna shape our destiny
Now we don't have any dollar or currency
But we can teach the world how to live in harmony
So move on up people, let's get it together
There's a new day dawning.

Move on up people, 'cause we're gonna shape our destiny
Now every knock from many quarters by adverse publicity
Some of our own have knocked us quite heavily
Let's get it together, 'cause we're shaping our destiny
We'll never fall if we're together.
No matter, no matter how stormy the weather
So move on up people, let's get it together
There's a new day dawning.
Move on up people, 'cause we're gonna shape our destiny
Oh yes, move on up people, let's get it together
There's a new day dawning.
Oh, move on up, let's get it together
There's a new day dawning.

8

Traditional Occupations

Sisal Farming

Sisal is a natural fiber contained in the leaves of agave rigida sislana plants. Because of its stiff, strong texture, it was used to make rope and twine. Significant amounts of money were invested in sisal farming by English companies. In 1908, sisal was the major export of the Bahamas. Five processing factories existed on New Providence, two were in operation on Inagua, and others were located on Little Abaco, Whale Cay and the Berry Islands. The Bahamas were unable to compete with Mexican growers, however, due to Mexico's better soil and cheaper wages. Government officials, in their reports to the Colonial Office, frequently complained that output from other countries, high United States duties and the practice of cutting immature fiber had caused the price of Bahamian sisal to drop.

Furthermore, in 1926, the industry was crippled by hurricanes, which destroyed the leaves of the plants. These misfortunes, and Philippine exports of a higher grade of sisal, resulted in the gradual closing of the fac-

*tories. Growing and processing of sisal had become a peasant industry by
1940. The failure of the sisal industry caused many thousands of Bahamians to return to subsistence farming.*

Carrie Lunn, New Providence

My father was a manager of a sisal plantation. He started from Turks
Island. There was a place called West Acres, and there was a lot of sisal
growing there. An Englishman came out by the name of Mr. Wilde, and he
got friendly with my father. They worked together with this sisal plantation. Then, after the sisal died out from there, they came down to the
Bahamas looking for sisal. Then, over in Whale Cay, the sisal got too low,
and they moved to Abaco, where they found a lot of sisal. And they opened
factories here in Nassau, down to the Caves. Then at a place called Chap-
man's, they had two factories.

This man, Mr. Wilde, had a yacht. My father was a navigator. He
brought the boat down into Nassau and they went to Whale Cay, where
they found a lot of sisal. It was growing wild. Like nobody cared about it.
Nobody took an interest. When they came, they took over this place. I
don't know who the place belonged to. All I know is that they started
cultivating the land, and then they would have the sisal.

They had factories over there. A factory to grind the sisal and a factory
to bale it, to ship it away to make rope. They hired local people. They had
men that would go into the sisal fields and cut the sisal, the long leaf with
a little brown prong. And they would cut it and fix it in bundles and put it
in a dray [wagon]. I'll tell you what a dray is. It is made of pieces of long
wood [that go] crossway and two wheels, one on either side and drawn by
a mule. They would cut the sisal, tie it in bundles and lay it on this dray.
The dray used to bring freight from the ships. They used to have drays in
those days. They had no trucks. And we had very few motor cars. Then
they would take it [the sisal] into the factory, and they had women to cut
those bundles asunder and fix it on a metal chain that would go through
the machine to take all that green off. They call it feeding the sisal. They
would lay it right on, and as they would start up the engine, they put the
sisal in, and it would go through just like that. Come right out into a big
trough. And the women used to take it and wash it in the sea and hang
it out.

The factory was built on the edge of the water. They would take it [the
sisal] to the sea to wash it. They had hangers, which they put them on. Just

like how you would fix it on a clothesline. It was like bleachers. You throw this washed sisal on these bleachers and you leave them there. If the rain came, all the better. It would wash it some more. Then, when it's dry, they pick it in. Fix it in smaller bundles and clip it. Clip all of it even. Then it would go through this bigger machine, which would bale it up to ship it to make rope.

They shipped it to the United States. I don't remember what state they shipped it to. My father came over here [New Providence] and supervised the factories. That was his work.

Joanna Bethel, Grand Bahama

Mrs. Bethel described how individuals, rather than businesses, grew, processed and used sisal.

People used to grow sisal for a living when I was young. They cut the leaves and strip them and tie them in little bundles and put them in the sea for them to rot. Then they take them out and they wash them off clean. And after that, they bundled them into bales and ship them into Nassau. And that was used to make rope and hats, shoes, slippers and all that. I don't think they do it anymore. They don't have the sisal to do it. You get the spotty areas. Ivy Simms, on Long Island, uses it for pompoms on top of the hats. But it's getting scarce. People used to help themselves get money like that.

Rafaleta "Goddie" Williams, Andros

According to Mrs. Williams, the entire preparation of sisal, including the cutting of the leaves, was done on Andros by women. This was not the case everywhere. She said that the men were out sponge fishing.

We go out to get some banella—some sisal, they call it. You see it out here. Cut they; that's what we live off in my day. Put 'em in the water; soak 'em. You used to sell 'em. They make rope with them. We, the women, were doing it. Ain't a man's job. It was a woman's job to soak it and wash it.

John Wilson, born on October 29, 1915, Bluff, Cat Island

I was talking with Mr. Wilson for half an hour before I found out that he was blind. This was because he "looks at you" when he speaks, wears clear glasses and has such an assured bearing. He is one of the elders of his settlement. When Mr. Wilson asked various people to show me aspects of how they processed corn, each of them responded instantly. He is obviously a very respected member of his community. His description of processing sisal and his explanation of the economics of the process were quite enlightening.

I was a farmer from fourteen years old. The first farm I went into was sisal, that's what we was growing. Sisal. That's the first living I started to work. Then I start farming corn, peas, potato, beans. Farm all that.

How we farm sisal, we burn the land and we get the small shoots of sisal. They like pineapple shoots. And we put them in the ground to grow. After nine months, we could cut them. Strip them open. Get a knife, you know? Some have side points and you got a point up top. You cut off those side points and cut off the bottom point and you take a knife and you cut the heart. You take scissors and you scrape the green off. After that, you sheaf a certain amount and you tie it up. Then you have to go to the farm. Put the bundles in water for eight to fifteen days. After that time, we go and we wash it. After it washed, after it dried, you pack it in one bale and it goes to Nassau. That what Nassau does sell. They shipped it away. And make rope and the rope come right back to Nassau again and we buy the same rope. I does made rope myself.

Bob Dean, Andros

*Mr. Dean pointed out a large field of sisal plants with big green leaves
that terminated in sharp, dark points. From his description, I gathered
that men did this work also.*

This is sisal. In days gone, you couldn't buy nylon rope, only the rich man.
So we used to cut 'em off down there, strip 'em open. Put one end on your
feet. And scrape it up. When we reach to the end we stop, get a piece of
wire or a string. String 'em up. Put 'em in a place where dead water is, and
in 'bout twelve days, we go and we shake it out like that and everything
come white, white, white.

The points is poison. Yeah, man, if they stick you, they won't make you
sick, but give you plenty burning in your skin.

Subsistence Farming

*Natural disasters in the form of droughts, hurricanes and insects have
plagued the Bahamian agriculture industry since its inception. During
the first decade of this century, major exports from the Bahamas included
sisal, sponge and pineapples. In spite of a prolonged drought in 1907, the
Family Islands produced the greater part of the food, including chicken
and meat, consumed in the Bahamas prior to 1914. The Family Islands
produced corn, fish, turtle, pineapple and citrus fruits. In addition, they
exported sponges, the shell of the hawksbill turtle, and sisal. Then, during the twenties, the blue-gray fly appeared and began spreading through
the islands. Within two years, the entire citrus fruit enterprise had been
eliminated.*

*In 1932, corn birds destroyed many of the cornfields of Grand Bahama.
It was reported that there were three defenses against corn birds: the
farmer needed to stay in the field from sunrise to sunset until the corn
matured; he needed to beat an oil tin constantly throughout the day; or
he needed to shout very loudly as the birds approached.*

*Tomato farming became a rapidly growing industry during the period
from 1911 to 1920, although the continued lack of rain during the summer of 1918 devastated many crops on Eleuthera. Because Bahamian tomatoes were harvested earlier in the season than those in Florida, exports
to the United States and Canada were profitable during the twenties
and early thirties. By 1934, the sale of tomatoes yielded the third highest*

export revenues for the Bahamas. Because the United States had raised tariffs, and Cuba and Mexico were competing in the market, exportation to the United States became unprofitable shortly afterward. Exports of tomatoes continued to be shipped to Canada.

Although Jamaica began competing for the United States' tomato market in the 1950s, Abaco, Andros and Grand Bahama continued to successfully export small amounts. The Colonial Secretary reported in 1951 that the Board of Agriculture and Marine Products continued its policy of furnishing seeds, fertilizer, inspection and marketing facilities to aid farmers on the Family Islands. He further described a steady increase in pineapple production. Sugar loaf and red Spanish varieties, grown in Eleuthera, were being shipped abroad. Through most of the fifties, major exports continued to include pineapples, crawfish and lumber.

By 1960, pineapple exports had diminished to insignificant proportions. Citrus fruits grown on the islands were sold primarily in Nassau local markets, and the use of sisal was restricted to the manufacture of local products. During all of these years, white Bahamian merchants were in complete control of the economy. The export of cash crops and marine products was determined by them.

In 1980, the Bahamas Development Bank reported that only 13% of its loans had been for agricultural pursuits. Similarly, the World Bank estimated that agriculture accounted for less than 5% of the gross domestic product of the Bahamas in 1986. This trend may be reversing, however, as a result of the Ministry of Agriculture Act of 1993, and the fact that almost 90% of land in the Bahamas is government-owned Crown land. In an effort to utilize these Crown lands to aid in the growth of the economy, the Prime Minister directed that 36,148 acres on Andros, Abaco and Grand Bahama be leased to the Ministry of Agriculture.

Andros, Abaco, Grand Bahama and Eleuthera are the main islands presently exporting crops. In 1994, they exported citrus, cucumbers, okra, avocado and papaya valued at $14.5 million. Ninety-five percent of this produce was shipped to the United States. Other governmental efforts to encourage agricultural development include the government experimental station's policy of providing budded citrus plants to interested individuals.

For some Bahamians on the Family Islands, agriculture remains their only livelihood. Packinghouses on Andros, Cat Island, Exuma, Long Island and Eleuthera store produce until it can be shipped to Nassau or exported. Freeport and Nassau have wholesale produce exchanges. Dairy farms are successful operations on Grand Bahama and New Providence. In 1993, poultry farms provided over fourteen million pounds of meat and four million cartons of eggs. Presently, about 1,800 such farms exist, but the challenge of getting young people to choose agriculture as a vocation remains.

Clementina Adderley, Long Island

I used to farm all over, down in the Bight, down to Pinders. I walk and had a donkey. And she coulda only bring the produce. Whatever you get in the fields, she bring a load. I teach my children how to farm.

When I coulda go, I'd rather take my feet, never worried about walking, never had a car. When we used to work on the farm, I used to leave from here in the morning, three o'clock, and I used to get to the Bight or Pinders and sit down 'til daylight to go to work. We don't wait until no daylight to left from home.

Fred Ramsey, Cat Island

Mr. Ramsey has two shelves near the ceiling of his house. They contain large unlabeled jars with seeds inside. He saves and dries some of his seeds and kernels each year. He plants these for the next crop. He guarantees his seeds!

I keep my corn up on shelves in those jugs. Put it in a way that people can't take it. People destroy it. It's for seed. Most people don't disturb the farm, you know. Once in a while, you may find some people pass around and broke a corn or so. These are lima beans. There's a big lima and a small. You can carry them back to New York and plant them. You can get a couple more. Put two in a hole. You can't eat the lima beans you'll get [laughter]. You'll get too many!

John Wilson, Cat Island

Mr. Wilson solicited the assistance of his wife and her friend to teach me how to make grits. Since he is blind, he touched each piece of equipment and the corn as he described the process. The women paced the speed of their activities to match his descriptions.

We only grow up eating guinea corn grits, lima beans, cow peas, pigeon peas, beans and sweet potato. Now, I'm going to tell you. In my time, we cooked rice once a week. That's on Sunday. When you get a pound, it was for Sunday. Sweet potatoes, yams, cassava, benne [sesame seeds], Irish potato, pineapple—all that we grow up with.

You want to know how we turn corn into grits? See the hop on top? You pour the corn inside. First of all, you crack it. Then you send it through twice more. You fine [grind] it to your perfection, right? Then you take it out and you sift it first. Take off the flour. Then you take off the husk. And that's your grits. We put a post in the ground and put the mill on it and grind the corn. We have two corn, red corn [Indian corn] and guinea corn [black and white kernels]. But the most we eat is guinea corn. I can call one of those ladies and let them give you a demonstration. We'll put an amount of guinea corn in there, and let one of these ladies show you. There's some grits in there. There's some flour in there. Take this and sift the flour. Take off the husk. Now the shaft empty. And that's grits. Ready to cook.

Go in the pot and cook. That's what we live off. We buy the corn from a farmer. This is only the stalk. Cut it here, when it ripe. Put it in a flour bag and beat it with a stick. You bring it home. You already cut your field, right? And then when you go to thresh, you thresh all at one time and then you put it in a drum until you're ready to grind it. Take it out of the drum and you go to work. Now, when you done thrash this corn, you put it right in the fanner [a sifter made from straw]. And your flour is ready. Corn flour is very good.

If you have mice, they'll go into it and eat it. But most of the time, when you're in the field, it's the black birds. Yeah, they'll eat the corn in the field the minute it starts getting ripe. You tie a piece of cloth on every tree. Then they eat, but not that much.

Benjamin Saunders, Andros

Mr. Saunders painted a vivid picture of subsistence farming. For example, in the old days, armed with a cutlass and a bag containing seed, he walked through the bush to "sight a good spot."

When I first got married, I was just doing gardening in Cat Cay. Well, it was different sections, different crew of men working in different direction. Sometimes they move you from one thing and put you to another.

But I spend about three months, and I came back. After that, I went back to the old system again, doing the farming.

Go fishing when I can, after the farm is set. Get on the boat and go fishing. We only farmed—just to have some produce for ourselves. It wasn't no farming being done like how it is today. We had to do that with your cutlass [a short, curved sword with a sharp edge on one side], support a whole family. But today, tractors is available, and they can cultivate some land for you and you can go out and plant a good crop. But it wasn't so then. We only had a little path to go through the bushes, you see? You could walk from here across the water with your cutlass and your bag and you go. Wherever you sight a good spot where you could make a farm, why then, you go and cultivate. But that was only for family use, not to sell to anyone. We farmed just to have some produce for ourselves.

After the Contract [an agreement between the United States and British governments], I went back to the old system again, doing the farming. Go fishing when I can. And I did that until I was listed as a constable [a member of the police force].

Gerald Dean, Cat Island

I have used a fictitious name for this gentlemen, because he requested that his comments be reported anonymously. Mr. Dean clearly described the "slash-and-burn" method of farming used by his father, who successfully grew an amazing assortment of crops. Mr. Dean, in his farming and training of others, uses techniques that are more advanced.

I work as a minister of the church down the road part-time, and I work part-time for the Ministry of Agriculture. I see about the farming in the area. See about the farmers. In the old days, my father just went out with a cutlass and cut the bushes down. When it dry, he burn it. If he want to plant a second crop, he would take a hoe and dig a hole. But if he was going to plant corn or cassava, he would just take a stick and put it in the hole and drop the seed in. He planted sweet potatoes from slip [root or stem cut from the plant]. You can plant them from seed but it takes a longer time to run, you know? Plant that slip. Just cut the tender end off and put that in, and that keep on growing. He grew everything, cassava, sweet potato, pineapples. He grew guinea corn. His farm wasn't that big, two acres, three acres, sometimes. He had a place to plant everything. Well, he had more than one farm. Put them all together and I guess he had more than three or four acres across on the sandy loam. He had a place over there, where he grew onions and cabbages and things like that.

There was a time when—it might sound kinda funny—New Providence, Nassau got the food from the Out Islands [Family Islands]. And Long Island and Cat Island were some of the major islands of that. It change. People began to open up large stores and selling like that, flour, grits. As things got sophisticated, the people didn't want our produce any more.

They wanted the chicken that came from the United States. They wanted the pork from the United States. They wanted all the meat from the United States. There was a time when all the chickens they had was from Cat Island and the other Family Islands. Now, they don't want the native chickens; those chickens gone wild. You see them all through the place. They still buy eggs sometimes. But they stop buying from the Family Islands some years ago.

You know, I went on Contract [worked on farms in the United States through an agreement between the United States and British governments] in '43, something like four years. And by that time, people began buying stuff from the United States. When I came back, I just start farming myself. But I farm little different from most of the farmers here. They—most of them—still use the cutlass and slash the bushes down, but I get a tractor. I sell my produce. Right now, I trying to sell some tomatoes.

I tell you, I used to pick strawberries in New York. They could grow here because in the summertime you have the same temperature. They grow quick. It doesn't take a long time.

We don't grow sugar apples [green sectioned skin, with very sweet, pulpy fruit inside] and other native fruit for sale, you know. You'll find that most people have a tree, but not enough for a sale product. A few people have mangoes. The old folks grew mangoes and pineapples to sell. Because all through the land, you meet an old mango tree, pineapples. The old folks used to grow that. But the young people today, they grow one crop: tomatoes. They want to make money. This is why you have so much waste in tomatoes. We bottle. We put them in bottles for our use and friends, you know.

It's easier to sell what you grow now. Before, you had to send it to Nassau and you had to take what you get for it. Now you carry your stuff to the packinghouse and they give you a ticket. And after a while, at the end of the month, if the commissioner is stationed here, you get your money much quicker. If he's not here, it might take a couple of months.

There's a standard price from the Ministry of Agriculture. What they paying for this and the other. A few months ago, tomatoes were twelve cents. You can get a lot of money for hot pepper [bird pepper, *Capsicum minimum*]. Many people don't grow that, but it brings a good deal of money.

Nobody grows flowers full time. I remember when every house had a flower garden, beautiful flowers. I guess the people who used to do it are dead. The young people, they don't stay here long enough to grow anything.

John Newman, Long Island

Mr. Newman's comparison between slash-and-burn farming and farming with a tractor is clear and informative. He was the only "absentee farmer" whom I met. It sounded like a perfect arrangement.

Before, we didn't have any tractors, so we couldn't raise bananas much. Only you had to find nature holes [natural recesses in the land], you know? You find holes and you clean them out. But now, they go through it with the tractor. And the tractor rip the land. Push off the black soil first. Then they rip up and get the white soil, which we call the quarry [crushed limestone]. Push that aside. And put the black soil back in. Use a little fertilizer and plant your banana down so it can get a little moisture. See, the banana needs moisture, but it can't stand too much moisture.

Now what happens, they raise about two different crops in there before reaping the bananas. When they plant bananas, they plant watermelons right to the same hole and fertilize. The watermelon will come and bear before the banana is ready. So they weed up the watermelon and maybe they plant the next set of watermelon or some corn. And by the time that is all over, nine months, the banana begin to shoot [push forth its new leaves]. The red bulb you see hanging from the banana plant is the last of it. You cuts that off. Then the bananas will full [grow] much quicker.

You find some plants have from ten hands down to one hand. That's an extra large one with ten hands. Some I know grow as high as twelve hands. That is with very rich soil. Generally, you get ten, six or eight. After that, the bananas is up and full and it's ready to reap. You cut that off and you cut the tree down. You cut it off level to the ground. You can cut it up fine, make manure, or you can throw it out. Because there's another one coming up right from the ground. From that same stock. They keep coming up. You don't have to replant unless you dig up the hole or something. That same first one you plant will continue on.

I have someone down in Deadman's Cay. He raise my bananas for me. What they do, they sell it and we share the money. I don't have to do anything at all to it. Just get what they're going to give me.

Many people on Long Island [have] reduced the area that they farm. What happened, you see, in general, they use the tractor. And using the tractor, you can't get that much land cleared, because it's expensive. They rent the tractor. What we used to do before, what I used to do, I must say, we cut the bush ourselves. Let it dry and then burn it. Some people still do it here. Then you have more land cut down and you grow more fields. People using the tractors, because I think it get to the spot where they can't manage cutting the bush like they used to. The help is not there. Most of the farmers are older and they really cannot cut the bush. So they can manage to hire a tractor.

Harcourt Stevens, Cat Island

It was a pleasure to hear Mr. Stevens' confident description of how he could feed his family without "depending on the food that come from away."

This corn [is] for my children. I have plenty children. Grind it up by the bushel and I ship it to them to Nassau. They like to have corn grits, what we call English corn grits, different from American, and hot peppers. My farm is a little bit far this way, and I got some over here. I cut bush and plant pigeon peas. Let me show you pigeon peas. This is beans. This is the corn what we're planting now. You're walking on 'em. Clean them out so that we have food to eat. We don't have to depend on the food that come from away. I could feed my family right from this. I could feed them from this and catch me own fish and raise me own goat. See, me own goat, I catch one and kill it and I got me own meat.

Kathleen Thurston, Cat Island

Mrs. Thurston's energy is limitless. Not only does she do extensive farming, she also operates a tomato factory in her side yard.

All me life, I worked me farm. Ain't no other work for people to do on Cat Island like people do in Nassau. I raise me tomatoes, send it to the packinghouse. When it [the tomatoes] ripe, I grind it and put it up in the bottles. And you could sell the bottles then. When people come for it or people want it in Nassau, they'll send and let me know. Then I'll send it on the boat to them. I just pick and grade them tomatoes out and I send them to the packinghouse. That's what we do. This what we put up [she showed bottles containing tomato products]. This the paste. All of these goes to Nassau.

My husband been to the commissioner's [high government representative] office the whole day most. He gone ten o'clock and he never come back here 'til one. He been to Miss Bain and them to get his money. It took all day; them be busy, you know. Them made payments yesterday but we didn't know. They didn't put it on the air [radio]. Yeah, see when they put it on the air, we does know. But I didn't hear.

We only needs money to buy clothes, flour and rice, lard, [things] like that, and sugar. I buy rice, you know, because my daughter have two children and they don't eat grits. See my corn up there, what we grow? Out in the field, I [do] dis work. We does sell the corn. Sell it to produce.

Feel that little spry [rain]? I get wet yesterday and I gonna get wet again today. Yesterday I was getting things, picking my tomatoes for the boat [to take produce to Nassau]. The boat come yesterday and it going back tomorrow. Now I'm going to plant some corn. I going out to plant my corn today. If you plant it in August, you start getting it in October. Takes two months to start to get green corn. You can plant it every month if it wet. I does plant it, just how I see one rain now. I done have me corn plant last month. My corn high, so I plant it in the tomato ground. Use a little fertilizer. 'Cause when you plant your tomatoes, you use fertilizer, and then you take that same tomato hole and plant your corn.

You don't have to fertilize for the beans. You plant it [beans] to the stump in the field and it bear. We have more soil than in Nassau. There, the ground is hard. You need a tractor to mash up the place.

This month—March—we plant watermelon and thing, mush melon, cantaloupe. You'll get them in May. It takes about two months. Put a little pot of lye; it come out quick. Me peas are drying now. Ain't no green peas here. It's according to the month when they planted it. Peas just grow every year. You pick this year; you'll pick next year.

We had a pear tree, but the gale broke it down and it died. We have dillie [sapodilla] trees about in the yard. Plenty dillie, but they ain't full yet. We have mangoes out in the land. We ain't have no oranges or grapefruit. I could sell them. I was gonna get some seed. We got one orange. Just started coming, you know? This a lime. That's a guinep [tropical fruit].

That's a fig tree. The birds does eat them. They ain't big, though. That's a plum tree. Plums on it now. See, they dropping all over. They ain't so good this time. They does be big. But there's been a drought. This [is a] soursop. They does be big. You need plenty of dirt to grow them.

This is where you make the fire to cook the tomatoes. You fill the whole thing up with bottles of tomatoes. If I grind it, with the grinder with the seeds, I have to put it in the bottle and boil it. Then I put salt to season it. You have to season it, less it spoil.

Animal Husbandry

During the early part of the twentieth century, stock farming was prevalent on the Family Islands. In 1932, Long Islanders raised 3,674 sheep, 698 goats, 555 swine, 368 horses and mules, and 21 cows. In the same year, the stock on Grand Bahama included 250 cows, 240 pigs, 4 horses, 12 sheep, 84 goats and 10 turkeys. Typically, the sheep, goats and pigs were shipped to the Nassau market, while the remainder of the stock was utilized on the Family Islands. Many Bahamians report that stock raising was discouraged by the government when the Bay Street Boys were in control, because these merchants could gain higher profits by selling meat imported from Australia and New Zealand.

This policy was modified during the fifties when the Agricultural and Marine Products Board was created to foster agriculture, animal husbandry and fishing. This board performed a variety of functions. Periodically, it supplied purebred animals to farmers on the Family Islands in an effort to improve native stock. By 1959, Eleuthera Limited of Hatchet Bay had begun to reclaim some of the animal husbandry industry from the imported market with a stock of 406,000 poultry, 22,300 sheep and 10,200 pigs. The Bahamian poultry industry is now protected from imports. But much of the meat in Nassau supermarkets continues to be imported.

Fred Ramsey, Cat Island

I ride my horse all the time. He carry me to the farm. It's right on the path. Go from here! [His horse had come into the house and was coming toward the table where we were sitting.]

He's about seventeen. Horses live a pretty long time, to [age] twenty-eight or so. He came in the house because he sees his food on the floor there. See it here? It's good for horses. He's plenty trouble. Always eating! He just like a child to me. He come in the house [because] he know [I] haven't fed him.

John Wilson, Cat Island

Before Mr. Wilson lost his eyesight, he raised, slaughtered, refrigerated and sold an impressive variety of animals. He even filled orders from Nassauvians.

I used to raise cows. I used to milk cows and sell the milk right from the steps here. Every morning I milked five cows. I put the milk in bottles. Strain it. You strain it for hair. All milk supposed to be strained. I used to scald the milk, but one doctor we have, Dr. George, say I must not scald it. Let the people scald it themselves. Who wants to scald it, let them scald it themselves. I just strain it and put it in the fridge. People would come or I send it out to them. The people from Nassau, they put in an order for milk for when they going back. See, my milk was right from the cow, you know. No doctoring.

I also had goats, sheep, horse, chicken. Well, you have to have that. I used to let the chickens lay and sell eggs right along with the milk. And we kill the goats, make meat and sell the meat right here. I slaughtered the sheep, too. Shipped them to Nassau, you know. What with Easter coming, I kill a sheep, hog. Everybody come and put in an order. They get their meat. So you kill a pig or kill a goat and some people come round and make souse [pickled pork in highly seasoned juice] to sell to people. We keep the meat in the fridge. We have a freezer and a generator. Can't let it [the meat] spoil.

John Newman, Cat Island

Mr. Newman's explanation of how raising sheep enabled him to farm more land than was otherwise possible was amazing.

I have sheep now. They're in Clarence Town, not many. I had up to a hundred heads and more. That was when I was able to turn around, do it myself. Now I have about thirty. It was easy raising sheep back then. But it's not easy now.

In those days, where you farmed, you fenced that in. And after reaping your crop, you turn the sheep in. The sheep cleared the field and the sheep clean it up for the next crop. What you had to do then was pull out the high weeds, and you planted. The sheep was a big help. And then for the next crop, you find somewhere else to put the sheep and you go and plant that same place.

We used to sell sheep. Sent some to Nassau as well as kill some here. The people here never buy much, because they always had their own creatures. But we shipped them to Nassau and sell them there. It got difficult for me because, you see, you can't hire people to farm because the wages went up so high. Paying them a high wage, you lose. So we just simply had to cut out that and only raise what you can farm yourself.

In years gone by, they used to use sheep wool to make baby pillows. Now, sometime we clean the skin. Sell the skin to the fellows in Nassau and we sell it to the people here. You know these drums they beat for the Junkanoo parades? The end they beat is covered with sheepskin. They have orders in here now, for August, I think. I have orders now. I asked the man who collects the skins, just asked him the other day, to get some for me. But now, what cause sheep raising to run down that much, people drop farming. Farming isn't so great.

Olive Ramsey, Long Island

Mrs. Ramsey has twenty-one animals, not counting her chickens. Although I tried, I couldn't convince her that it was unnecessary to "put them [chickens] up for three weeks" before she kills them to eat.

I have a few goats and one black sheep. I'm trying to get two more now, because that one is old. I like sheep. I so like my animals. I hardly kill my goats. I like my creatures. I have thirteen dogs, ten puppies and three big dogs. Everybody is asking me to give them one, you see? I have five bulldog puppies and five lady puppies and two mother and one bull and four cats.

I have plenty chickens. When I gonna eat the chickens, I have to put them up for three weeks. They running in the yard. We don't eat chicken when it's running like that. They pick up, eat, worm or centipede. Boy, chicken run! They [are] birds, you know. They eat all kind of stuff. But you put them up in the coop for three weeks to get clean. That's how I does if I gonna eat anything. I got a big coop in my daddy's yard. We close them up. All the folks on the island, that's what they do. People tie it by the leg, so they know what it's eating.

I eats all kinds of meat. Some is mutton, chicken, turkey, pork chops, spare ribs, all of them. I send to Nassau and some of it, I get right from Tony's [a local store]. My children kill a goat when they ready, but I don't like to kill my creatures what I raise. I love my creatures.

Sponge Fishing

Sponges are multi-cellular aquatic animals. They live in colonies at-tached to the ocean floor or to other objects. Because sponges are full of holes and can soak up large amounts of water, they are used for washing and bathing. The waters surrounding the Bahamas are so clear that fishermen traditionally used glass-bottomed buckets to locate sponge beds. The main areas for sponging were found off the coasts of Abaco and Andros. "The Mud," located on the west side of Andros, was one of the great sponge beds of the world. There were smaller sponge beds near Long Island, Bimini and Eleuthera. During the first decade of the twen-tieth century, sponge was the most valuable export. It was shipped to the United Kingdom, Canada, the United States, France, Holland, Ger-many and Russia.

The life of the sponger was a challenging one. Although the sponge broker companies that provided equipment, supplies and food to the spongers generally made profits, spongers themselves often ended up in debt after a harvest was completed. In 1905, an act amended the previous law in an effort to protect spongers. The new legislation provided that pay was to be in the form of cash, rather than goods or credit. Many sup-pliers blatantly violated the new directives.

Soon after the turn of the century, the Bahamian sponge trade began a precipitous decline. Hostilities during World War I caused the loss of 88% of the Bahamian market for sponge. The situation was so serious that sponge brokers did not even bother to outfit fleets during the winter season of 1914. Hurricanes further contributed to the decline of the sponging industry. In 1926, numerous vessels of the fleet were damaged or destroyed when three serious hurricanes hit the islands.

Despite these developments, most men and many women who lived on Grand Bahama during the early thirties were still involved in the spong-

ing industry, harvesting sponges from the Little Bahama Bank or prepar-
ing them for export. Spongers were also still active on other major is-
lands, to a lesser degree. In November and December of 1938, however, a
disease caused by a microscopic fungus attacked the sponge beds. The
sponge industry was literally wiped out. As a result, many thousands of
spongers lost their livelihoods.

The sponges did eventually recover and during the 1950s, the prospect
for the sponge trade began to improve. A number of sponge beds were
opened in 1956, 1957 and 1961. Independent captains from Long Island
and Abaco sold sponges at auction to be exported to Israel, Canada and
Britain. By 1962, many of the remaining sponge beds had been reopened.
Most fishermen, however, were no longer interested in working the beds,
because prices were so poor. The development of synthetic sponges had
helped to render sea sponging unprofitable.

Clementina Adderley, Long Island

My husband used to fish and sponge. He would go sponging and I would
work in the fields. Then, when time for him to come, I'd go and carry his
food. He'd throw those sponges on the beach, and when it was time for
him to go back, I'd place those sponges on the shore for them to die. Then,
the next day, he'll scrape and take care of them. He cleaned them hisself.
And the man would come and buy them. That's how you [we] got money.

Benjamin Saunders, Andros

Mr. Saunders explained why the sponge fishermen—because they had to
deal with the outfitter who was also the storekeeper—were often caught
in a cycle of poverty. He was the only person who alluded to the fact that
the sponges died and how that affected the spongers.

Back in them days, you ain't making no money if you don't fish. Different
from when the sponging was going on. That was the only industry in the
Bahamas when I was a young man. Sometimes you go sponging and you
come back and you don't get a shilling! No, the man who outfit you to go
was working as an agent. He supply all the foodstuff for the men on the
boat to eat during the sponging season. When you come back and after
you done sell the sponge, you only make sufficient to pay him for the
groceries that you carry. That's how it was. Sometime you be lucky, accord-

ing to the merchant who buy the sponges. Most of the time after you come back, if you want some more groceries to bring home, you go to the same agent. That's a "borrow," and you owe him. So you go back on a trip and collect some more sponge—I mean, to pay for the groceries that you got from him. Well, things were hard in them times. It ain't all that hard today to get money.

I used to get on the boat and go fishing. That's all we did. We only farm and fish. We go crawfishing or scale fishing. When the season is on and you can catch crawfish, well then, you do crawfishing. I didn't have my own boat. But sometime, I go captaining out on other boats. I used to do that. Sure enough, that's when I come down to the places where there wasn't nuttin' else to do but sponge dive. I begin from farming as a young man. And when I got a full age to go to sea, I then began as a seaman. Oh, things was kinda tough when the sponge died, very, very tough.

Conch Fishing

In the Bahamas, the word conch (pronounced conk) usually refers to the edible pink conch. This conch, strombus gigas, is a univalve or gastropod that produces an external shell composed of a limy material, calcium carbonate. Conch are plentiful, and their importance as a staple in the Bahamian diet cannot be overstated. They are used to prepare conch fritters, conch chowder, conch salad, cracked conch and steamed conch. Many people go down to the local dock to buy their conch, but conch are also sold in the markets. In 1958, in an effort to keep prices down, a law was passed prohibiting whole conch exports. Approximately fourteen tons of conch were sold in the Nassau market that year. That quantity had increased to over 215 tons, with a value of $741,932, in 1981. By 1990, both output and value had doubled.

Joanna Bethel, Grand Bahama

Shell boats used to get shells in my childhood days. My father and two brothers had a job of doing that. They used to get these big conch shells. They used to ship them for cameos [jewelry—a piece of conch shell with a figure carved into it]. We had to drain them and let the conch die. Then they pull the conch out and they clean the shell out clean. Bring them into Nassau. They got paid what the merchant give them, what he like.

How they do the queen, king conchs to get the shell in one piece—they stretch them, and then when they die, they pull them right out. Then they wash the shell properly in the sea and pack them up and bring them into Nassau. They bringing a good price now. The regular eating conch is the one with the pink lips that they use for the cameo.

On some of the islands, they use the conch shells for building. They use them for sub-floors, where there is a shortage of rocks. They make limestone out of the conch shells. They get the wood when they cut down the field. They take all the big wood out of the field and they save that. They make a big round circle. Heap the wood on top of each other until they get it high off the ground. Then they put the conch shells on top of the wood and they heap more wood on top of the conch shells. They have some small pieces of wood on the top. When they're gonna light it, they light it from the top part. After all that burns down, catch the wood underneath, all that turns to lime. Mostly, they used to build houses with the lime and sand. They would take the lime from there after all that stuff was burned and mix it with the sand.

I guess conch is the same basic structure as limestone after it's all burned down, because they call it lime. The shells and all those things, they come from the coral formation and all that. Limestone is a porous, soft rock. It grows in the ground.

Crawfishing

The Bahamian crawfish is a spiny lobster. Because it lacks the large, meaty claws of the North Atlantic lobster, generally only the tail is exported. By 1934, crawfish tails were being exported from Bimini, Grand Bahama and Abaco. Since World War II, crawfishing has become the main occupation of many Bahamians. It was estimated that 2,000 individuals were actively engaged in the occupations of scale, crawfish or conch fishing in 1958. During the fourth quarter of 1977, 334,063 pounds valued at $1,405,472 were exported. By 1992, this number had risen to 5,215,382 pounds, with a value of $52,169,440.

Since the advent of exporting tails, size has been regulated by the government, and a closed season exists during the breeding period. While visiting Grand Bahama in the summer of 1985, I observed these regulations in action, as two blonde, suntanned ten-year-olds industriously measured crawfish tails against a painted strip on their work bench.

Those tails that were too small were put in a pail. Ones that were as long or longer than the painted strip were carefully wrapped in plastic and neatly placed in a cardboard box.

Joanna Bethel, Grand Bahama

From listening to Mrs. Bethel's description of the processing at the seafish factory, I was baffled that others didn't keep the industry going when the owners abandoned it.

The bootlegging [the selling of alcoholic liquor to United States citizens during Prohibition] caused the American people to find out how rich our waters was with crawfish and fish. And the people used to come to Grand Bahama—we used to call them party boats—on a cruise. My father and my brother was known for that [crawfishing]. For crawfish they used to get $1.00 each. They thought they were making plenty money. They used to catch them in a ten-foot boat. They had staff with nets on the end of the staff, like a basketball net. They put that over when they see a crawfish. They have a peg on the end of the staff they used to get under the shelf where the crawfish was. They would push the peg under there and root it out. When the crawfish ran out, they put the big net over it and lift it up. It can't get out. As many as the people wanted, they could get. Plenty of crawfish there.

When they used to get stone crabs, used to get a dollar each for stone crabs. They only wanted those big biters off the stone crabs. No meat inside a stone crab body. Well, every now and then, they used to make out very well. Beside that, we did other things. Make a little money around using pilot boats and fishing. After the seafish factory opened up, all the people turned to catching crawfish and fishing.

People had jobs in the factories, packed them and canned them and stuff. The factory isn't still there. Just like everything else. It just closed up for a season and then it goes out. People, other people, get hold of it, you know? They weren't doing so well. It [the factory] came up here to Nassau and it just slipped. That factory down there [in Grand Bahama] used to sell the whole crawfish and package the tail. Down there, they used to can. Women and men, young people, would cook the crawfish and pick out the meat. In this factory here [in Nassau], they freeze them. And then they shipped them over there [to the United States].

Herman Sawyer, New Providence

Mr. Sawyer's description of the first Christmas he and his wife spent to-gether is the most romantic narrative I have ever recorded.

I just got married at six o'clock in the morning, and by eight o'clock I was on the boat going to Andros to make £3,10 shilling [$16.80 U.S.] a day. I just left one little job that wasn't doing. I was working for General Hardware, making £1, 10 shilling [$ 7.20 U.S.] a week. That was November 2, 1943. At that time, we had something like a barge that we used to go on and go crawfishing. A company that run the crawfishing season hire you to work on the barge. The small boats would go and catch the crawfish and bring it to us. We pay them every day. The people who owned the barge used to give us the money that we used to buy the crawfish from the small boats. Every two weeks or ten days, a boat will come there with ice. Take the crawfish tails from us and take them to Miami or bring them to Nassau. I guess we bought the crawfish for three [about 75¢ U.S.] or four shillings each. Sometime you could get a crawfish for three pence [laughter]. They would come and dump them to us and we would put them in the kraal.

See, the boat had like a house on this side and a house on the other side, and in the middle was what we call a kraal. It was filled with water. So we'd keep the crawfish alive there. When the boat come, we have a group of people we call "wring 'em." They wring the tail off [laughter]. Push the tails in the ice and the heads, we throw away. Then the ice boat take off and go to Miami or Nassau. The same company own all the boats. I think we had about five different stations, Berry Island and such. I only did it for five months.

My wife didn't feel good about it, but I had her come down to me in seven weeks. We both stayed on the barge. The first Christmas was the most wonderful Christmas we ever spent. Everybody went to the mainland and it was just she and I. We got married on November the second and she came down on December the seventeenth. All that moon shining. See the fish passing and we jump in the little boat and go over to a little island. Wonderful time. It was wonderful. Then, after we came back to Nassau, she went back to further her nursing. And I came right back and went into plumbing again.

Boat Building

Andros, Harbour Island, Abaco, Grand Bahama and New Providence have a history of boat building that dates back to the early settlements. Boats were the only mode of inter-island transportation during that period and were used both for passengers and to deliver mail.

Today, mailboats continue to visit sixty Bahamian ports on a weekly or biweekly basis, delivering mail, transporting passengers, and carrying cargo such as food, construction materials, domestic gas cylinders and cars on trips from Nassau. Return voyages typically transport agricultural produce and passengers. Most mailboats can accommodate up to twenty passengers.

Despite the continuing use of mailboats, the boat building industry has declined, because boats are no longer the primary mode of inter-island transportation. At present, the industry's main functions are to provide made-to-order boats for regattas and to provide service and repairs for existing vessels.

Earlen Nathaniel Knowles, born on February 12, 1938,
Mangrove Bush, Long Island

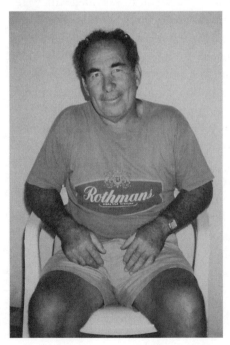

I had intended to interview Mr. Rupert Knowles, who was born in 1914 and was one of the most famous boat builders in the Bahamas. But his son, Earlen, informed me that his father had died in 1988. Earlen owns a restaurant and bar, the walls of which display pictures of the boats built by his father and the family. My initial reaction was one of disappointment. Because of his age and the fact that he was working, I was sure that I would not get the information I sought from him. However, he took me to a quiet spot in the restaurant and showed me how

totally wrong my perception was. He provided a complete history of his
family's role in the boat building industry. His description of preparing a
ship and crew for the regatta was particularly interesting.

My daddy and my Uncle Bert, his older brother, got started boat building
at a young age. In those days, things was really bad. Wasn't no boats
around.

They started with an old one they got from somebody. They started by
repairing boats. This would have been in the late twenties, 'cause at that
time, my father and his older brother was getting in their teens. So they
started in the late twenties, early thirties. My uncle, he worked along with
an older man named Hilton Turnquest. He used to do ship repairs in
Nassau. He was no designer. He just did repairs. And when they started at
that age, Uncle Bert, he got into it more than my father.

What my daddy did, he went on Contract to the States once or twice.
When he came back, he did freight hauling from here to Nassau. He had
experience. He sail boats for other people, toting freight back and forth.
Because in those days, there was no motors. So what he did, by going to
sea, he had experience of what kind of boat he would need. He built a
larger boat. As he was going along, he was building some smaller boats. In
those days, mostly they use that yellow pine, really heavy. You get Bahamian yellow pine in Andros and Grand Bahama. They got the timber from
the trees in the bush. Cut it out the bush. Mainly, it was a tree we have
called wild tamarind that every Bahamian knows and madeira, and also
sea mangrove that grow by the sea. That's very hard wood, but it is heavy.
So he use that type of wood for the frame. But the rest of the wood came
from Nassau, like the planking and the decks. He would order it, but he
would get the frame right on the island.

They [Rupert and Bert] kept on, going along as the time went on. Now,
the first bigger boat they built was about a twenty-six footer. They built
that one together. And also built one for some people. After a while, in
1951, a friend of his own, Bert Cartwright, had an order to build a fishing
boat for his brother-in-law and a fellow named Percy in Nassau, them two
together. They was doing insurance business together, so they decided to
build this boat. That old navy base in George Town had a lot of lumber
there, good, heavy fir. They decided to build the boat in George Town. If
you ever go to George Town, Exuma, where the Out Island Hotel is, she
was built right there. 'Cause I went over there; I was young then. She was
fifty-two feet. They built and rigged her themselves. That was one of the

biggest; that was the biggest one he built. After then, he still kept building boats for the local people, smaller boats, fishing boats, him and my uncle.

When this racing started in George Town about 1953, he used the same model for all the boats he had at that time for racing. As the years kept going on, they were looking for more speed, you know? In 1957, he built his first—what they call now—an A-class boat. She was actually twenty-nine-and-a-half feet on deck. We use her for fishing out of Nassau, between Long Island and Nassau. I used to go along. She was fast. And the year after he built her in 1958, we took her to George Town for the regatta. He was racing before that. But he was racing smaller boats. She performed! Our problem was we didn't have a good mast; we only had a pine tree, which is no good. We performed good, but you know, we didn't have a good mast. We had to get a better mast for her. The year that I got the mast, my father went and sold the boat. And I didn't really have a chance to perform in the next regatta. But he sold her and she wound up with Wally Granger. In '59, when they sailed in George Town again, Prince Philip came down to visit, and he sailed with Wally. So we was mad about it. Daddy said, "Well, we can build more boats, what you want?"

He built a boat for a man who came down to watch the regattas from Milwaukee, Wisconsin. Her name is the *Margaret F.* He built her a little smaller, about a foot and a half smaller. The owner says, "Will you keep the boat and sail the boat?" He spent all the money and treated all the boys good. He said, "If the boat make any money, just take it and don't worry about it." It was a conflict—handicap—which means that if a boat is smaller, I'm twenty-seven-and-a-half feet and you twenty-nine-and-a-half feet, you have to give me a handicap, which is ten seconds a mile. So even if you beat me and I close to you and the handicap can't make up, I still be ahead. So it was Reverend McPhee. He died now. He was a good sport. He owned the *Thunderbird.* And he always talking about our boat shouldn't be racing. She belong to an American man. He didn't want us to win.

Daddy had also built some smaller ones in between there, which was fast. In 1964, Daddy say, "Okay, let's stop this talk. Let's forget about this boat and let's build a new one." He got up on the platform and said, "I want to talk to you all. We coming back next year and we'll win. We'll build the same size boat and we'll win a race." Everybody laughed.

We didn't make big money building boats. Daddy didn't charge enough. Couple boats he built for some American people, he made some money. They paid him good, because they were good boats and good wages. But for the local people, they didn't worry about cloth and time and everything like this. What they got to pay him, they paid. So really, in their profession, they didn't make no money. His boats were so much better than other people's because of the design he came up with. His brother and he came up with their own design. He tried to keep to the Bahamian tradition of the Bahamian work boat, the same design, the model, you know?

But we had to go into different designs to get more speed. It's just like the design of airplanes, right? It's what you got to push and what you got to pull. That's friction. It's what you got to drive and what you got to push. So you got to put the design where you have less to push and less to pull, and that's where you get all of the speed you have to have. I could tell you a lot of things, but you wouldn't understand them.

Well, a lot of it takes good men, too. You need a good hull [the main body of the boat]. The hull gotta be there first. Good rig [the way the sails and mast are arranged]. And you need good men. But the hull must come first. A lotta people think they put a crew on a boat and all they need is design and the crew. But that ain't true. Respect the crew and the rig must be right. But the first thing gotta be the hull.

Daddy named that one [he pointed to a picture on the wall] after my mother, the *Lady Muriel*. She won the regatta and other races a good many times. Well, I put the good spar [the heavy pole used to hold up the sails] in. When they went to race, they had a good mast. She performed properly. That's where she start to win. So, when we built the next one, we had to build to beat her.

What we does, we make a mold. When we design the boat to set the boat up, we make a mold out of wood. Say one by six. You take your drawing. We do a drawing. You have a floor, concrete floor, any good floor. We make a drawing first. If we have the molds of this boat, we take the molds of that and use them. So we'd know what to take out and add. Each one gets better and better. He kept these molds of everyone he built. Then, if he sell the boat and he want to go back into it, he could design one. He know he'll be on top. If you happen to let those molds go, you've got to be good to get back. You think you right some time and you ain't right.

Now, we got a few that are class boats. It's an expensive sport, real expensive. You know, they say only a rich man or a fool owns a sailing boat, which I think is true sometimes. You never stop spending on them. Now, we did it because we were brought up in it and we think we shouldn't let it drop. It's something that should be taught in school. It's an art. We had a couple faster ones, *Ocean Wave*, that my daddy built for my brother Bert. Bert wasted a lot of money into it. He wouldn't go about it in a strict head, you know? He also worked along with Daddy for a good while, too. The *Ocean Wave* is a real fast A-class boat, but he let her deteriorate. That hurt me bad, you know? I said, "We should have kept her in memory of him. And look at it."

There's a lot of talk at all the regattas that we go to. I hardly miss a regatta, 'cause I like it. So they say that we can't build another boat to beat these boats. Two years ago, Daddy was still living, so you know how it is, me and my brother Mark and my younger brother Rupert, decide we gonna try one. We start models. Daddy couldn't get around to do nothing, but he could look. We did the drawing, made the molds, and set it up. Said to Daddy, "Would you take a look at it? See what you think." He looked at it. He wasn't as good as I'd have liked him to be. He lost sight because of his age. He said that it looked good. I tell him, "Looking good is one thing, but we got to beat what we built before." He says, "That's true." So after looking around a little while, I said to Daddy, "Just my ideas. I may be wrong, but hear what I got to say. We're staying to the same design. We don't have to be even or behind, we want to be in front. And we got to prove something. How about changing some of the design?" He looked at it and he said, "I think you're right. Go do it." I said, "We're spending the money and doing the work, so we have to do something different." We did some redesign and she came out perfect. We named her *Rupert's Legend* in remembrance of him. He was a legend in boat building.

She proved when she went to George Town last year, the first race she run in, just a test run. I couldn't do the test here, because I was short of time. I went over there to do it in time over there. Some bad weather came down and the boats wouldn't come out for me to try them. The day of the race, the first day sixteen or seventeen boats, which was a big crowd, tussled up together, and we starts with anchor down. We had to pull anchor to start. I had a bad start. I came in second that day. Next day, I bust a sail. I took it in first position.

So, in the Long Island Regatta, we came back in early June. I could have won every one clean, but I had a green crew and a young crew and they can't, they won't, understand. They won't listen. They wouldn't take orders. So I wound up splitting first between me and another boat. But this coming regatta, I getting prepared for it. My crew is ready and who don't want to listen, can stay home. That's all. They have to take orders from me and the mate.

Racing takes concentration. You got to keep at it, you know? Too much talk gets it fouled up. So this one is—not because we built her, but everybody knows, I think, they'll have to come up with a real different design to beat us.

The reason I run this restaurant/bar is that, like I said a while ago, there isn't that much orders for boats. People don't want boats. If people wanted boats, we intended to open a shipyard. We would like to go into it, you know? It would have to be enough to keep us busy to pay off. We would have to work at least nine months a year. What we were thinking over the years was to build some of the big boats, like some of the mailboats that go to the United States. They could bring business to the Bahamas.

But the government should have supported us, too. Then I'd be encouraged to make it. Because, what happens, this could die out eventually. If you had support to keep you into it and then some of the younger ones get into it, it's something to create jobs. It's a skill to be handed down. You see, about eighteen, twenty years ago, they asked my daddy to teach down at the high school, N.G.M. He told them, yes, he would teach. But they never came to make it work. Never went through. And it hurts us, too, 'cause to see it die out, it hurts. You know all the skills that the older people had, like in boat building, is dying in the Bahamas bad. Harbour Island, years ago, used to be a big, big boat building island. Abaco used to do a lot of boat building. They slacking down; they stopping. Abaco is doing dinghies, small fishing boats, but all the big, larger boats, it's all dying out. Yeah, we should have support. The government should look into it.

We shouldn't have to pay duty on our logs and materials for these sailing boats. This sailing, the regattas, brings a lot of money into the islands. And the government should know, because they know what happens. During the regatta in George Town—Regatta Week—millions of dollars are brought into George Town and the Bahamas. Money is made from airlines, different people, all kinds of things. So these are the things that need to be done.

This is the last generation of boat builders now. My uncle's son-in-law, he can do some building, but he's more into construction, building homes in the construction business. But he would do it if he had people who wanted him to build [boats]. But, like I say, the money is in construction. But he could build boats. There's only a couple left. That's why we built this one [he referred to another photograph on the wall]. To show them that Daddy died, but the art is still here. Like some of the people come and visit and look at the boat. They say Rupert ain't dead; he's still here. You would be surprised to see how many people came to look at that boat. They want to know about the design and like that. It shouldn't die out. They shouldn't allow it to die out. Even if they come down and see my brother, my younger brother, Mark, who did most of the work on this one, *The Legend*. He was head of it. I worked along. I like to give a person credit. If it belongs to them, I give it to them. He has more ideas than me. He spent more time with Daddy. But I know, too; I know when things are right or wrong. We worked on it together. We took our time building this one. We built this one spare time. It took us about sixteen months. If we got right into it with power tools and equipment, we could put one out in four months. Four to five months, we'd have her ready to go.

With sailing boats, you got to take your time with certain things, not like a work boat, where you might not be that particular. When we put that thing in the water, the design has to be right. The finishing has to be as smooth as glass. We spent weeks on just sanding alone, you know? Just getting a polish. She looked like a piece of—like she came out of a factory somewhere. Right now she's in Salt Pond. We have the mast out. We're trying to get it in line. See, we have a disadvantage in Long Island. In Nassau, they have good dry-docking facilities. They bring the boat in, the ballast is in place, all the rig on it. They lift it up and put it on the dock. We have a dry dock to the north, but we can't use that. We can't lay it on the dock that long. We got to take the mast back out, which is a job. Got a sixty-foot spar in her, high spar. And then we got to try to get her out of the water. We trying to get her out this weekend. Dry and polish back up to go. Need time to get her straightened out.

We making a set of sails. One sail alone is $3,600. She's expensive. It's an expensive sport. We earn money, because we have a fishing boat. We were trying to get a sponsor to help us, 'cause it's hard. We could take that money and do something else. Go on vacation, do something else with it. Some of the people, the folks in Nassau, sponsor a lot. We trying to get a sponsor now. Although things tightened up a bit since this Gulf War, I think that, she being the kind of boat she is, we'll pick up a sponsor. At least get sails, like that. It's expensive. We built our boat out of the best material we could buy, you know? The wood in that mast alone in the States cost eight dollars a foot. That mast cost us nine thousand dollars. But when you go into it, you go into it to win. It's light wood. It's spruce pine, grown in Alaska. It's very light and strong. We built everything ourselves. We made the sails ourselves, everything. My sister did the machine work, stitching, and we do the cutting and the redoing. We had her [the boat] in the water since April. We had her out of the water in dry dock for two days in May.

Well, some of the boys come visit the boat from Nassau and say, "You all do the finished work before you try it?" Well, my brother Bert, he be kinda sure. He say, "Well, we know it be good, okay? We know what we have." She's really the talk of the town in sailing. They fear her; they're scared. We looking to the future to build some more. We don't want to stop there, you know? We want to keep going.

We holds our regatta on the weekend of Whit Monday. All the Long Islanders have time to come to the regatta. It's a three-day event at Salt Pond. We have a site for it, which we built over the years with the help of the Long Island Association in Nassau. They're our same club. With their help, we got a good site.

Straw Work

Handmade articles produced from the fiber of the fronds of palm trees [raffia], sisal or dried tropical grasses have been made in the Bahamas since the arrival of African slaves. By plaiting narrow pieces of these fronds in various patterns, long strips are formed, which are then sewed together to create bags, hats, dolls and other articles. Platting continues to supply a valuable source of income for many women in the Family Islands. Although all artisans use sisal and/or palm fronds as their basic raw materials, some have unique, easily recognized styles.

Most tourists to Nassau include in their sightseeing a visit to the Straw Market on Bay Street. Because most of the straw work sold there is virtually identical, each vendor vigorously tries to attract tourists to her stall with a warm greeting and an offered discount. The vendor immediately makes a judgment about which item might interest the potential customer and suggests a particular article. The older vendors stated that they have regular customers who come back to them whenever they visit Nassau. Some of the vendors are affluent and well respected in the community.

Clementina Adderley, Long Island

I plait [braid dried strips of palmetto leaves or coconut fronds]. I was plaiting just now. See, I got a box of plait right there. Only now, you can't get it sold. Ain't nobody wants to buy it. They can't get no sale, that's what they say. Well, you see some of the people does order the plait. Have somebody send what they want. Sometimes somebody will come and say that they want a couple of rows.

Rafaleta "Goddie" Williams, Andros

Mrs. Williams was the only person who said, "I used to make good money selling balls of plait." When I asked her how much money she made, she didn't answer.

I used to do straw work. I get blind doin' straw work. The dust from the raffia get in the eye. You gets the raffia from off the palm. I used to make good money selling balls of plait. Can't do it now. I blind.

Ivy Simms, Long Island

This is the saga of how Ms. Simms became involved in straw work. The moral of the story could be, "Never trust someone in the military," or "Every dark cloud has a silver lining."

I took a trip to Toronto in the year 1939. I took with me a little envelope bag from the market, a multicoloured, embroidered thing that everybody thought was so beautiful. But I was determined when l came back that I would do something better than that. So, that is how my interest in straw work started, and it started not as a business. I started with gifts for my family and friends.

Then when the war started, not started, because that was in '39 and I was in Toronto. During that time, they had a United States Naval Air Base at Exuma. I invited one of my cousins to join me in helping to do the work. We might be able to make some money. So we got four girls at that time, and we did some pretty nice work, I would say. We sent them to George Town and the servicemen bought them.

From that, there was an airman who used to fly back and forth from Palm Beach to George Town to Mayaguana, where they had another base. He thought that after he came out of the service, he could make a fine thing of it. So he came in here one fine day while the war was still on. He put his plane down. He shouldn't have, because in those days there were quite a few casualties on the water. When we saw this little thing on the horizon, I got all excited thinking that someone was out there and perhaps needed help. My brother, Arnold, he said, "Go on, do your business. That's nothing for you to be bothered about." Anyway, I was not content with that. I got the local constable and my foster brother to go out in a boat to see what it was. And they found it was a plane out there wanting to come in, but he was afraid of reefs. So he was very cautious. Well, you know, he should not have done it, anyhow. When they got out to him, he said that he was interested in seeing Ivy Simms, who did the straw work. We had a laugh on that one. Anyway, he came in and he said that he would like to see if, after he came out of the service, he could get us to do this work for him.

Well, it turned out to be a disaster. He said that we would have to cut our prices, because he would be ordering thousands of bags. We said we really couldn't do that, because we didn't have the people to work. Plus, the fact a thousand bags sounded like more than a thousand. In those days, we had no machines to do this work. We had the ordinary hand machine. How we did it, I don't know, since we graduated to foot machines. So we told him no, we couldn't do it. Well, he wasn't satisfied with that. He came another time. Still in his little airplane, but he was a little braver this time. After much consultation with my brothers and family, they said, "Well, it could do no harm to try." So we told him we would try.

The first thing he did was to cut our prices. Therefore, we had a strike, the first strike in Long Island. The girls wouldn't work. We had four girls working for us then, and they said they couldn't work for that. We got that patched up and started on this thing. By then we had about thirty people working for us. Anybody who had a hand machine, we asked to bring it. We had to teach them how to do it and we did not know too much ourselves what we were doing. We were still learning. My cousin, Myrtle Knowles, was in charge of the raffia work at that time. But we always had patterns that you stamped onto the straw and did a little more sophisticated type of work than the market. But I guess they were more artists in that way and they could do without patterns. I was in charge of the sewing and we had thirty people. That was pandemonium. I could tell you! We worked at the Simms No. 1 Burial Society Hall. They let me use the building. It went free. That helped, since the guy cut prices. So, we carried on. I guess we did about a thousand bags for him. I don't know how he sold the first ones at all, because they were a mess. Some of them were so crooked, you had to pin them. My cousin said, "Well, he cut us so in price, pass me the pin, let me pin it. I'll pin it in place after it's finished." These were just plain envelope bags. So that was quite something.

First of all, we were known as Simms Handicrafts, and his name was John Sorrentino, and he wanted these bags named "Tino Bags." He said that would sound so much better. He lived in Palm Beach, but he had his factory or sales place in West Palm Beach. We shipped them to him, and when we shipped them, he sent the check. Well, after having done the thousand, this fine day, he sent a letter asking if we would ship the bags and he would send the check after. That was the trick; but it did not work. We poor fools on the Out Islands did not know what this meant. Anyhow, city slickers, I guess. So, he supplied the lining and the zippers. After asking us to do this order without getting the money first, he sent back and said that he could no longer take the bags and we would have to seek our own markets. Before he paid us for that lot, he wanted to find out how much material we had for him, how many zippers, whatever. We had to give an account of that, and he deducted that amount. It turned out to be, we were left with one thousand bags. He wanted us to stock them here, as he said stocking them in the States would cost so much money and this and that and the other and a bunch of foolishness.

Anyhow, we had them packed up in cartons in the back of the Burial Hall. We had the different models all numbered, so we made up so much of each one. And then the disaster started with mildew. You know straw will mildew, especially if it rains. Well, luckily, a friend of mine who was a chemist came over from Exuma, Felix Bowe. He said, being a chemist, you know, "Sulfur will whiten. Give me one of your old bags and we'll try it and see what happens." It actually removed the mildew. You had to put it into a little container, light it, and then it takes it off. Not if it is a longstanding one. It has to be fresh mildew. So, we didn't lose the bags by constant sulfuring from time to time. It took us two years to unload, because that was after the war.

We didn't make any more bags after that. We couldn't. I owed for the bags. I had to borrow money to make up for those bags. Gilbert Dupuch was then in the House of Assembly for Long Island and, of course, you know he was part owner of the *Tribune,* and he decided that he would make up some cards advertising these bags. We put them all into the hands of the hotels and the taxi people and the shops in Nassau. We tried to sell them in Nassau and that helped a lot. He was very helpful. Also, my friend, Thelma Bowe, had a shop in Nassau called Teen Togs. She took some and my sister, Eva, had a shop called Joyce's, named after my sister Joyce. So they both tried to sell, and we put them anywhere that anybody would sell. Some we had to sell on commission and others we sold outright. It was a very distressing time.

If this air force fellow had not come, I would never have done straw work on such a huge scale. I would have done it on a smaller scale, in Nassau. He really changed my life to a disaster. After we got rid of all those bags, then we became well known and in demand and so we never have been able to supply the demand since then. Do you know, he had the nerve to come back here after that and ask me would I buy plait for him and ship it to Palm Beach? He was going to make them up over there, so I said, "Not on your life. I'll never do anything for you again."

What made me so angry with him was that one of these times the plane came in, and only my foster brother and I were here and we had a little eight-foot rowboat, and it was blowing an offshore wind. It was fine going out, but we couldn't get back. Oh no, it wasn't my brother, it was Myrtle, my partner. She was a two-hundred pounder, and when she sat in the middle of the boat, the two of us couldn't row. When she sat in the bow, it was impossible. When she sat in the stern, same thing. So, she said, "Well, the only thing I see to do is to give up. We gone drown right out here." But my mother got all upset and sent for Myrtle's father and another friend who had a boat. He went out and rescued us. We would have drowned there, because we were way in the sea. Way out, because he wouldn't bring the plane in. It was fine going, you know, but coming back you couldn't buck that wind and this was in the wintertime, too. So, when we got home, I'm telling you, the lectures we got from my mother and her father. He said, "Well, Myrtle didn't know any better, but I expected that you would." We came in like drowned rats. Our hair was all wet and we were so nervous and everything, frightened to death. And so, to get out of it all, I went over to the workplace to settle my nerves. My work has been my therapy [laughter].

I don't do any plait. They all have different names. I buy it from the people who work here. I tell them what I want and they do it. At one time I used to ride to Deadman's Cay every week and collect plait, also in the north end. But at the moment, my production is so down, I don't go to Deadman's Cay anymore, just get from around here, north end. My production is down, because I can't get people to work and because it takes a little while for them to learn. There are many of them that I taught. They thought they were making me rich, so they decided to go on their own and do their own thing. They knew how to do the bags. But if I must say it, I don't think they look like mine. Well, the one thing I did do from the beginning was to get labels. I knew copies would be made, and I wouldn't mind having my own faults, but I don't want to take those of other people. They do, however, have a nice copy these days, very good. But I sell to Logos Book Shop, and also to Johnson Brothers. Well, Johnson Brothers started the turtle sale [tortoise shell jewelry] just about the same time that I did the straw work, so they have been carrying my bags ever since. Logos is just a late thing.

My family was glad to see me starting the factory. Before I started that, I used to do dressmaking. I did not do dressmaking as a business. I did it for people who needed something done. And I would do it, but they said that I was so fussy about it. One girl, she fainted. I had her fitting so long. I always believed that something worth doing was worth doing well.

I always lived here with my mother—not that she was an invalid then. She was quite lively and sprightly. She didn't help me in the factory. None of my family did anything in the factory but my sister-in-law, before she married my brother, Cecil. She was his second wife and she knew the business quite well. After that, she became the telephone operator at Simms. She was with them for thirty-six years and then she retired. But even though retired, she does not fancy straw work. She likes a little gardening. Everything she touches, it grows. Now with me, I can't grow anything. I am not a gardener. The only farming I can do is that lowly silver top palm tree.

I think we are going to have to plant them, too, because the people are destroying them. Some people are not careful about the trees. The way they cut the leaves is killing some of the trees. I think eventually we will have to have a planting spree, a plantation, although it's a wild plant. And you know it's called "silver top," because one side is very silvery, especially in the moonlight. You see it waving and you know how people talk about spirits? They think they see a spirit because of the little palm tree. It's the smallest of the palms.

The tan part of the straw is the leaf, which is not opened yet. And they cut that from the middle. Like this beige or tan, whatever you call it. That's the middle. You cut that green, put it in the sun, dry it and it becomes that colour, beige or tan. The brown is the same thing, only it is the leaves that are already grown. They cut it and singe it over the fire, put it out to dry in the sun and it becomes brown. And you know the way they found that out? A fire caught in the top trees, and after this fire they went there and found that this brown colour had come up. Now the women who plait do that.

I don't do anything in the plaiting line. But I do work on the bags in the evenings. My eye is telling the tale of that. I often work at night to try to keep up with what they do all day. They don't do any of the finishing off. I do all of the finishing. They do all of the stitching. I do the marking out. I cut the cardboard for the stiffening of the bottoms. I make all the linings.

Lady Pindling [the Prime Minister's wife] visited here once. She told the children, if they really knew just how much this craft meant, they would be here begging me to teach them. But how can you change them? At one time I did have quite a lot of schoolchildren come in, and that's how most of my girls started their work. They came out of school afterward and they stayed a while and did a little work. I guess my time for work is nearly over. But it gives me great pleasure to give to people. My family tells me that I give away all of my profits. That pleases me to give something that I know I have some part in. It feels a part of me.

None of my family want to do it. I have two nieces and they wouldn't do it. One ended up as a teacher and one was a mortician. My niece's children are not interested. None of them are interested. Not a soul. But it was very—what's the word I should use?—I just can't think of the word, but it makes me feel good that I could do something that no one else has tried.

Ena Lee Major, born on September 4, 1934,
Lower Deadman's Cay, Long Island

Mrs. Major is an active, enthusiastic, friendly woman. I met her in her airy, well-stocked grocery store, where she also sold straw work. I was amused as she explained how she could acquire goods as a young person with no money. She recognizes that children are no longer interested in straw work and fears that when these older people are gone, the craft will be lost.

When I was little I start to doing straw work, little baskets and hats, like that. There wasn't hardly anybody to sell it to. It was just a matter of practicing. Sell to the children or persons around. You could sell a basket to use for shopping or a hat to use every day.

I also did plaiting at home. At that time, there were two persons in south Long Island who bought the plaiting—that was Arch Darville and Mark Knowles. We would always go after school and on weekends and take the plait there. Then, they had something to sell that we could buy in return, food or cloth to make clothing. You could get money or whatever you want.

Now, I'm selling straw work for about eight different people. They all bring straw work. Olga Major is the only one who makes these "all-in-one hats." The crown and brim are made from one continuous piece of plait. I'm trying to encourage her to teach someone else, but the young people today don't seem interested in things like that. These are all older people who are doing this. But the young people aren't interested.

Midwifery

In the thirties, notification of the birth of every child was instituted, to be performed by the midwife in attendance no later than forty-eight hours after the birth. Midwives reported that the greatest number of deaths of newborns occurred in the first week of life, and more than half of the total deaths occurred within the first month of life. The main contributing factors were said to be malnutrition and the diseased condition of mothers, which reportedly stemmed from poor diets.

All Bahamian hospitals are located either on New Providence or Grand Bahama. As a result, most of the babies born on the Family Islands are delivered at home by midwives.

Midwives provide care to women during pregnancy and childbirth, as well as delivery. They practice natural childbirth procedures. Midwifery training is acquired through apprenticeships or nursing education. Most pregnant women choose their midwives based on word-of-mouth recommendations or proximity. Family Islanders with whom I spoke expressed a high degree of satisfaction with midwife care and deliveries.

Enid Sawyer, New Providence

I was involved in midwifery. In later years, I worked with a gynecologist and an obstetrician. But I delivered many babies myself. Most of the nurses are midwives. If you became a nurse around here, you had to do the midwifery. There was a time when the midwife did all of the work herself. She went to the home and took care of the patient and delivered the baby without the aid of any doctor. I've done a lot of that. I went in and examined the patient. Then you process her. You prep her. And you just wait. You wait and keep checking her to see how she is progressing until the time for the baby to be born. If things aren't going right, you call a doctor or you take her to hospital. But when you are working in hospital, you aid the doctor.

There was a time when the nurses did all of that, even in hospital. Now, as soon as the doctor comes and the head start showing, episiotomy. The nurses don't do that. They let that head crown and they deliver it without you getting a tear. You get a normal baby with no marks.

I worked until it was time to retire. I retired because my father took ill. I couldn't find anybody to take care of him. You hardly can find anyone to go to a home to take care of an old person. I left my work and I stayed home to look after him. He was living with us. That's the funniest thing, when you have an old parent and they live with you, the rest of the family don't worry about it. And when he needed them to do, they can't do nothing. Say, "That's your job. You a nurse." So I took the full responsibility. He was sick for about a year. He still wanted to go out walking to the docks, so you had to watch him. After he died when he was ninety-three, I find that I was worn out. I found out that I had diabetes. And was kinda stressed out. I didn't go back to work right away. I found that I was not well myself, so I stayed home. I didn't go back. It was nearly time for retirement [laughter].

Olive Ramsey, Cat Island

The usual procedure for pregnant Cat Island women is to have their babies at home, assisted by midwives. I was surprised at what Mrs. Ramsey attributed as the reason babies get pneumonia and bronchitis.

Mrs. Hepburn and I deliver babies. I deliver ten and she deliver a couple. I deliver one for my daughter. The baby is two years now. Two more died when they get a size, six or seven months. When we cut the baby navel, after nine days, the only thing you can tell the mother is to take care of the babies. You see, when we leave them, they healthy and strong. They go to the doctor; the doctor check them out and they good. Now, if you don't take care of your baby and let them get wet and dribble, it give them pneumonia and bronchitis. Then that's it. They get that bad fever. Some people don't take good care of their babies. Like me with my babies, I wouldn't let them be bare. In the afternoon, I keep them with socks to keep them warm.

Dressmaking

During the first half of the twentieth century, many Bahamian men and women were tailors and dressmakers. In addition, older family members sewed clothing for themselves and younger siblings. Most Bahamians regularly used these sources for their clothing needs. At present, more affluent Bahamians tend to purchase clothing in the boutiques in Nassau or to fly to Miami and to New York to obtain the latest fashions.

Eva Williams, Nassau

Mrs. Lofthouse would ask me to come to her guest house and do dressmaking. I took care of the tourists who would bring these lovely dresses from New York and Chicago. That fit in nice, so I went up there. She used to curse. She was a American woman. She say, "These damn drunken people. Instead of they get out of the bed and have their breakfast, they stay in the room all morning and you sit here and give them all your time until they decide to come down and bring the clothes. Eva, you never thought of trying to get a little store? Then you wouldn't have to come all the way from home and waste your time. They'll come to you. Find a little shop."

I went to look for one right next to Mr. Reuben. The owner say, "Yes, I could rent you a section, but it will take me too long to renovate it proper for you to carry on dressmaking." So I went around to Frederick Street. When I got there, I saw Mrs. Deal. She was the older sister of Bishop Eldon's mother. She was doing dressmaking and she say, "Oh, you looking for a shop to rent? Let me tell you something, my dear. My husband been nagging me to death to give up this dressmaking and come home and mind Sylvia. I been out sewing quite long enough and he could support me. So you can move into this same shop. You go on Bay Street. When you see the sign, R.H. Curry Steamship, you go in there and tell them you come to see Mr. Curry. Tell them that Winifred Deal send you and that Mr. McPherson is your father and that Mrs. Deal say she's stopping sewing and let you rent the shop." And that is how I got established on Frederick Street sewing for years. That was in 1939.

Mildred Campbell, New Providence

This conversation took place while Mrs. Campbell was making uniforms for a group of Girl Guides. Using scissors, straight pins and a smaller sized uniform as a pattern, she placed the material on a flat piece of cardboard and cut it, without a tape measure, compensating for the larger size from memory. As she did this, she explained exactly what she was doing. Without stopping work for a moment, she also reminisced about her family and philosophized concerning one's responsibilities to other human beings.

I was very young when I started sewing, because my older sister used to sew. And then my aunt was always sewing and my daddy was a tailor. I worked in my daddy's store a long time. 'Cause he used to call me his eyes after he couldn't see. I stayed with my father for a long time up to the tailor shop. My dad sewed for men and women. He would make skirts and coats for women.

Now, you see, this is a fourteen size and what I want to make is a sixteen. So I must cut this a half-inch bigger. And the hems have to drop. The hems are about two inches. See what I'm doing here? I have to fold this, so that I can get that half-inch, because I don't want to waste the people material. [She was working on the front seam]. So instead of wasting it on the front here, I'm going to eliminate that. Cut two inches here for this hem and leave two inches here for that hem. And here I go up a half-inch, because the neck have to be bigger and the sleeves have to be bigger. I have to come out here a bit. Here it is now, I'm getting sixteen. I'm going to mark the dart. This is the dart for the bust. And when I get one sixteen cut, I will cut all the other sixteens by this. I have to make six sixteens and six fourteens. So here I have a sixteen. I need to cut some fourteens, but I cut the sixteen first.

I had a woman who used to come to just watch me cut freehand, you know. She said she couldn't understand how I could cut freehand without a pattern. But I know the measurements for a twelve and this is how I got the others, the original ones. I know what it is the yoke; across the shoulders, the arms, everything. So here it is now. I'm going to put the zippers here. This is where the zipper goes. But it's a double seam up the front. I venture now, that's fourteen inches. If it is not fourteen, it's not far from fourteen. [She measured it with the tape measure. It was fourteen inches.] You know how long I was sewing? I was only fourteen when I was making dresses for people for two shillings [48¢ U.S.], you know?

My daddy, he always wanted us to have an education. So, after we went to the public school, he took us out and put us in a little private school. Cecil Bethel, Cyprianna's father, ran it. We all went to his school. And after he closed his school, he said those who wanted to go on to school, he would send them to Government High School, and they would either be teachers or this and that. But I told him that I wanted to sew. So, I didn't go on to Government High School. I came down to my aunt. Between my aunt and my father, I learned to be a dressmaker. Everything just came natural to me.

I always wanted to play the piano. And it was so difficult. Maybe I didn't have a musical ear. My dad had bought me a piano. I took piano lessons, but I never lasted to learn the piano. That wasn't my forte. But sewing was something that I did naturally. I enjoy sewing, because even if I had a difficult pattern or something to make, it was another thing that really inspired me. Someone would bring a picture and say, "Mrs. Campbell, I want you to make this dress for me." And I would say, "But you know, I don't know how to cut that dress." And I would go to sleep with that dress on my mind. And you know, during my sleep, I would be cutting the dress. When I woke up I knew how to do it [laughter]. When I got up that next morning, like I cut the whole dress during my sleep. I was working in my sleep. And here it is the next morning, I knew how to cut the dress. So I knew there had to be some supernatural spirit trying to help me.

The Girl Guides [a club for girls that teaches service to others and outdoor activities] started off paying me ten dollars for each uniform. But look, I have to pay a dollar-something for a zipper. I have to buy thread. I have to pay electricity. Now I get fifteen dollars for each uniform. I have thread to buy, buttons, zippers, electricity. What they told me was that they have more underprivileged children that want to be guides than children that can afford these things. In order for them to sell the uniforms at a rate that the underprivileged child can pay, I wouldn't charge them more for these uniforms. Once I suggested that they send the children to me and

I would teach them how to make their own uniforms. But the parents wouldn't send the children. They had so many other things to do in the evening, going to ballet, music lessons, studying for exams and all that. The children didn't have any time left to make their own uniforms, so the parents didn't mind paying. And it costs me all of five dollars after I get through those four things. It comes to at least five dollars. Ordinarily, I would only be getting ten dollars a uniform, which is sewing for charity. Look at my time! I've been doing these uniforms for the past forty years, so it doesn't take me long to do them.

I think they were recommending me for an award for doing this for the Girl Guides all these years. Because when they called, they said, "You know, Mrs. Campbell, we were watching you for a long time, all your charity work." So I said, "All my life, since my children were grown, I was doing charity work." Instead of working for myself, I were working for other people. I accepted that because I felt like . . . you know? Gosh, give me some flowers before I die. When they called and told me that they were honoring me, I felt really happy about that. My mother always told me, when I was catching so much hell behind my husband, "Millie, pray for long living and everything will work out for you."

See this one? I just go by the pattern that I made. Now I have to cut two twelves. I have to cut the sleeves and the collars. It don't take me long to sew them. Every hour I could make one of these after I get all of them cut out.

I got sick the other day. And I asked the dressmaker around the corner here if she would help me do some of these uniforms. She said, "Mrs. Campbell, I know there's a lot of charity work and all that kind of stuff. But I could never sit down and sew a uniform for ten dollars. They would have to pay me twenty dollars for each one of them uniforms." I said, "Okay, then. They'll just not have any if they can't find someone to do it for charity. They'll just have to wait until I feel better."

Let me show you now how I put them together. I'll cut out four at a time. Here's where I put the zippers. Now I'll put the pieces for each dress together. Once I get them this far, it don't take me long. I could sew four of these in one day. This pin determines what position I put my dart in. See, some people have to mark a dart before they can put it in. All I need is that pin there, because I know this is where it starts and this is where it ends, see? This is where the pocket is supposed to start. This is where you mark the pockets. I don't baste. A lot of people baste. I just go ahead and do it!

Ena L. Major, Long Island

While Mrs. Major was discussing sewing, her voice was relaxed and quiet. Then she began talking faster and faster. After I heard all the things she used to accomplish each day after moving to Clarence Town, I understood why! Just thinking about it had evidently caused her to speed up her speech pattern.

In school we had someone teaching us sewing. So I continued on with that, and then I went to Mrs. Liz Turnquest. She helped me. I continue on with the sewing, because I'm really interested in that. Then I helped Mrs. Meryl Saunders; she was a friend of my mother. She would help me and she would give me ideas about making different things. We had other older people who were around. They would give you ideas on how they would make underclothes. There was something they called the shimmy and the other parts, the legs. I got right into it, you know? And I kept on. My mother had six girls, so me learning to sew was something to help them. We learned the needlework. We learned to do spider web and all the different designs. And we shared with persons around. Well, I don't have time any more to do sewing.

I came to Clarence Town in 1955 in June to stay with my aunt, Mrs. Hazel Newman. In fact, she got to work at the office and I took care of the children, the whole house. I stayed at her home from 1955 'til 1958. In 1958, I got married. So I left her and continued on with sewing. Even when I lived with her, it was just like when I was home. What I did in the day, took care of the children and would cook and when they would go to school and whatnot, I would sew. At night I would iron and clean the house while they were asleep. So, I would make some money in the day and keep the housework going in the night. Just like I was home. It didn't make any difference, you know? It was real nice being there. After that, I went home and I got married and I did more sewing at home. I sewed for pay.

Bread Baking

Frequently, on Cat Island and Long Island, I observed outdoor ovens made from rocks, sand and limestone. They varied in size. The largest were approximately five feet in height, four feet in width and six feet in length. Each was a woodburning oven.

Fred Ramsey, Cat Island

I bake bread in that rock oven. But I ain't use it for a good while. You put wood in the oven and let that burn down. After that done burn down properly, you haul that coal out. You get leaves to clear bottom and you put the bread right in there. That's it. We close it up. I got a door right inside here. It's made of tin. And you leave that there for about an hour and when you open it up, your bread is brown from bottom to top. I got a cousin and another man to make the oven. We bake the bread and then we sell it all the time in the market. We send it on the boat. If boat going tomorrow, I would bake today and get it ready for in the morning. I does make fourteen or sixteen loaves. You bake all that one time. It holds twenty-four because of the size, you know? The larger it is, the more it holds.

Storekeeping

In the Family Islands, "the store" usually sells everything from Alka-Seltzer to yeast. Because such stores generally have a generator and refrigerator, they can offer light in the evening and cool sodas. As a result, stores are a popular gathering place in many settlements.

Joseph Carroll, Long Island

I did a little farming, not much. I wasn't a very good farmer. I didn't like it. I didn't like dirtying my hands. However, I did a little farming and then I used to go off and on to Nassau, worked in the hotel in the season. Then come back and farm. You never really made enough money to take care of the whole year. I got sick in Nassau. I got a double pneumonia case. And I came here. It was our own foolishness. I used to drink, you know. So Saturday night and Monday morning, we used to go back in the cold storage and take stock. I never put on anything. I got a case of pneumonia and I came here and it really got bad. I had pain and fluid and that fluid last so long. It was something, me being out of action. So I had to rest for three years. You know, it was so long. I had a spot on my left lung and that put me out. In those days, you had to rest, you know. That being around 1950. I came back in 1950. And after I came back home, I still couldn't do much hard work.

Anyway, since I couldn't work hard like I would have liked to, I decide I would go into business. It wasn't nothing then. It was thirty-two years ago. Nothing here at all. So I had a friend of mine back a note for me to the bank for £300 [$1,440 U.S.]. I started with a little business in that same little building next door. And, of course, it grow. It was a grocery. There was no jobs or nothing. You had to depend on the farms. Sometimes you would credit the people and wait for the things to grow for them to pay.

I went along, and the bank manager told me that should I need another borrow, I wouldn't have to get nobody to back me. I could just come in. So later on, I borrowed another £500 [$2,400 U.S.]. I don't like borrowing. You got to pay so much interest on it, you know? Then I went along, I don't know how many years. I stayed in there until I could have built a bigger place. Just before I decide to build a bigger place, some boys come from Abaco to build the airport over there. They came down to the store and asked me to recommend people for the job, you know. And I did that and then business came in, you see?

In the late sixties, I decide to build this store. Then I went along for years. We didn't have any roads then. People had to come from north and south, so the business prospered. What you might call prospering on the island. So, as I saw an opening, I embraced it.

Ten years ago, I built the furniture store, because there's nothing much in groceries. Everybody who came in after that, they decided to open a grocery store. Nothing much in groceries unless you had a certain amount of customers. But you catering to the same people every day. There's no influx of people, you know what I mean? So I had in mind to expand in something else. None of the boys [his sons] were interested. They were doing well for themselves. And I didn't want to take more on than I could have handled. I had it [the furniture store] in mind for a long time, but I couldn't make up my mind to go ahead with it. I didn't realize that the business would prosper—not any furniture store on the island, you know? So how it started off, my brother Ralph, who has the Imperial Mattress store in Nassau, asked me one day, "Joe, why don't you sell beds?" I said, "Man, beds don't sell fast, hey?" He said, "Well, they sell fast down here." I said, "Yeah, down there. But Nassau a city, you know, you have an influx of people in and out." "Well," I told him, "I'll try." I wish I was in ten years before. You sell plenty of beds.

What encourage me to open a furniture store, everybody who come for a bed, they want a bureau, dresser drawers to go with it. So I thought about it for a couple of years, and then it wore on my mind. But about four years ago, it came strong. I say, I'm going to do something before it goes forever.

I went to work and I built the building. I put in furniture to prompt the grocery business. 'Cause there ain't too much in groceries, you know? Thought it'll be a back up for the grocery business.

I didn't intend drawing any money. I didn't have to, really. I borrowed another $30,000. I had a plan. If I'm fortunate, the business will pay the money back and it will work out according to plan. Last year, I paid it all back.

The other building where you staying downstairs [the guest house] was a garage. But I had a chap, Griffin, from Eleuthera, he was up here for five years. He was a mechanic. After he left, I intended to go on with the mechanic, but I couldn't find nobody. I had three or four of them, but as soon as they made a couple thousand dollars, they left. I got fed up. It [the garage] was standing there for three years. So one night I said to my wife, "You know what I'm going to do? I'm going to renovate this place and put it as a guest house, you know?" She never agreed. I went ahead, because the people were coming and there was no place for them to live. Some people who were coming had to go back. That's what gave me the idea, because I used to rent one of my homes here to them. So I converted it into some rooms and did fairly well. One night, I said to a guy who worked here, "I think I gonna put a second story on the building." My wife said, "You talking foolishness!" I said, "Was the guest house foolishness?" And I did that. I already had this thing up, the rough work and the plumbing laid. A friend of mine, he was a contractor, came along. I intended to make one two-bedroom apartment. He said, "Why don't you just make two one-bedroom apartments for people like that?" Only had to change the plumbing around. I did that and that proved to be successful.

I cater mostly to Bahamians. They come, like government people and people who come up here for a couple of days. Especially a couple, or one person. They want to come for a couple of days. They get one of the one-bedroom apartments.

Now, I'm hoping, one chap came in here, a mechanic. He's going to work in the store. He's going to use one of them, and I think I have the other one rented to somebody else. If I had it to do all over again, I would have gone in for a guest house, you know? I would have really gone in for a hotel if I had it to do again, because it proved out to be really successful.

Ena Major, Long Island

Mr. and Mrs. Major's acumen in knowing how to start and run a store was absolutely fascinating. I doubt that a business major could have accomplished the task with greater success.

I think it was in 1961, we formed a community store and I ran it. In there I also did sewing in the spare time, because there was a lot of time when I wasn't busy. The community store isn't still in existence. Most of the people who invested wanted their money back. They wanted to do other things, so we didn't have any capital. My husband and I kept buying out shares until we owned the majority of shares. By 1972, we owned the majority of shares, so we bought out the rest. It was down on the corner. At that time, it was being rented from Mrs. Gibbs, Mrs. Hazel's mother. They owned that building. The building was where they lived. We used a portion of the downstairs as a store and they did baking in the other part. They lived upstairs. The building was deteriorating with termites. It was coming down. So something had to be done sooner or later [laughter].

From there, we needed some money to buy out the business and to build a building. With the bank, you have to be worth so much. They said they would lend us six thousand dollars. The property, the three lots together, was valued for nine thousand dollars. So, we said, "This is something!" What we decided to do was to buy the front lot, which had an old building on it. Now, the building wasn't worth anything. But it belonged to an old gentleman and you couldn't tell him it wasn't worth anything. You just had to—if you wanted the land—take it. So the building on the front lot was for five thousand dollars. The one in the back was four thousand dollars. But you have to buy the front to get the back. We needed the front. What we did, we got six thousand dollars from the bank, and we paid the gentleman off. We paid on time to the lady in the back. We made a down payment and we told her that we would pay monthly. By the time we had finished paying the bank, we had finished paying the lady in the back as well. We got a six-month supply and put it down. Then we got another six-month supply and we were able to put the building down. On the twentieth of December 1976, we moved in here, and we were here ever since. It was a struggle. But if you have faith, you will make it.

Salt and Shrimp Production

Residents of Inagua and Long Island have a history of involvement in the harvesting of salt by using salt pans to evaporate sea water. An island must have low levels of rainfall in order to produce salt. Inagua presently has a successful operation. In 1992, the Bahamas exported 896,973 tons of crude salt valued at $8,163,808.

Diamond Crystal Salt Company opened in 1962 and was located at Hard Bargain, Long Island. The operation proved to be unsuccessful, because of an abundance of rain. Consequently, the site was sold to World Wide Protein, Limited, which presently operates a shrimp and fish farm at the location. In 1988, the name was changed to Maritek Bahamas, Limited.

George L. Roberts, New Providence

I went to Inagua about 1943. It's a big place. When I went there, all they had was a big salt mill. Make salt there. They had these big salt lakes [ponds]. Morton Salt, they own it. They let the salt water in and they close it, sorta like the Panama Canal. Then the water evaporate. And they get these big bulldozers to scoop up the salt. That was the onliest [only] thing they got there. The whites established Morton Salt on Inagua.

Patrick Darville, born on February 14, 1941, Deadman's Cay, Long Island

I interviewed Mr. Darville at the airport in Long Island, because he was flying to Nassau on the next plane. He was headed to Nassau to take a course. Mr. Darville had been employed previously by Diamond Crystal Salt Company. He enjoys his present position as accountant and office manager for Maritek, and is looking for-

ward to the next phase of his career. He expects to become a deacon in his church.

My father was sick and I had to leave school. So I went to work for A.C. Knowles Farms as a farmer, helping to grow vegetables.

Then I got a job to Diamond Crystal Salt Company. That was the salt company that started operation here in 1962 at Hard Bargain. They called it the Flats. When they started, this area was mainly shrubs and bushes. They started building houses and made a community. From then, they started to build ponds for salt. Pump the water up through a canal from Deadman's Cay Sound area. When it got into the ponds, the wind and sun evaporated it. It became salt. Each concentration pan was several acres in area. We had fourteen crystallizers. Big operation, but still they could have stand to made more money. Well, our only hindrance was rain. The rainfall was too high for salt. We'd have a good crop up for harvesting and the rain would come down and destroy the whole thing. We thought about putting some kind of protection a lot of times, but it cost too much money. It couldn't work. But at the highest season, we got about 320,000 tons. That was one of the highest yields we had. The Diamond Salt Company was a very good company. It had a lot of respect for its employees. They got up to about 104 employees. One time they got to 115. So, we had a good many people employed. If it was not for the rain, we could have still been in operation. The expenses was overpowering, the profits too little for the company to survive. It was very difficult, and in 1982 they decided they couldn't survive anymore.

And then in June of 1983, World Wide Protein (Bahamas), Limited, bought the company out. They reorganized the operations for shrimp farming and raising fish using the same ponds. They had to change things around a little bit because of the water. Other than that, it was almost set up for shrimp farming. They have a struggle. They almost gave up in 1986, because of financial problems. The mortgage was a little too high for them, so they let loose for a while. In 1988, they started back again. Changed the name to Maritek Bahamas Limited. And now it's progressing.

We only have twenty-five employees. In the first stages, we employed almost seventy people. That was during the construction period. We could have gone up to eighty. Now, we have the shrimp farm itself and we don't need that many people. In the processing and the care of the ponds, we have thirteen people. But in just a few months, we expect to expand. It could be, if we get the finance.

It's very difficult to care for shrimp, because the water has to be at one temperature at all times. We have to bring our larvae, the baby shrimp, from South America. The next step is that the company is going to build a hatchery to improve the shrimp. Instead of purchasing the baby shrimp from away, we'll raise them ourselves. We do have a red fish hatchery and it's doing very well. The red fish is similar to the red snapper, but it's different. It's a very delicate dish, very expensive. We get a good price for our fillet in the markets in Nassau. And we now export fish to the United States.

The only problem with the shrimp is if there's a disease. Every time you have a new set of larvae, the ponds have to be cleaned out. From the time you put the babies in until you ship the shrimp could be about six or seven months.

We have to import the fish to feed the shrimp from away. Imported feed costs are very high. We cannot grow enough food on the island to suffice them. The idea about the baby shrimp—once our finances get clear, that's one thing we will have to look into. We'll have our own hatchery. It's pretty much together now. It's only small. In the next few years, if we keep growing, we could supply half the United States and the Bahamas.

Maritek is in the process of trying to build a huge luxury hotel. We're trying to develop forty miles of waterfront right here. If we can put together a marina and golf course with the hotel, Long Island will be able to compete in the tourist industry. I'm an accountant, office manager at Maritek.

I'm also training to be a deacon. If it's God's will, I have two-and-a-half more years. It's a four-year program. I go over to Nassau once a month. When I retire I can qualify. As of now, I still have to work.

Government Structure and Services

During the colonial period, the executive branch of the colonial Bahamian government consisted of the Royal Governor and a nine-member advisory Executive Council. In addition to the Executive Council, the Governor relied on the colonial secretary, the attorney general and the receiver general. The legislative branch was made up of the House of Assembly—with twenty-nine elected members authorized to pass bills, over which the governor had veto power—and the Legislative Council of eleven members. In 1929, the chief requirement for House membership was that a citizen-candidate had to possess real or personal property valued at £200 ($960 U.S.) or more. Until the middle of the twentieth century, voting was restricted to those adult male citizens who owned land valued at £5 ($24 U.S.) or more in New Providence, or £2.5 ($12 U.S.) or more in the Family Islands. House members representing the Family Islands generally were and continue to be residents of Nassau. The secret ballot was initiated in New Providence in 1939; the practice reached the Family Islands seven years later.

By the end of the 1920s, although most House of Assembly members were descendants of white colonial families, almost a third of the House consisted of black members. By 1935, however, only four black incum-

bents were reelected. Some Bahamians attribute the decrease to an up-surge of anti-black racism—which, they say, was instituted to please United States tourists.

In 1942, black Bahamians seriously began to challenge the power of the Bay Street Boys in the House of Assembly and in the streets. The Burma Road job action is the most dramatic example of this.

The Duke of Windsor (Edward VIII) had arrived in Nassau on August 17, 1940, to serve as Royal Governor of the Bahamas. The Duke had abdicated the throne in 1936 because Prime Minister Stanley Baldwin and members of Parliament objected to his intention to marry Wallis Warfield Simpson, a twice-divorced American. Historians have specu-lated that the decision to appoint the former King of England to this post was made because the British government wanted him away from Europe. In particular, the government was concerned about the Duke and Duchess' sympathy toward Hitler and their rumored desire for Ger-many to win World War II, which, they thought, might have resulted in the Duke's being reinstated as the King of England.

Many older Bahamians think that the Duke of Windsor exerted a positive influence during his stay. They say that he tried (unsuccessfully, due to the Bay Street Boys' opposition) to force reforms to benefit poor black citizens. Although he could not get the Bay Street Boys' coopera-tion, the Duke pushed for the enforcement of building codes, attempted to eradicate the slums in Nassau and started the Windsor Farm as a training camp to prepare young men in the field of agriculture.

Burma Road Job Action of 1942

Under a 1942 Lend Lease Agreement between Britain and the United States, the United States supplied Britain with fifty destroyers in return for the creation of four United States bases in the Bahamas. Two of the bases were to be constructed by the Pleasantville Company of the United States. They were to be located in New Providence and to be used for training of United States airmen. One was an extension of the existing Oakes Field and was referred to as the Main Field. The other was lo-cated in the Pine Barrens near the western end of the island, and was called the Satellite Field. Construction of the bases greatly assisted the Nassau economy, because between two and three thousand men were employed. Workers referred to the construction of these air bases as "The Project" and named the road between the two bases "the Burma Road," after the route through Burma the Allies were using to transport supplies to the troops in Asia.

Although the Pleasantville Company was prepared to employ 2,400 Bahamians at $2.00 a day (the rate that black United States employees received), the Bahamian and United States governments agreed that Bahamian workers should be paid at the local prevailing wage of four shillings (approximately 96¢ U.S.) a day. White United States workers received significantly higher salaries. For example, Bahamians were driving trucks for 1 shilling (about 24¢ U.S.) an hour, while white United States citizens working at the same jobs received at least $1.50 an hour. On June 1, 1942, hundreds of Bahamian workers made an effort to have their hourly wage increased. The most serious disturbance on record in Nassau occurred as a result. These activities are referred to by the participants as the Burma Road Riot.

The Government forces available in Nassau to control commotions consisted of a force of 200 members of the the Cameron Highlanders, who had been stationed at Fort Montagu Beach Hotel since the start of the Project; the Bahamas Volunteer Defence Force of approximately 146 members; and the police force, numbering 150 men.

Work on the Project had begun on May 20, 1942. On May 31, a Sunday, a group of frustrated Bahamian workers gathered at the contractor's office and demanded to be paid at the same rate that the United States workers on the Project were receiving. Nothing was resolved. The next day, June 1, the Bahamian employees struck the Project.

Under a system intended for use in emergencies, when a certain siren was sounded, all people in Nassau were to clear the streets. Despite the angry crowds that gathered on Bay Street on June 1, the siren was not sounded. Some citizens were later critical of that fact, feeling that the imminent injuries to people and property could have been prevented. Instead, attorney general Mr. Hallinan spoke to the crowd from the steps of the colonial secretary's office. He instructed the protesters to disband and to send representatives to present their grievances to the colonial secretary or the Governor. The crowd ignored him. Mr. H. G. Christie and Captain Sears next addressed the growing crowd at Rawson Square, unsuccessfully requesting that the laborers go home. The Royal Governor (Duke of Windsor) had gone to Washington, D.C., on May 28th and was not on the island at the time.

The resentful crowd on Bay Street was getting out of control. The police reaction was to form a line across Bay Street just west of East Street and to walk west down Bay, hoping the protesters would retreat. The angry workers began throwing bottles and stones at police and developed their own plan of attack. As the police cleared an area of Bay Street, groups ran into the side streets. When the police had passed, the crowds would return to Bay Street. Finally, the company of Cameron Highlanders was called in. With their help, the police eliminated the workers from Bay Street before noon. The ensuing quiet, however, was merely the eye of the storm.

The crowd that had gathered on Bay Street moved over the hill and began looting bars in Grant's Town. One of the Cameron Highlanders was struck in the face with a stone. As a result, Roy Johnson was shot and killed. It was reported that another one of those killed, David Smith, might have lived if the crowd had not refused to let the police touch him. He was later taken to the hospital, where he died. A few police and some of the workers were treated for minor injuries.

By afternoon, the crowd was totally out of control. After stopping at some local bars to drink, the workers and their supporters headed to the Grant's Town police station, where four unarmed officers were on duty. The crowd burned an ambulance and a fire engine in the station next door. The police on duty fled. For unknown reasons, the Executive Council did not send other police to Grant's Town for the next twenty-four hours.

The following day, the government established a curfew for the hours between 8 P.M. and 6 A.M. However, the violence and bloodshed continued. On the morning of June 2, a crowd of about 100 people armed with sticks, machetes and other implements started up Blue Hill Road. When the men approached a store owned by Richard Holbert, Holbert's son Clifford told them to leave. When they refused, Clifford shot and killed Donald Johnson, who was at the front of the crowd holding a hammer. Citizens later reported that Clifford never went to jail, because the court determined that he acted in self defense. The same day, a crowd of over two hundred men went from Grant's Town to Shirley Street to continue the disturbance. Once again, there were no police in the area. Cole's Pharmacy was looted.

Work resumed on June 4, 1942. Two weeks later, the Royal Governor announced that a midday meal would be provided to the workers free of charge. His justification was that the work was very strenuous. In spite of the obvious need for concessions, the Bay Street Boys continued to demand that workers' wages remain at 4 shillings. It was finally agreed that

workers' salaries would be raised to 5 shillings a day. The curfew was
·lifted on June 8. For a raise of one shilling (24¢ U.S.), six people had
died and over sixty-seven had been convicted of crimes.

Four weeks later, on the morning of June 28, a fire destroyed some of
the stores on Bay Street. Some elder Bahamians reported, in glowing
terms, that the Duke worked in his shirt sleeves to help put out the haz-
ardous fire. Whether the fire was the result of an accident, started by a
proprietor whose business was not producing profits, or a continuation
of the Burma Road disturbance, has never been firmly established.

A parliamentary inquiry was convened on October 5, 1942, with Sir
Allison Russell, K.G., serving as its chair. After a thirty-three-day hear-
ing, it was concluded that the disturbance was not based on the racial
situation in the Bahamas. Rather, the report suggested that labor prob-
lems needed to be addressed.

George Roberts, New Providence

The Pleasantville Construction Company built the airports. That was at
the beginning of World War II. I worked at both of the airports. I was
working for the Water Works [Department] then, but the construction
company was paying more money, so I went for the biggest money. I quit
the Water Works and went and worked for them [the Pleasantville Construction Company]. We were in the accounting office under an American. The head supervisor was an American. I was getting something like £5
($24 U.S.) a week. The common laborers, unskilled people, only got £1
($4.80 U.S.), but people like plumbers and engineers, they got higher pay.
The higher-ups like Arlington Granger, they were drawing big money. I
think Sir Harry Oakes negotiated all of that. I think it went through him.

They started work in 1942 and I left in 1944. They were not finished, but
they were completed enough for planes to land and take off. See, when the
planes came from the States, they came and they fueled and they went to
the Azores. From the Azores, they went to Africa.

There were a lot of plane crashes at the army airport, the place where
they refueled. 'Cause they would send these fighter planes through there.
They were crashing and carrying on there. They were coming in too fast
and those planes weren't put together so good. They were building them
fast. They were fighter planes. The Air Transport Command [ATC] would
bring them in.

Me, Philip Worrell and George McPhee, the three of us, worked together. We did all of the streamlined bookkeeping. We was the timekeepers when they were building Oakes Field. It was the Satellite Field. But when they turned it into the airport, which they use now, they changed the name of it to Nassau International Airport. The Satellite Field was for the army. Oakes Field was for commercial. All the commercial planes came to Oakes Field and all the army planes went to the Satellite Field.

They [the United States] got a lot of airstrips on the islands. I work on Mayaguana; they built an airstrip there. The United States government got to build all the airstrips, 'cause they gave Great Britain fifty destroyers. They built one in Eleuthera; the one they use now in Savannah Sound. They went into Grand Bahama too, I think. Those were for emergencies. They stored bombs and stuff. The Caribbean was a buffer against Germany for the United States.

You know about the riot? Mr. DeGregory shot a retarded man, Mack, during the riots. He was the only person killed during the riots that I know of. The government called the Bahamas Defence Force [BDF] out when the workers were attacking Bay Street. They went up to Government Hill to the Duke of Windsor, 'cause he had to straighten it out. During all this rush through Bay Street and stuff, Vincent DeGregory—he was head of the Defence Force—shot Mack. Mack couldn't have done anything anyway because he was retarded. Nice jokey guy, go around talking all kinds of nonsense. He shot him dead. That's the only death I know happened.

They break up all the stores on Bay Street, Cole's Pharmacy, Pritchard's. There was a lot of looting. That was on their way coming off of Bay Street up George Street going up to Government Hill. So they came from over East Street into Bay Street. Went down into Bay Street, straight up George Street past Cathedral Church. Quite a few people got arrested.

The American construction company had two different salary schedules. They had the native salary at 4 shillings a day and the American salary at $1.50 an hour for the same work. So it was a big difference.

Which you couldn't help that, no way, because the Bahamian government only allowed you to get a certain salary. America pay the government a big amount of money, but they only allowed to give the workers so much. That cause the riot.

Alfred Love, New Providence

Because Mr. Love was speaking from the perspective of someone actually involved in the riot, as he described the events I could feel the excitement and fear the soldiers and the crowd must have experienced.

The riot was in May '42. I was working on the base preparing it for the soldiers, Royal Air Force, different army units. We were working out there at what they call Oakes Field at that time. We were hired to expand that field and to construct Windsor Field. It so happened our wage was far less than the American wage. When I went to work there, I got what we'll call a little less than fifty cents an hour. But the Americans were getting far better paid than us. Well, that was a Lend Lease concern. America furnished the bases and Britain paid later. It happened that the Americans [employees from the United States] told us that we could get more money. So we started to agitate for more money. The Bahamas government was afraid to give more money than our regular pay here, because after the war was over the Bahamian wouldn't want to revert back to the old wages. We workers decided to go and protest to the colonial secretary's office. We walked from where the airport is now to town. While we were there, the colonial secretary told us that we cannot get more money. And on our way going back from the colonial secretary's office to over the hill, there was a Coca-Cola truck delivering Coca-Cola out on Bay Street, and one fella took a bottle and threw it into one of the showcases. That was the beginning of the riot.

Police came out and the soldiers were here. They had to come out and try to quell the riot. People smash up quite a bit of buildings on Bay Street. Loot, took people's bolts of cloth. You might have heard about doe skin, blue serge, gabardine; they were the top. Looted them by the bolts. After the police chased us off of Bay Street, we went over the hill right up to a place called Dillet Street and Blue Hill Road. There was a barroom there, and they carried, must have been, fifty gallons of rum. They opened the barrels and threw the rum down the drain. It was running like a river. They had just decided to carry the riot right on through. Some nutty heads! One probably would say today, "Well, the people over the hill didn't stop them from getting anything, so why they bother them?" In those days, they just decided to get what they could get free. That's what I see. They start brokin' up the barroom; throwing away the liquor.

I witness two fellas got shot. The soldiers shot two fellas in Grant's Town. One of them, I knew him well, 'cause he was living down here in Chippingham. I saw his guts out on the ground. I followed the mob right from town, but I saw a soldier with a steel helmet on. A fella threw a rock and knocked that soldier right down. Hit him in his head and knocked him right out. When I saw that, I started to run. The soldier was a Canadian soldier. When I look, I came about twelve or fourteen inches from his bayonet. And he said to me, "Get on the side, buddy. Get on the side, buddy." He saw that I wasn't taking part in this. But I believe if it was an American soldier, I would have got that bayonet. He would have said, "Well, you there, so you was taking part." But I wasn't. And I got on the side and ran from there right home. When I reach to the step on my porch and I sat down there, I see how close I was to death. I decided no more for me.

Herman Sawyer, New Providence

In Mr. Sawyer's judgment, the workers made a serious mistake by creating this disturbance. He explained why "the damage they did, we're still paying for today."

The common laborers used to make four shillings a day. In those days, we used to call four shillings a dollar. But four shillings in that day was ninety-six cents. Our money was almost equal to American. A pound, we used to call five dollars. It was really four dollars and eighty cents. After the war started, we went from four shillings to five and six. That was when we had the Burma Road. "The Burma Road Declare War on the Conchy Joe" was a song about the riot. Workers were at war with the government [laughter]. That was when they were building where the airport is now. The road between the construction sites was referred to as the Burma Road. They [the United States] came over here and start hiring the people for four shillings a day. The government was controlled by the Conchy Joe. They did not agree for the Americans to come here and pay the people more money. They said, "When the war is over, we will have to pay the same money." So that's the time men working there got together and declare war, the strike.

They got a little more money, but the damage they did, we're still paying for today [laughter]. Because that's what caused everything to go up. At that time you could go and get a penny lard and a three-cent butter. That penny lard went up to four cents. Just like today, we're making a hundred dollars, but look what we have to pay.

Murder of Sir Harry Oakes

The most sensational event in the forties was the murder of one of Nassau's most prominent residents. On the morning of July 7, 1943, Harold G. Christie found Sir Harry Oakes murdered in his bed at his home in Nassau. Oakes had owned the Lake Shore gold mine in Ontario, Canada, and was a multimillionaire. Upset by the amount of taxes the Canadian government collected from his income, and on the urging of Christie, he moved to Nassau in 1934. He bought over seven thousand acres of prime land on New Providence and provided employment for many Nassauvian laborers.

The day after the murder, the police arrested Oakes' son-in-law, Alfred de Marigny, and charged him with murder. On November 11, 1943, after a twenty-two day trial—during which the defense practically obtained an admission that de Marigny's fingerprints, supposedly found on the scene, had been forged by the Miami police, whom the Duke of Windsor had brought in to solve the case—the jury acquitted de Marigny of murder after less than two hours of deliberation. However, they recommended that he be deported. Alfred de Marigny sold his property and left with his wife (Oakes' daughter Nancy) for Havana, Cuba. He has always maintained his innocence.

Although the murder has never been solved, many theories exist concerning the cause of the killing and the failure of the subsequent investigation to find the murderer. One is that the Duke of Windsor, concerned about possible world attention, first tried to squelch information concerning the details of the murder and then handled the case without the assistance of the mostly black Bahamian Police Force. He imported two police officers from Miami to manage the investigation. It is alleged that their analysis was faulty and that they invented evidence against de Marigny.

A second theory is that H. G. Christie hired a black hit man from Florida, who did a black-magic type slaying (Oakes' head was battered and the body was partially burned) as revenge for a business double cross. The Duchess wrote to her aunt (Higham, 339–340): "We are endeavouring to keep as clear from this awful case as is possible. I am afraid there is a lot of dirt underneath and I think the natives are all protecting themselves from the exposure of business deals—strange drums of petrol etc.—so I wonder how far it will all go. Most unpleasant as I do not think there is a big enough laundry anywhere to take Nassau's dirty linen. . . ."

Another theory attributes the slaying to the Mafia. It is alleged that reputed gangster Meyer Lansky orchestrated the slaying because Sir Harry had refused to allow the Mafia to run the gambling casino in Nassau.

A fourth theory was reported by Dr. Doris Johnson (Johnson, 26): "Many Bahamians say that Sir Harry was killed because . . . [he] had vowed to bring about the downfall of one of the Bay Street Boys."

Eva McPherson Williams, New Providence

Harold Christie was young then. He was a white Bahamian. Born right here in Nassau. He was a land developer. Was one of the men who started Bahamas Airways in the forties. He was the first chairman of the Development Board. And if it wasn't for him, Sir Harry Oakes would never [have] been in the Bahamas and brought all those millions. You heard about him? He got rich [from] gold mining in Canada. But child, you know how these rich people are. He got angry with the Canadian government because they taxed so much of his money. H. G. Christie got him to move here because we didn't have any of them taxes. And he was good for the Bahamas. He bought the New Colonial Hotel and started calling it the British Colonial. They used to say that he bought it because some employee was rude to him and he wanted to fire him [laughter]. He built the old airport and did other things.

Wenner-Gren was another millionaire Christie brought in. But in 1941, the Bahamian government told Wenner-Gren he had to go. He was a Nazi. He was a Swedish multimillionaire who had a mansion on Hog Island [Paradise Island]. We ain't had nothing like hotels over there then. We used to go with your basket of peas and rice, fried fish and guava duff, and spend Easter Monday and all like that with your children on the beach.

But then Sir Harry Oakes was murdered. His wife used to go to Maine in the summers and he'd stay here. In the summer of—let's see—1943, H. G. Christie found him dead in his bed. He had been beaten up, murdered and set on fire. Boy, was that a scandal. Everybody had a different idea of what had happened. They tried to pin it on his son-in-law, but the jury didn't buy that.

The Duke made a really big mistake when Sir Harry was murdered. He didn't think much of our police force. They were always recruited from Barbados and other West Indian islands, so they were all coloured. He called in the chief of Miami homicide [Edward W. Melchen] to conduct the investigation. His detective [James D. Barker] decided that Count Alfred de Marigny had committed the crime. At the time, it was said that the captain made up evidence to make it look like de Marigny was the one who was guilty. The jury didn't believe the evidence and found the Count innocent, but they suggested that he leave the island anyway. He came back recently, just for a visit. I think he wrote a book about the whole thing. Other people have written books about that murder too, 'cause it was never solved.

Name Withheld, New Providence

This is a version of the murder I had not read or heard from anyone else.

You know Christie had him killed, hey? He got killed in the back of Paradise Island. And he was brought to the house and burnt. He was on a yacht out there. They went on a yacht. I know about this. It was a Saturday night. I remember it real good. They all got together and they went out on this yacht. Sunday morning we heard that he was dead.

This person who killed Sir Harry Oakes was shipped out of Nassau. They tried to pin it on the Count, 'cause he was the only one who had a motive. But you see, what happened, the Oakes had the wrong lawyer. If A. F. Adderley had taken that case, Marigny wouldn't have got off. Their lawyers were Toote and them. Christie didn't want Adderley on that case. 'Cause all of them woulda went to jail, too.

General Strike of 1958

In 1955, Wallace Groves, the founder of the Grand Bahama Port Authority, and the Bahamian Government signed the Hawksbill Creek Agreement. The Port Authority promised to develop a deep-water harbour at Hawksbill Creek in return for the rights to purchase 50,000 acres of Crown land at an extremely generous price and to be exempt from customs duties on nonconsumable goods, excise, stamp and export taxes for a period of ninety-nine years. Another stipulation in the agreement gave the Port Authority the right to bypass immigration regulations when bringing in needed "key personnel" [expatriates].

By 1960, when it seemed that Wallace's dream of establishing an industrial city on Grand Bahama was not to materialize, he added the goal of creating a tourist center in Freeport. The government, once again, cooperated completely. In return for a commitment to build a 200-room hotel, the Port Authority was allowed to purchase 50,000 more acres of Crown land at a trivial sum. And, on April 1, 1963, the government granted Bahamas Amusements Limited a certificate of exemptions allowing the introduction of organized gambling. A large number of non-Bahamians were employed in Freeport working on jobs that Bahamians could have been trained to perform. It was not until a new government came to power that this problem was addressed.

An event that profoundly affected black political awareness was the general strike of 1958. In many ways, it was the culmination of a series of political developments throughout the 1950s.

The first political party in the Bahamas, the Progressive Liberal Party (PLP), had been formed in 1953 by Cyril Stevenson, William Cartwright and Henry Taylor, three members of the black majority. In 1958, the Bay Street Boys and other Bahamians, as a reaction to the formation of the PLP, formed the United Bahamian Party (UBP), consisting mainly of members of the white minority. The UBP was headed by Sir Roland Symonette.

At this time, certain schools, private clubs, charitable organizations and some businesses were still segregated. Also, blacks were barred from hotels and most movie houses. Some legislation was beginning to break down racial barriers. In 1956, Sir Etienne Dupuch managed to get an anti-discrimination resolution accepted by the Assembly. It opened all public places to all citizens. This bill helped to arouse political awareness among members of the black majority.

Out of this context arose an important conflict involving the majority-black taxi union. The taxi union had been fighting privately owned tour companies over the conveyance of tourists between Nassau and Windsor Field Airport. Most of the taxi union drivers were members of the PLP.

The union understood that its members' livelihoods were threatened by competition from the newly formed tour companies. Therefore, Clifford Darling, president of the union, organized a blockade of the airport roads for twenty-four hours in November 1957. The one-day blockade failed to produce progress in negotiations, so a strike was called for January 11, 1958. On January 12, the Bahamas Federation of Labour, led by 33-year-old lawyer Randol Fawkes, called a sympathy strike. Because laborers, hotel workers and garbage collectors had now joined the cab drivers, hotels were forced to close. This show of solidarity revealed the mounting frustration of black workers, who complained that living costs continually rose faster than their wages.

One of the workers' major concerns was the Trade Unions Act of 1942, which had been signed into law by the Duke of Windsor when he was the Royal Governor. This act banned hotel workers from organizing. Mr. Fawkes and the Bahamas Federation of Labour were demanding recognition of collective bargaining rights. A second irritation was the inflexible position of the Bay Street Boys, who wanted to wait out the strike until the workers' hunger forced them to reject their labor leaders and to return to work.

The airport was closed for nineteen days. Anticipating the worst, the governor, Sir Raynor Arthur, obtained an armed contingent of the Worcester Regiment from Jamaica. The strike ended peacefully and the troops did not participate in any action.

The strike resulted in a number of changes favorable to black workers. Secretary of State for the colonies, Mr. Alan Lennox-Boyd, visited Nassau in April 1958. He stressed the need for labor legislation revisions, electoral reforms, an extension of the franchise to all adult males and the creation of additional seats for New Providence in the House of Assembly. The General Assembly Elections Act of 1959 gave the black areas of New Providence four additional Assembly seats and extended the franchise to all males age twenty-one or over. Subsequently, the Trade Union and Industrial Conciliation Act was passed. It made possible the growth of trade unions and the development of the trade union movement on modern lines.

Rita Wood, Nassau

I remember there was a taxi strike. I know that there was a taxi-cab driver by the name of Clifford Darling. He was head of the taxi union. The drivers parked their cars 'cross the road to the airport. The government had to close the airport, because the entrance was blocked. Other unions sided with them and the taxi drivers won.

And later that same taxi driver, Clifford Darling, became a member of Parliament. Then he became Speaker of the House. And he ended up as the Governor-General. Sir Clifford was best of all; he never lost the common touch. Sir Clifford went to say his farewell to the Queen, who had knighted him in 1977. You know, that's protocol. I think he did very well for himself. It's a fairy tale, because most of those people in Parliament are lawyers or doctors.

Political Parties, Independence and Beyond

Through the efforts of Dr. Doris Johnson and others, women were granted the right to vote in 1961. On November 26, 1962, women went to the polls for the first time. Universal suffrage had come to the Bahamas.

On January 7, 1964, the Fourth Bahamian Constitution became effective. It granted the colony of the Bahamas a greater degree of internal self-government. The Legislative Council became the Senate. Its fifteen members were appointed: eight by the Governor, five on advisement of the Prime Minister, and two on advisement of the leader of the opposition. A cabinet was created, which consisted of members of the majority party of the Assembly. The first Premier, chosen by the ruling UBP, was Sir Roland Symonette.

April 27, 1965, is referred to by many Bahamians as Black Tuesday. On that day, Lynden O. Pindling, a young PLP member of the House and later the first Bahamian Prime Minister, threw the 165-year-old gold-plated mace (a club that was the symbol of the speaker's authority) out of the window of the House toward the black crowd in the square below. He said, "This is the symbol of authority. And authority on this island belongs to the people. And the people are outside." His action occurred because, in the previous election, although the PLP had received 44% of the vote, they won only 8 of the 38 House of Assembly seats, while the UBP, with only 36.6% of the vote, had won 19 of the seats. The PLP attributed this to unfair election boundaries. After much pressure, the boundaries were redrawn and the UBP set a new election date of January 10, 1967.

Michael Craton, in A History of the Bahamas, reported, "An enterprising Nassau preacher reminded his congregation that it was on the tenth day of the first month that the Israelites were led out of captivity in Egypt, and the PLP voters went to the polls singing the theme song from Exodus as their anthem" (290).

The 1967 general elections resulted in a tie between the PLP and the UBP. Two members of the House, Randol Fawkes, Federation of Labour (BFL) President, and Alvin Braynen, former deputy speaker of the House, joined forces with the PLP. As a result, political control was transferred from the white minority government to a PLP-led black majority government. The Right Honorable Lynden O. Pindling was named Premier.

Dr. Johnson (Johnson, 89) eloquently described the reaction of many Nassauvians to the PLP's political victory:

> *The polls closed at 6:00 P.M. Quiet continued until 11 o'clock that night. Just before midnight, the island of New Providence awoke with one wild, almost incredulous, raucous cry of jubilation. The PLP had won twelve seats out of seventeen on the island! Men, women and children, many in bedclothes, streamed out of their homes and began to dance in the streets. They clapped hands, threw hats and posters in the air. They seized banners and began triumphant shouting, singing, caught up in one irresistible wave of rejoicing. All over the island the frenzied beat of the goatskin drums and the clatter of the cowbells sent up a happy din. The black man's day had come.*

The Constitution was again revised in 1969, officially creating the Commonwealth of the Bahama Islands. The Premier became the Prime Minister. The Commonwealth government was granted increased responsibilities for internal security and certain external affairs. This was as far as the Bahamas could move forward until their people chose complete independence. And the PLP, with these increased powers, was now ready to go "all the way!" Large numbers of Bahamians had caught the fever and embraced their motto.

The problem of sizable numbers of nonBahamians being employed in Freeport came under serious criticism by the PLP. In 1970, the government succeeded in amending the Hawksbill Creek Agreement to include a provision that Freeport was now under the jurisdiction of the Immigration Department.

Also in 1970, eight House of Assembly members were suspended by the PLP for acting "contrary to the interests of the party." They formed the Free Progressive Liberal Party (FPLP). The 1971 elections delivered both the UBP and the FPLP embarrassing defeats. The Free National Movement (FNM) party was formed in 1972, when the UBP combined forces with the FPLP and the National Democratic Party (NDP).

Some Bahamians rejected the idea of independence for the Bahamas. Particularly resistant were many who took pride in their roles as British subjects and/or considered themselves to be white. Those sentiments were especially strong on the Abacos, where many residents (and chiefly those living on the Cays) are white descendants of Loyalists and Eleutheran Adventurers. Until recently, the community of Man-o-War did not permit blacks to remain in their settlement overnight. In July of 1971, a majority of the voters of the Abacos petitioned the British government to grant them the right to secede from the Bahamas. By ruling that Britain could consider the petition only if it was submitted by the Bahamian government, the British government averted a potentially divisive conflict. The Abacos continue to be part of the Bahamas.

After the general election of 1972, it was clear that the PLP government had received a valid mandate. Consequently, representatives went to London to draft a new constitution for an independent Bahamas. On July 10, 1973, the Bahamas became the Commonwealth of the Bahamas, an independent, autonomous member of the British Commonwealth of Nations, with Sir Lynden O. Pindling serving as first Prime Minister. Sir Milo Butler was appointed as the first Governor-General. Butler had fought for social and political justice throughout his career. The new government structure provided for the Governor-General, as representative of the Queen, to appoint the Prime Minister—always the leader of the majority party in the House. The Prime Minister would then select his or her cabinet. The Prime Minister was responsible for the general direction and control of the government and was accountable to Parliament.

The function of Parliament under the new system was to pass laws and examine government policy and administration. Of the sixteen members of the Senate, nine were appointed by the Governnor-General with the advice of the Prime Minister, four by the Governor-General with the advice of the leader of the opposition, and three upon the agreement of the Governor-General, Prime Minister and leader of the opposition. The majority party in the House of Assembly would therefore always have a majority in the Senate. The forty-three members of the House of Assembly were elected by the districts of New Providence, Grand Bahama and the Family Islands. This framework remained essentially intact after the Bahamas became independent in 1973.

The structure of the judiciary has been largely unchanged. The judicial branch of the Bahamas includes a Court of Appeal, which is the *highest court, followed by the Supreme Court, the magistrate's courts and the Family Island commissioners. In the Family Islands, local government is administered by the Department of Local Government. The cabinet member responsible for the Ministry of Transport and Local Government oversees this department.*

August 19, 1992, witnessed an end to the PLP's twenty-five-year majority in the House. With an overwhelming victory at the polls for the FNM, Hubert A. Ingraham became the second Bahamian Prime Minister. Sir Orville A.Turnquest became the fifth Governor-General.

Family Island Commissioner

In an effort to improve Family Island administration, the position of commissioner had been created in 1908. The commissioner's functions included serving as the official revenue officer and warehouse keeper on the island or islands to which he or she was assigned. The commissioner is still the highest government official on each of the Family Islands. This official's role has increased vastly, however. In 1992, the Local Government Department employed eight senior commissioners, five commissioners and ten assistant commissioners. Two women were involved in this service. All but two of the commissioners were assigned in the Family Islands.

"Lock-ups" on all Family Islands remain under the supervision of the respective commissioners, who also supervise all local constables. If a person is found guilty of a serious crime, he or she is transferred to the prison on New Providence.

Joanna W. Bethel, Grand Bahama

The real commissioner was at Eight Mile Rock. There was one at West End that we called acting commissioner, one who entered and cleared boats. But the real commissioner who could settle the cases for you was at Eight Mile Rock. The commissioner could marry you. We had him marry us. He was a justice of the peace. Most people had a church wedding. But we didn't wait [laughter]. We really wanted to get married.

Rudolph Moss, Nassau

Mr. Moss served briefly as a commissioner.

First of all, the commissioner is the official representative of the government on the island. He is the highest ranking officer on the island. His duties entail serving as a magistrate and a coroner for the district. He is chairperson of the town planning committee, chairperson of the Port Authority and a justice of the peace. Once a month he or she makes government payments, which include paying for educational janitorial services, for agricultural services and postal services. The commissioner is the finance officer who is the principal receiver of revenue and principal expenditure officer.

The local committee keeps abreast of all the people who have to be paid. They keep the records right there in the commissioner's office. They have a record of every one of those persons whom he pays. They know who worked. Let's take the janitors, for example. The principal of the school would keep the records. Other than that, if there's no complaint, they know that the worker was there. Otherwise, they will get a report saying that he or she did not work.

The people who do the farming take their produce to the packinghouse. They get paid for the quantity of their produce, not for the hours they put in. The ones who get paid by the hour would be the clerical staff and the workers at the packinghouse.

Family Island Constable

The Royal Bahamas Police Force is under the jurisdiction of the Ministry of National Security. In 1917, the Colonial Report listed the staff as consisting of one officer, one sergeant major, 83 rank-and-file staff members and one constable. By 1929, the force had grown to four officers and 125 of other ranks. Most of the police were stationed in Nassau. Because of the low crime rate on the Family Islands, these islands were generally policed by local constables.

Dating back to the 1800s, a minimum of recruits were obtained locally. Most came from Barbados, British Guiana, Trinidad and Jamaica. It has been suggested that this policy was based on the assumption that foreign workers, without local family ties and friendships, would be more objective and dedicated to their work. By 1990, 1,507 constables were employed. At present, there is a total law enforcement staff of 2,200, which includes commissioners, superintendents, inspectors, sergeants, corporals and constables.

Benjamin Saunders, Andros

I became a constable in 1952, on the first day of June. On the Family Islands, local people serve as constables to keep order. Most of us still work on our regular jobs, too. They used to pay in pounds, shillings and pence. They started me out on a salary that was £21 ($100.80 U.S.) a month. They wanted a man who had his ability. I mean, was capable of doing the job what was needed. Well, in those days, I think I was very active. I had a little schooling, anyhow. And after I was enlisted as a constable, why then, they called me into Nassau for a little bit of training. I spent three months in the barracks. Got some experience there as to how to handle matters in my district. Well, I definitely spent thirty-five years in the postmaster duty at the same time I took up the office of constable. From that time then [at the time], I was thirty-five years old.

John Newman, Long Island

1951 was when I was sworn in as a constable. I was in Nassau for a few weeks training. After coming back, I took my post in Clarence Town. I worked with several commissioners, I think sixteen commissioners, one after another. Some put in three months and some put in three years. Well, more or less, I was the senior constable. And my work was to go through the island with the commissioner. As well as I go when he sends me twice a week [to check on each district]. That is from south end to north end, the whole entire island. He did have other constables, but I was the senior one.

We didn't have much problems. The most of my work in going through the island was, at that time, Stella Maris [a tourist resort]. It was beginning to develop and they were buying the property. It wasn't named Stella Maris. But after Mr. Fox bought it, he named it Stella Maris. So I used to go backward and forward taking papers by the commissioner and by lawyers to get them signed. I did that sometimes twice a week. It take them quite a while to build Stella Maris. I really couldn't tell you how long, but it was a few years for it to get off the ground.

I didn't have much problem with any of the people. Several times we had some land scrape [difficulties] with some of the Knowles. I used to have to go down and get that straight. Spend the night when I used to go down there. I had to get the facts straight and the land dispute settled. It was settled in a way that each person hold onto where they were living.

Just what they used to occupy before, they occupy now. They never try to take anyone else's. It was settled that each person get what was theirs. One time there was a shooting. One person did fire up a gun. I think he went to prison, but not for so long. That problem settled down quite easy.

And in the south, we don't have much problems here. Only a sheep go into the next one's farm. And they have a little dispute. Can't settle it themselves, well, the commissioner would send me out. I would spend a couple days backward and forward until I get the matter settled. There was plenty sheep at that time. The areas were marked off, but just in a way that the sheep could always jump over and go in the other one's farm. When they do damage, sometimes I go and value the damage. That is, you walk along the farm. You see how much the sheep took. How much corn he eat down. How much potatoes he dig up, cassava he break down. Then you value it. See if they'll come to an agreement that they will pay off. That matter settled right there. If they don't get it straight, we take it before the commissioner. But seldom does that happen, that they have to go before the commissioner.

I liked being constable. It was something that I really did like. I worked with the high commissioners. What you didn't know yourself, they would help you with. I used to deal with the post office, too. In those days, we didn't have a postal clerk. We only had someone come in on that day when an issue arrived. After that, there was only me there and I take care of them. When selling stamps, I sell the stamps and stamp all the letters and have them all prepared. When the postal clerk comes in, she only have to seal the bag. So I keep busy.

Apart from that, when the commissioners have money, in those days, you never keep no money here. The commissioner has a safe and they sends money from Nassau. When they want to pay off people, he sends to Nassau for the amount of money he should have. That comes on the mailboat. So I goes to the boat and pick up this box, a big wooden box. A key left in Nassau as well as a key here. So I can count the money. Get it straightened out. See, mostly it be the first Tuesday in every month. Well, they were paying some grant-in-aid teachers [who worked at schools where parents also contributed toward the teacher's salary] as well as they were paying some people who worked for BATELCO [Bahamas Telecommunications Corporation]. And then different people do local work on the road, weeding, farming. Government pay them. In those days, you have wells. Some people take care of the wells. Keep them clean. We had them all cemented round. No water could run in. No dirt could get in. But they just simply stand by and clean them once every month. They had to clean them properly. They do have those wells now, but they stopped that payment. I think there's a few of them that are still paid for it. The grant-in-aid teachers don't get paid that way anymore. Some of them are paid through the bank.

Education

At the beginning of the twentieth century, the government supported 44 government schools and provided partial support to 11 grant-in-aid schools. Teachers at grant-aided schools were supposed to receive most of their income from school fees, but many parents had no cash and usually paid the fees in field produce and/or labor. By 1918, the number of elementary government schools had grown to 50. However, there was still no government-supported secondary education. Over and over, the Colonial Reports described a scarcity of qualified, competent teachers on the Family Islands. These Reports also expressed concern that Family Island settlements were so spread out that most students, in order to get to school, had to walk through the bush. Paved roads did not exist. Consequently, attendance was poor.

By 1920, the problems of illiteracy and lack of secondary education were so acute that the government passed the Secondary Education Act. The act provided grants to assist any school that provided secondary education and met certain requirements. There was a serious flaw in the program. These schools were operated by religious denominations, none of which accepted students of colour. Consequently, in 1923, it became necessary for the government to deal with the secondary education problem again. Government High School, in Nassau, was established. Its goals were to train teachers and to provide secondary education for a limited number of gifted students. There were entrance examinations and fees. An integrated Government High School, charging minimal fees, had finally been created. Students from the Family Islands, after passing the examination and being accepted, made arrangements to board with relatives or family friends in Nassau.

The schools in the Family Islands continued to be plagued with problems. A typical Family Island school might contain 100 to 200 students, ranging in age from 6 to 14 years. The school would be housed in one room, with the possibility of a balcony where younger students were edu-

cated. School staffs usually consisted of one teacher and three to five pupil-teachers or monitors, who were supposed to receive five hours of instruction per week before or after regular classes. Since no substitute teachers were available, when the teacher was sick, schools were closed. In 1932, it was reported that the school at Smith's Point, Grand Bahama, was closed for seventeen months due to the illness of the teacher.

In 1929, the wife of the Governor (Sir Charles Dundas) established the Dundas Civic Center in Nassau to provide general domestic training. Beginning in the thirties, the Dundas Civic Center received government subsidies to assist in the training of cooks, housemaids and hotel waiters. Male students who were considered to be incorrigible attended the Industrial School in Nassau, where they received training in elementary education and agriculture. The Colonial Reports from this period continued to express concerns about the number of poorly qualified teachers in the Family Islands.

Although most West Indian colonies had provisions for technical education, such training was not available in the Bahamas. This lack meant that immigrants often had to be recruited from the West Indies or Florida to perform such skills as carpentry. A school for technical education was constructed in 1938, but it was never opened. The building was finally designated the Wulff Road Junior School, which did not provide technical education. In 1950, the Training College and Training School opened at Oakes Field for 30 teachers and 260 students. It offered a two-year course of study.

Because institutions of higher education did not exist in the Bahamas, many wealthy Bahamians maintained a policy of sending their children abroad to British, Canadian or United States universities. This trend increased as more Bahamians earned higher incomes. For example, during the school year of 1963, a total of 135 students were matriculated at foreign universities: 62 in Britain, 16 in Canada, 54 in the United States and 3 in the West Indies.

In 1963, the legislature passed the Education Amendment Act, which barred discrimination with respect to religion, colour or race in the admission of students to any school receiving assistance from the Bahamian Board of Education. This legislation had the effect of integrating the independent and religious schools that had previously been racially segregated.

The College of the Bahamas (COB) was founded in 1974. In addition to its two-year programs, COB offers courses in association with the

University of Miami. The University of the West Indies also has a hotel
and tourism management program in Nassau.

At present, the Bahamas has a total of 216 elementary and secondary
schools. One hundred sixty-eight (77.8%) are fully maintained by the
Ministry of Education, and forty-eight (22.2%) are independent. The lat-
ter are usually operated by religious denominations.

The total student population is over 61,000. Approximately 46,500
(75%) attend government schools, while 15,350 (25%) are matriculated
at independent schools. Over 3,000 teachers are employed.

Clementina Adderley, Long Island

Contrasting Mrs. Adderley's description of school days in the early years
of the twentieth century and the atmosphere and equipment I observed
at an elementary school indicates that education on Long Island has un-
dergone important improvements.

The government never was so particular about paying for your schooling.
The parents had to go and work for the teacher two days out of every week.
My ma used to have to go and work for Mr. Ritchie in the field. Some days
he used to be okay, and other days he used to be on missions [drunk].
When he's on his missions, he got to come home. The school was where
the Baptist Church is up here on the Cay. That's where the first school
was. Well, after the hurricane—I can't remember what hurricane that
was—broke the school down, we built the big school up to Buckley's. The
government take it over. We walked to Buckley's and ran every step of the
way. We only had one slate, one pencil. For all the children, one slate, one
sponge. You wet that sponge. That sponge had a line [string] on it. You tied
it to your slate. You couldn't even spit on it to clean it, 'cause you'd get beat.
All my teachers was white men. No women teachers. My elder sister, she
didn't get no education. My two brothers, they used to teach. They was
monitors at Buckley's school. And when they big enough, they left and
went away, you know, sponging.

N.G.M. Major, Long Island

In 1920, I took my first exam. Go into Nassau to get out of the monitor
stage and to get into the teacher program. Timmy Gibson and I were
teaching together. He came first. I came second.

Mr. Albury held the exam. In his report, he wrote, "While Gibson got more marks than Major, it strikes me that Major is an intellectually brighter boy" [laughter]. Well, I liked that. But Timmy didn't argue against it. We always had plenty of fun. We had the exam in August and I didn't know anything about what happened until the next year in June. We would have gotten £20 ($96 U.S.) a month as a teacher. They would have had to pay me more money. They didn't say anything, so I decided to apply for a grant-in-aid school. We had several of them.

The inspector came after the examination was over, finding a teacher for this grant-in-aid school down at Gray's. I had applied; three other children had applied. And when he came to my name, he said, "Do you mean the teacher?" And my teacher told him, "We don't know that he's a teacher. We haven't heard anything about the results of the exam." He said, "No, we haven't sent out the results, but he passed. We're calling him in January for the Training School." I was glad to hear that. But they didn't pay me all those months. I still hold that against them. Because a dollar was worth so much more to me then.

I went in January to Nassau to the Training School. The first month I was there, they sent to ask for someone to go to Andros. Mr. Thompson [the person in charge] told them that I could go. But afterwards, he told me, he said, "Now, if you want me to talk for you, I can talk for you. Because where they're sending you, they believe in Obeah down there." I said, "I don't want to go down there!" So the second month, they wanted to send me to Eleuthera. Well, my friend Timmy, he say, "Boy, don't go. I know that school down there, those children. Those boys bigger than you." So I went to the office and I wouldn't answer one of their questions. And they said, "We understand. You don't want to go." So I didn't go. That was two.

One day in June, we were getting lunch. We were all standing looking out of the window. We heard Mr. Thompson mention Major and Rum Cay. By then, I wanted to get away from Nassau. The water that I had to drink made me sick all the time. Every day I got weaker and weaker and smaller and smaller. He didn't ask me. He said, "We're sending you." So he told me that I would go on the mailboat to Rum Cay. Told me to get ready. I went.

The government was reviving the salt industry in Rum Cay. The commissioner had to oversee the project. So the commissioner, who had taken care of the school, couldn't do that any longer. He had to take care of the salt.

184 . . . BAHAMIAN MEMORIES

I was the only teacher at Rum Cay at first. The senior monitor had been in charge. When I got there, I found out from her that she was eighteen. At that age, you decide whether you want to become a teacher or not. She didn't want to become a teacher. They preferred you to leave at eighteen so someone else could have a chance if you didn't want to become a teacher. So she left. I spent a year there. At the end of that year, when the salt pond was completed, I left.

I did very well. At the end of the year, the students took the exam and the school made 81%. We were 28th that year. I didn't want to leave. The people liked me so much. I got them to help me with everything. Began to get some money from the salt that I used to help the school. I used to put on little fun nights every other month. But a new commissioner was appointed and he brought his son to take care of the school. So I went back to Nassau.

I stayed in Nassau, waiting until the holidays were over, and while I was there someone at Inagua took sick. Mr. Albury said, "You ain't doing nothing around here. You're the only available person to go to Inagua. Get ready." And I had to go there. It made me sick. I was so lonesome, you know. Hardly any people. I wanted to go back on the return boat. But I decided to make it. Mr. Alexander, he was a Baptist preacher, had six or so in family. He kinda took me in. Had me to tea there every night and to dinner every Sunday. So I wasn't lonely anymore. I was an Anglican, but I used to go to his church every Sunday night. We became good friends. He was a very helpful man to the community. He was very Christian. He helped me well.

When I went to Nassau again, I told my younger sister, Lillie, to come. I needed her help in Inagua. She came. Mrs. Richardson and Mrs. Symonette [two residents of the community] came to my place one evening and asked me to let Lillie go and spend the evening with them. I told her to go and that I would come for her at nine o'clock. When I went to pick her up, I heard [a] little tinkling upstairs. They were dancing. I hadn't touched a piano for a long time, so I went upstairs and there was this lady at the piano. I wanted to get behind it to see if I could handle it.

She said to come. I stayed for about two hours playing the piano. The commissioner got it in for me for that. He sent for me to come to Nassau. He asked me to come and I went. I brought Lilly with me and that was the end of that, my teaching days.

I came here [to Deadman's Cay] in 1929. I built a little store right up the road here. And I carried on a little grocery business. I was [had been] doing that kind of work in Nassau. Anyhow, I'd been out of teaching for sixteen years, I think.

I went down to Nassau and saw Sir Alvin. And when he saw me, he said I had to go to the education office, because I was going to teach! The following year, I applied. I asked to go to the school in Roses at South End, to teach where I was born. But they said, "You stay right where you are [Deadman's Cay]. You go right in there. We got lots of children going down." Everybody knew me so well, the children knew me so well, I thought they wouldn't give me the respect that I deserved. But he said, "No, you go in there, go in." I went and decided to make a success.

I was at Deadman's Cay for thirty-one years. I chose my monitors myself. I should tell you something about how I got along in the school. The people seemed to be glad for me to be the teacher, because I started to do some of the little things that made them feel that their children were going ahead, you know. And that's all that people want. I started in September. I remember that, in October, we were taking up a collection to send away to the sick people. Each child would bring in a penny. There were a hundred and eighty students. So they brought me a hundred and eighty pennies. It came to my mind that maybe I could do a little something there to earn a little marks. I said, "I don't think I should send pennies to the office. I want more than that." And I went to work to think of something to raise some more money. I sent in £ 7 ($33.60 U.S.). The priest's wife called me from Clarence Town and said that I made the headlines.

I like teaching and they, especially C. I. Gibson, made me feel that I was doing well. I was under him. He kept me at certain classes that needed pushing. I noticed that they were moving others around and he left me. A good teacher who knew what he was doing would always be assigned to grade three. We had an A section, B section, C section. C section was before the children went into grade four. That was the tricky class. If you had good grade threes to send into grade four, you were getting somewhere. He kept me at grade three for years. I taught for forty-one years.

My task then was how to make children like you. We would read history and we would come across well-liked officers. And we find that the ones that are well-liked are those who used their soldiers to win battles. Those who know how to win battles. And so the soldiers would do anything to win. So I thought, I am an officer. These are my solders. I'm going to make them win. They believed and they would do what I say. They didn't want to fail anything.

Many of my students become teachers. The first exam was at Government High. Sent for the cream of the schools in the Out Islands. I sent six. They gave the students a test. Forty went in from the Out Islands. Ten passed. Four out of the ten were mine. That was forty percent of the total!

I enjoyed teaching and I didn't have a problem with the students. In teaching, discipline is the main thing you must depend on. So you become firm in that.

I saw a report on the teachers recently. It looked deeply into the results of student exams. Sixty percent didn't do well. What we've been hearing about the discipline in the schools in Nassau, it's terrible. Because never mind how good a child is—if she spends her day among others who are getting by with some things that her parents had taught her to shun, some of that will rub off on her, too. They found that they had to do something to promote it [learning].

Joanna Bethel, West End, Grand Bahama

Throughout Mrs. Bethel's narration I was enthralled by her determination to obtain an education.

Some of us children went to Eight Mile Rock to school, but things were very tough. There was only one school on the whole of Grand Bahama. That was in Eight Mile Rock. We had a church school after I went back home. That's where I attended. And then we had a grant-in-aid school. The government paid half and the parents paid half. Sometimes that wasn't working. The grant-in-aid wasn't going on. My mother used to hire people to come in the house and teach us, and people from around the neighbourhood would sent their children also. You used to pay three pence a day to be taught. And you'd give the teacher a good meal. Once my mother asked the tide waiter, in his spare time, to give us lessons.

I was sixteen years old when the public school came to West End. I was sixteen, but I wanted to go to school. So I went. It didn't bother me at my age or how grown I was. The problem with that was, I was just good enough, after going to all these other grant-in-aid and church schools, for standard one [the equivalent of the second year of school]. I was quite comfortable in standard one, but I had to teach. I wanted to be in the class. Because, after you finish teaching, the head teacher is tired, and so are we. Monitors are tired, and we want to go home, too. We weren't getting what we should have gotten had we been in the class.

Carrie Lunn, New Providence

*Mrs. Lunn's description of the differences between educational goals
for boys and for girls when she was growing up is another factor in the
"double standard" that existed in Bahamian society.*

I went to school right here in Nassau, Bishop's Eastern School. That was
the name of it. It was a place right up by the Eastern Parade. There was a
house right in there. It was a private school. My parents had to pay, and
they had a lot of nice children going there. You just sent in your application
and you could go. You know Hilda Thompson, who used to be at G. R.
Sweeting? Hilda Thompson used to go there. And the Haxtons, who lived
on Bay Street. They were light-skinned coloured people. The Smiths, they
were light-skinned people. The Stewarts and who else now. And you know,
if you don't know of them, Dr. Farrington's mother used to go there. She
and I grew up like sisters.

In those days, you know how it was. When you finished that school, you
just go and do fancy work [embroidery] and things like that. It was not like
it is today. I was pretty good in school, but none of the girls went away to
school. They stayed right here and they got jobs. They got jobs in stores
and they got jobs in different, various places. Not like today. When you
finish your school, you go away. Well, Mr. Adderley and Mr. Toote went.
But, in those days, what I talk about now is in my day, when I was a young
girl, most people didn't go. There were lots of boys who went and studied
law. Some went and studied to be doctors. But no girls among all of them.
Some years after that, girls would go away to take up nursing. Some would
go to England, and then they would come back and assist in the hospital.

Eva M. Williams, New Providence

*Mrs. Williams was one of five girls who were admitted to Government
High with forty boys, including some of the sons of the Bay Street Boys.*

When Bishop Roscoe Shedden came from England—all the priests came
from England in those days—he found that there was a school going by
the name of St. Hilda's School. The children who looked like me were not
accepted, only whites. I guess he wanted to advance the Anglicans and
pull more people in, so he organized this school to be held in a small

building next to St. Matthew's rectory. It was called Bishop's Eastern School. He didn't use his own name. Our parents were so anxious for the better education that we could get rather than sending us to public school, they sent us up there. Mr. and Mrs. Russell sent their three girls. I was an only child. My parents sent me. It was an average-size school. They had one schoolroom, which is still visible on that side of St. Matthew's church, and another that we used as small children. We had three teachers. We had Mary Wilkinson, who was the daughter of the English priest, and two other young women to help, by the names of Linda Eldon and Miss Rahming. She was a dark lady like myself. We went there for a few years and when I was eleven, Poppa sent me to Government High School. I had to take a test to go to Government High. Only the students with potential went there.

My father was very keen on education. He fought for it, although he wasn't a college man himself. Government High School was in the city by the British Colonial Hotel. My favorite subjects were arithmetic and geography. This English master used to call it general knowledge. So now, I think it was forty-five of us, about five girls and forty boys. The Bay Street Boys took their sons out of the Methodist Queens College and sent them to school with us. But they kept their girls at Queens College, even though they knew Government High was better.

Ivy Simms, Long Island

It is deplorable that the outrageous behavior of one teacher could deprive Miss Simms of a public school education.

I went here to this primary school for two years only, and then I was privately tutored by my cousins. At that time they started some games in the school, and the schoolyard was a very rough place, like the sea rocks. Every time we came home, we were all bruised up, fallen down, broken up knees. My father said, "This is foolishness." Well, he went to the teacher, talked with him, and the teacher said that if we did not come in the morning for the games, we would have to do them in the afternoon. After that teacher left, a letter was found in the schoolyard where they had written to him, saying that if Mr. Simms objected to his children playing the games, they were only to make school more enjoyable; they were not compulsory. That is why Joyce and myself were taken from the school and privately tutored. In those days they did not do much about exams. Thank God! I don't think I would have passed one.

Benjamin Saunders, Andros

Poor Mr. Saunders. His mischievous friends led him astray!

What I remember about school is that I didn't go every day. I did like school, I mean, when I was a child. But I can't say I been every day, because some of the times some of the companies [friends] was mischievous like myself and we made different plans. I leave for school all right, but I didn't go. That's true.

Alfred Love, New Providence

It seems that corporal punishment was alive and well at Western Senior School.

I went to Western Senior School. I went because I had to go. I didn't say I hate it, but I went to school because I was frightened of the truant officer. I was very talkative. The teacher used to send me to get some cane [stalk from a sugar cane plant] to cut me in the hand. I used to chat a lot. And he would hit me in my hand as punishment. I left school when I was sixteen years old. I could have gone back, but after repeating the sixth grade a couple of years, it wasn't no use going back. At that time, they never used us to teach the younger ones. On the Out Islands they had monitors.

Lawrence Smith, New Providence

When I come outta school, fight just start. 'Cause when I come outta school, they trying to tease me. They saying, "You dumb, this and that." And so we start fighting. After that, well, I tell you, Miss George [his guardian] beat me for it. She used to taught us, you know? Teach us at school. So she say, "I teaching you at school, don't fight." She just beat me when I get home. I say, "Mommy, I ain't gonna fight no more." I used to call her Mommy. But I had sense to know that wasn't my main mother. But she beat me. Teacher beat me even when I try to spell my name and all that kinda thing, something like that, you know? We get beaten for that. Wasn't right.

And mostly, after I started growing up larger, she start to send me over to work. She wouldn't keep me in school. She send me to go weed yard. Instead of her [taking] her time to taught me. My life coulda been better if I coulda stayed in school, learned to read and stuff.

After listening to Miss Simms, Mr. Saunders, Mr. Love and Mr. Smith, I had to admit that we teachers fail to meet the needs of many of our students. I have always been a proponent of individualized education, because I presumed that, if each student could progress at his/her own speed after being assigned to the proper level of instruction, the majority would succeed. I came to this realization after listening to my father discuss his role as a monitor at an all-age school in Palmetto Point, Eleuthera, during the first decade of this century. Some elementary schoolteachers in New York employ the technique of creating small groupings within their classroom to insure that students are working at an appropriate level for their capabilities. Using different texts, methods and hands-on materials, many succeed. How different lives could be if teachers cared for all students.

Iris Dillet Knowles, born on December 25, 1938, Nassau, New Providence

My cousin, Iris, is one of the "youngsters" whom I interviewed. She now operates Dillet's Guest House on the property where she and her sister grew up. I conducted five interviews at the guest house. As Iris overheard these, she was often able to add a different perspective. Her important discussion of high school education in the '50s and of the changes that followed juxtaposed with the descriptions presented by older narrators, and those who were educated on the Family Islands completes the pic-

ture of the evolution of public school education in the Bahamas during the twentieth century.

I attended Government High, starting in 1950. There were three terms in the year. Even though it was a government school, you still had to pay to attend. There was an admission of some fifty children every year. You were really very, very select to gain admittance when you reached the age to go to high school if you were black. You had to be one of the top fifty who passed the examination and have the ability to pay to get into Government High. So what I am saying is that it is a fairly recent phenomenon, if you are black in the Bahamas, to be able to get a free high school education. Black people who are now in their seventies would have been the first to be able to go to high school in the Bahamas.

Back in the old days, they took the brighter students to help with the younger ones, because you would have had one teacher in each all-age school. So they took the brighter children and made them monitors. And then the monitors would go to evening classes to this one teacher, who would then constantly upgrade their education so that they would be prepared to help with the teaching. Eventually, they would be prepared to sit for the British External Examinations. There were two examinations— Cambridge Junior and Senior.

When I was in high school, you took the Junior first. It was kind of a preliminary. Then, the following year, you took your Senior. And then, if you were smart enough and your parents had enough money for you to stay in school, or you didn't opt out to go get a job and what have you, you could stay in and take your matriculation. Now, I always remember Cecil Wallace-Whitfield. Cecil took his Cambridge Senior Examination, and he got such high marks that he was exempt from taking the matriculation examination. But he was unhappy with his mark in something or the other. So he went back and resat the examination [laughter]. And we all thought he was a fool. "Boy, suppose you fail the examination and you're already exempt from the matriculation." He said, "No. I have to live with myself, and I know that I can do better than what I did." Well, he took it over and he did get the exemption from the matriculation again.

Now, when I was in high school, they had just discontinued the Cambridge Junior Certificate and it was only the Cambridge Senior Certificate. And by this time, you had a choice to take a second foreign language. Everybody had to take Latin, so I opted to take Spanish. There were two other subjects that you had to choose. This was the first introduction of having optional subjects. Prior to that, everybody who went to school had to take all of the subjects whether you had the aptitude for it or not. When you took your examinations at the end of a four-year period, you had to take all of the subjects. And if you failed maths or English or both, you had to take all of the subjects over again.

What happened is, they discontinued that system and they implemented what they call the General Certificate of Education. This was something that came into place because the British decided that Great Britain was poor and it wasn't going to be underwriting all these external examinations. So, they then came out with a different examination. The governments of the colonies had to make an arrangement with the University of Cambridge in England for them to still monitor these examinations. Once they put that in, they went with the present situation. And what we have found is that a lot of the children opted out of the English and maths classes. And so, we have ended up that the standard of education has just gone totally out of the window. You will find children graduating from high school over here who have passed one subject in the General Certificate of Education and that will be, say, art. The Ministry of Education policy is such that once you have completed four or five—whatever number of years it is—if you are not up to standard to take the examination, or you take the examination and you fail, you get a piece of paper from the school saying that you have completed five years and you have been exposed to these subjects at these levels. You've got five, six thousand children graduating each year. A thousand children coming out of the high school system every year just here in Nassau.

Now, what the Ministry of Education has come out with is a certificate BGCSE—Bahamas General Certificate for Secondary Education. The first is at the level of the Cambridge Senior that existed when I was in school. It [the graded certificate] works its way through to the General Certificate of Education. Now, you know that the children have actually passed an examination at these different levels. If you come out with "A," then you have completed the equivalent of a Cambridge Senior. If you come out way down around "E" or so, it means that you are a candidate for learning a trade or this kind of thing. You were exposed and you absorbed what you could, but it wasn't enough for you to pass the exam at the level that was set. This is good, because with the certificate of attendance in the past, you didn't know what people knew.

Telephone and Electricity Services

After several private initiatives failed, the government established a tele-phone system in Nassau in 1907. By 1992, there were telephone facilities in Abaco, Acklins (twelve subscribers), Andros, Berry Islands, Bimini, Cat Island, Crooked Island (government offices only), Eleuthera, Exuma, Inagua, Long Island, Mayaguana (only for Bahamas Telecommunications Corporation), San Salvador (only for Bahamas Telecommunications Corporation), New Providence and Grand Bahama.

By 1909, an acceptable system of electricity had become operational in Nassau. The Bahamas Electric Corporation, however, did not begin operating in any of the Family Islands until 1973. Some of those islands have now been completely electrified. A few other settlements are served by franchises regulated by the Ministry of Works and Utilities. On Grand Bahama, an independent power company serves Freeport and neighbouring communities.

During my visits to Cat Island and Long Island in the 1990s, some communities were still relying on personal generators and kerosene lamps. A number of residents expressed the opinion that their region had been ignored because of a lack of enthusiasm on the part of their representatives, or because the party in power had not won the district in previous elections.

Clementina Adderley, Long Island

Most modern conveniences don't impress Mrs. Adderley. She will hap-pily live without a telephone until the problem of "people gonna listen in and they gonna know what you say" is solved.

I ain't got no generator now [laughter]. But I does get the light from my son. He got a big generator and I gets it. Got everything wired from there here. [Her son lives next door.] I got my lantern in the house and got two lamps in the house. The generator could go bad, too, you know. I don't have a telephone. I put in for a telephone and I ain't even got that. My son from the States, he tell me, he say, "Momma, put a phone in the house. When I call, I could call direct to you." But after he tell me, I tell my grandson to put in one for me. He promised me that from last year. November gone make one year. Haven't got it yet. Now this what he tell me. He say they was to put the lights through here. And they gonna give them the telephones. You see, when these people call now, just as soon as they ring, if it's your ring, people gonna listen in and they gonna know what you say [more than one person shares a line]. And they say, when they put them in now, only you will know your business and nobody else. So I guess I'll be dead before I get it [laughter].

Ena Major, Long Island

They ain't run electricity on this end of the island yet. The information that I got was that Mr. Ed Knowles was trying to get the neighbours here in the south to put in money to get it going, right? Buy shares. He started a self-help thing going. 'Cause like he said in meetings that he held, the government would take over. Private people start and the government takes over. If the government doesn't start here, it means that someone else would start, but they will eventually get their money back. I was told that when they made allocations for the money in the north, they didn't include the south. The south had already started on its own. This was what I was told. I don't know how true it is. I know it was started, because people put in money. Because they felt it was important. But they [Mr. Knowles' group] didn't get [raise] enough money to get started.

After a year or so, everybody got their money back with interest. They didn't get the amount that they needed to proceed. This happened about a year ago. Everybody got their money back last year. But it's on its way to the north. And they say after the north, then it will be the south. There were some people here from that department getting information on what all you have using electricity. They're working kinda slow.

Hurricanes

No other natural occurrences create the level of concern among Bahamians than is generated by the news of a hurricane headed toward their islands. Hurricane season in the Bahamas extends from June to November. Hurricanes begin as tropical depressions and, when conditions are favorable, they gain strength and become tropical storms. These develop strength and energy over warm ocean waters. When their sustained winds become greater than seventy-three miles an hour, they are called hurricanes. These huge storm systems can extend from five hundred miles in diameter to over three thousand miles. Generally, they weaken as they move over land areas. Although winds are usually responsible for most hurricane damage, in the Bahamas, waves and storm swells of tides caused by the wind also cause some damage. Many of the islands have suffered greatly, as entire settlements and cash crops have been destroyed. For example, the year 1907 witnessed hurricanes destroying the sponge beds on the north side of the Exuma Cays. The same weather systems devastated many orange trees whose fruit had been a major export during previous years.

From 1925 to 1929, a succession of five serious hurricanes hit the Bahamas. Three of these struck between July and September of 1926. Every island was hit by at least one. Whole settlements were washed into the sea, and thousands of people were left homeless. Because some of the inhabitants of the Family Islands found themselves without housing and without crops to harvest, they prepared to move to Nassau in the hope of finding employment. But Nassau had also been heavily damaged, and the government posted notices throughout the Family Islands assuring residents that help was on the way and cautioning them that, by coming to Nassau, they would forfeit any government help. Cat Island and Andros were the locations where the storms were most serious, but the damage to property was widespread.

Commissioners were authorized to provide free food to the needy and to employ men to rebuild the houses of widows and those who were unable to work. Limestone was provided to aid in the repair of the homes. Owners of damaged ships and boats received assistance from the government. In addition, the Bahamas branch of the British Red Cross and the Imperial Order of the Daughters of the Empire assisted in providing relief for victims. The devastation continued as the hurricane of September 1929 destroyed sixty percent of the new citrus trees that had been planted to replace those previously destroyed.

During the 1940s, severe hurricanes again plagued the islands. In October 1942, New Providence and many of the Family Islands were hit. Then, in 1945, a severe hurricane destroyed boats, houses and crops on Mayaguana, Crooked Island and the southern part of Andros. There was also hurricane damage that year at Governor's Harbour, Eleuthera. In August of 1949, a hurricane destroyed certain areas of Nassau and fruit growers' properties on North Eleuthera.

On September 7, 1960, the eastern Bahamas experienced winds of 150 miles per hour as a hurricane completely destroyed three settlements on

Mayaguana. The Red Cross, the Bahamian government, a United States base on the island and the United States Air Force provided assistance to the inhabitants.

In 1965, hurricane Betsy caused extensive damage requiring additional aid. During the next two decades, hurricane winds and tide surges caused some damage. But the destruction they caused cannot be compared to the devastation that occurred in 1992 with the arrival of Andrew. That hurricane struck North Eleuthera, Bimini and the southern Berry Islands on August 23 and 24, 1992, causing unprecedented economic losses.

Currently, the United States National Hurricane Center in Coral Gables, Florida, provides the Bahamas with improved weather forecasting, starting twenty-four hours in advance of an impending hurricane. Boaters receive five-day coastal weather forecasts. Hurricane Center predictions include satellite and Doppler radar reporting. Presumably, the assistance of the Hurricane Center will lead to fewer lost lives and a reduction of property and crop loss.

Clementina Adderley, Long Island

And oh, my dear, when she [the church] was up to the belfry, the hurricane come and level her down to the ground. The same length that she was, that was on the ground. Father Pyfrom come and the people were there mourning. He tell them, he said, "The good God what put it down; the good God gonna help us put it back." They worked hard. In no time, they had it back up.

George L. Roberts, New Providence

I was surprised to hear Mr. Roberts' tales of pilfering and little thatch houses.

In Nassau, when I was young and a hurricane coming, everybody go and look for the building that blowing down and steal everything you could steal [laughter]. I know about that 'cause I was part of it. If a hurricane came seriously, there was a big blow, and it would last a day. So the building blow down, and you have—what you call it—pilfering. People go and take what they want to take. Even steal coconuts. Everybody had a coconut tree, but yet they steal coconuts.

Plenty wooden houses was destroyed in hurricanes. Little wooden houses, they'd blow away. When Chippingham first opened, Mr. Chipman built plenty these little three-, four-room houses. And this the time of the three-day hurricane, 1938. After these houses blow down, it's a flood. Flood the whole of Chippingham. People whose houses didn't blow down had to drill holes in the floor to let the water out. People didn't get hurt. They may stick their leg with a nail or something. But everyone ran to people with the biggest house. Stayed there 'til it passed.

Poor people whose houses got destroyed built them a little thatch house. We used to build them when we were small. You take and put a leaf on top of a leaf [for the roof]. You use sticks for the sides. Just like you do in Africa. You go in the pine barren and you cut a pine. You get long lumber, you know. And they build them and put them up together.

Most of the houses in the poor neighbourhoods was thatched roofs in Governor's Harbour and those Out Islands. Just like the Indians used to build. They use thatch and lap them over. The thatch roof last five, eight, ten years. If it leaks, you just put another leaf on top of that part. If you scratch a match in dry season, they went [burned]. We had horse-and-carriage fire engines. They didn't have no motors. They got the water out of wells to put the fire out. Everybody had artesian wells. They'd pump the water out of the well. Did it with buckets, too. Sometimes they couldn't put the fire out. 'Cause a woman I used to call Grandma Effie, she got caught in a fire like that. She died in the fire in her house.

Rita Wood, New Providence

It's not as bad in Nassau when there's a hurricane as it is on the Family Islands, 'cause the government, hospitals and supplies are all here. But we're still hurt by the bad ones. That last hurricane took so much sand from some of the beaches, and people's trees were pulled right out of the ground. So much fruit was destroyed.

The government sends out all kinds of warnings on TV and the radio telling you to put up storm shutters, get lamps ready in case the electricity is out, stock up food and water. And when it's over, the government, Red Cross and Friendly Societies try to get everyone back to normal.

After that hurricane Andrew hit in 1992, we had to collect clothes, food and money for some of the people on Eleuthera, because three people died and so many lost everything. Some Bahamians living in the United States tried to help out, too. It takes a while to recover from a hurricane, because crops, trees and land all get messed up. And it's really hard for poor people living in wooden houses. Some of them lose everything. But the government does whatever it can to help.

Drug Interdiction

The history of the Bahamas is replete with examples of smuggling and piracy on the high seas. These include the legacy of Blackbeard and his comrades, the illegal transportation of guns by Bahamian citizens during the United States' Civil War, and transshipments of liquor during the bootlegging period. But none of those ventures devastated Bahamian society to the degree that the transshipment of drugs has. During the 1970s, marijuana was remarkably available on the beaches and in the nightclubs of Nassau. South American traffickers made frequent air-drops of drugs. Although destined for the United States, much of the marijuana, never left the Bahamas. And as United States citizens increased their use of cocaine in the mid 1970s, that drug also was airdropped on these islands. Many young Bahamians began using drugs during that period, and some continue to be addicted today. As a result, crime and violence have increased significantly.

In 1980, in an effort to control the drug problems, the Royal Bahamas Defence Force was assigned the task of patrolling the waters of the Bahamas. Prime Minister Pindling appointed a Royal Commission of Inquiry in 1983. Its findings were made public in December of 1984. The report stated that the drug trade had permeated Bahamian society. Several government ministers, senior officials, and employees of the Police Force, Customs, and Immigration Department were implicated. The report stated that the domestic drug trade had reached epidemic dimensions.

In 1986, the government started the Drug Abuse Rehabilitation Program, which was partially funded by the United Nations Fund for Drug Abuse Control. Its purpose was to aid in the prevention and treatment of drug addiction. In addition, legislation was enacted to provide stiff penalties for drug traffickers.

Beginning in the mid 1980s, the Bahamas also became involved in international efforts to turn the problem around. The Bahamian and United States governments formed a joint Drug Task Force. Additionally, a Sea Rider Program (also known as the Ship Rider Programme) was established, which enabled Bahamian officers to authorize the use of

United States helicopters and Coast Guard vessels in Bahamian waters
for drug interdiction operations.

These and other efforts had a dramatic effect. The United Nations
International Narcotics Control Board, in its 1993 report, praised the
Bahamian government for spending 15% of its national budget on drug
issues. From 1983 to 1992, the annual supply of marijuana passing
through the Bahamas decreased from an estimated 732 tons to an esti-
mated 10.6 tons. In addition, between 1987 and 1990, cocaine shipments
decreased by approximately 59%, from 83 tons to 34 tons. Bahamian citi-
zens are hopeful that this plague is now behind them.

Many Bahamians expressed deep concern about this—and the hope
that drug trafficking and drug use will be reduced and/or eliminated.

Clementina Adderley, Long Island

My dear, today, the people is so rich. They so rich that they don't know
what to do with it. They say they don't want no fish. They don't want no
peas. They don't want no conch. They don't want no lobster. They only
want pork chops and steak.

People get so rich since this thing you call marijuana come in the
world. They got so much money. Some of them, they hardly don't want to
speak to you. But, thank God, I think the bottom of that drop out. If it
ain't, it very near out.

'Cause that put too much people to destruction. It make too much
craziness in people. My dear, right here, all about. 'Cause when they use
it, they got no sense. And if it's my own, when they catch them put them
in jail and don't let them come out.

Joanna Bethel, South Beach

Then, because Grand Bahama was so close to the United States, it got
involved in the drug trade. Oh yes, Grand Bahama got involved. That's for
sure. I heard about that. It's so easy for them to get there. Right across to
Bimini, and then right across to Grand Bahama. From Grand Bahama to
Palm Beach, it's only about sixty miles.

Rafaleta Williams, Andros

In days gone by, you coulda walk any hours of the night. You coulda done anything at night. But you can't do it now. It's the drugs. I don't know how to look. I don't. We never used to hear about them things. Where they come from? Yes, some Bahamians are getting rich. They get this, that and the other. I can't see it.

I just talk to an old lady, talking to her on the phone. I learned in my church; I learned, my parents learned me. A slow dollar is better than a fast one. Because when it's slow, you work and they mightn't pay you what you are worth no how. But it's still better than if you get one thousand dollar quick as that and don't know [dishonestly]. When you come look, the man come grab you. Now see, you should have been satisfied with the two dollars you was getting. And enjoy yourself. Be free. That's what you call an honest piece of bread.

Sit right down and go weed my grass. Sun hot for true and jook up the bush in my hat to keep me cool over my head. When I finish, somebody put one three dollars in my hand. I go to buy one bag of flour. I come in and sit down and eat one bread I bake. Eat it. Nobody ain't come to arrest me for that. But soon as they hear, Mrs. Williams, I hear she get a load of money last night. When you look, you see one big thing parked out there [a stranger's car]. That's what I say now. That's what they will do. They'll come and say, "You got thus and so here? Well, I bring this paper to search your house." Now, what you call that? That's a fast dollar. That ain't no life. When you look here, you trembling. Earn an honest piece of bread and weed that grass and you pay me a couple of dollars. That's honest. That's what I call a slow dollar is better than a fast one. But these today, they want fast dollars.

Ivy Simms, Long Island

Latterly, we got into this terrible mess of cocaine and that has ruined so many people on this island. Many, many here have gone into it and so many pushers. This place has quieted down now because it's at its lowest ebb, I think. They have got it a bit under control, but some is still coming in.

You see those little planes coming in? They don't care, you know, those planes that bring it in. They don't care if they get killed. That's a mission. It's a terrible thing.

Alfred Love, Nassau

Drugs started getting bad in the Bahamas around '72, '73. I can't really say whether the situation is better now. But I know for sure that the effects of it are still on. You get a lot of people walking like zombies. They stealing. They only skeletons from cocaine and whatnot like that. Rocks [crack] is here, too. Like in the States. People were freebasing here before they started in the United States. You see, I don't worry with it. I know for sure now it did a lot of damage to the country.

I know, because I built a house for a cousin of mine in a place called South Street. He live over forty years in the United States. He built this home to come over and spend time. I used to leave every bit of the lime, cement, blocks, lumber, you name it, I leave it right in the open yard. And come home down to Chippingham, which is over a mile, sleep, and the next day, not a piece of it gone. After this drug came on the scene, doggone, they take my three-foot-wide and six-foot-high steel gate. They take it and sold it. Right here last week sometime. You got a private road. It had a car gate. They unbolt the wire off the gate and gone with it. When I built it and put that wire there, that been there for years. But after this drug thing come on, you can't keep a thing. I used to have bananas by the bunch. Come home and leave them on the place. Cut them when I want to cut them. Now, when I look, I can't get a banana. They take them, and today they cut your bananas before they ready and sell them. Two-thirty in the morning, young men jumping over six-foot fence and up in the tree, stealing guineps and mangoes. Just to get a hit [drugs]. It's really pathetic.

One thing, you have to blame the Colombians, 'cause they're the ones who brought it here. If the citizens of America wasn't using it, there would be no need of them bringing it. It's so many islands here, they coulda come in and set up a depot to transport it from there to America. Many times you didn't even know they were there. I believe that's where plenty of the guns started coming in. Colombians bring the guns to protect their stuff. The government have an amnesty [to hand in illegal guns] now. But it won't work. You see, the majority of the guns is in the possession of criminals. They bought those guns to commit crimes. So they are not going to turn them in. They might find a few people who bought guns for protection. That particular individual might be more inclined to turn his in, 'cause he is not a criminal-minded person. For that reason, he wouldn't want to go to prison. But the criminal, he don't mind. He go to jail. He spend his time. He come out and commit crime again. And he ain't gonna turn in his guns.

Israel "Bubba" Saunders, born on August 6, 1919,
Behring Point, Andros

> *Mr. Saunders was the first person I interviewed at Small Hope Bay. He*
> *is the fisherman who supplies fish for Small Hope Bay Lodge. I thought*
> *we would discuss his job, but most of our time was spent discussing poli-*
> *tics and the drug problem.*

I don't bother with sponges now, because the West Side of Andros is very dangerous. The fellers with that dope. I don't wanna go there. A lotta fellers gone down there yesterday crawfishing. They ask me was I coming with 'em. I tell 'em, "No. I ain't coming!"

Enid Sawyer, New Providence

I think the drug thing is getting a little better, because the government is beginning to crack down on it. I think they're trying to curb it. They have quite a few places for addicts to go. The people off the street don't have to pay to go there. I think it's good. There are some other places where you do have to pay if you can afford it. After they get into this habit, it take a long time to get out. Many of these people who get addicted to drugs are intelligent people. It has nothing to do with intelligence.

Herman Sawyer, New Providence

Dope start coming on the street and it ruin things. Bad. It's better now. It's controlled immensely. 'Cause a few years ago, there was more dope than tourists. That's all we had in the treasury, dope money. All these million of dollars they trying to find. They didn't have to give the accountability or nothing, 'cause all this dope money was here. I [a government representative] want to get myself ten to fifteen hundred thousand dollars, a quarter of a million dollars, I just take it. Nobody write up nothing. The Commission of Inquiry going on now just trying to find out what was going ahead. The ordinary man didn't know nothing. People like me, I wouldn't say I knew, but I had a good idea. But, at that time, everybody was in that, and when people like me speak about it, [they say,] "Oh, you're an Uncle Tom." [Laughter.] And black man say, "The white man had it all the time. Now let the black man have it." Now, it come right down to the place where the black man have it. Black man going to jail. Can't hold their heads up. In days gone by, we [blacks] could always hold our head up.

When the white man do these things like dope and stuff, nobody knew anything about that. To tell you the truth, this thing [dope] was going ahead since the time I know myself at the age of six or seven. But we didn't know, because the other people transfer by banana boats from Cuba and Haiti. That was dope running right there. But it was controlled by the white man. That's why the white man was always on top. I can remember when dope really got out of control here. I can't remember the year. The first black millionaire we had was named Ferguson [laughter]. Everybody know. After he came, they start transferring [drugs and money] back and forth. Then so many got millionaires overnight. Those people ain't never worked.

Kathleen Thurston, Cat Island

The drug situation in Nassau had to become less. Else, it would be just a few people left in Nassau. You know, it came to a point where a boy was killing his own family, his father and stuff like that. A little baby, they throw in the bush and all like that. Things was bad.

5

Departures and Arrivals

Emigration

Throughout the twentieth century, Bahamians—and particularly Family Islanders—were recruited as laborers in North, Central and South America. During the early 1900s, Hamburg-America Lines steamships traveling from New York en route to Gulf ports, Jamaica and Haiti stopped at Long Cay and Inagua to recruit laborers. Bahamians were hired to serve as stevedores in Central America, as railway construction workers in Cuba, mahogany cutters in Mexico and in the construction of the Panama Canal. These emigrations were typically for brief periods of employment, and most Bahamians returned home when the contracts were terminated.

During the same period, a steady flow of Family Islanders to the United States also occurred. By contrast, however, many of these emigres never returned. Most Bahamian immigrants worked as farm laborers in southern Florida and construction workers in Miami. By 1911, many of the immigrants had been joined by their families and had established permanent homes in Florida. Some of the Family Islands lost a majority *of their able-bodied men to the United States during the first two decades of the last century.*

By 1914, steamship companies ceased to call at the Bahamas, attributing their new policy to the outbreak of World War I. Nonetheless, emigration continued throughout the war. The years from 1914 to 1918 witnessed the exodus of thousands of Bahamians involved in various war-time capacities. These primarily included serving in British, Canadian and United States armed forces.

On September 9, 1915, the first contingent of Bahamians known as "The Gallant Thirty" left the Bahamas for service in the British armed forces. It was decided that these Bahamian volunteers should be sent to Jamaica for initial training. They became a machine gun section. When the first contingent subsequently arrived in England, they were assigned to the Second Battalion of the British West Indies Regiment. Two successive contingents followed and were also drafted into the British West Indies Regiment. The second contingent consisted of 105 men, and the third totaled 87 volunteers. Five additional drafts brought the number of Bahamians of colour who served in the West Indian Regiment of the British armed forces to 700. Meanwhile, most Bahamian whites served in the United States, Canadian and British forces rather than in the West Indian Regiment. In addition, although not utilized, 225 fishermen volunteered to act as crew members for the Royal Navy.

In 1918, the emigration of over 2,500 Bahamian contract laborers to Charleston, South Carolina, to work on port installations there had a serious impact on the population of some of the Family Islands. By 1924, the United States' Johnson-Reed Act virtually excluded Bahamian entries into the Florida labor market. In 1934, Dutch steamers called at Inagua, once again seeking stevedores to unload cargoes at South American ports.

World War II began on September 3, 1939, when Britain declared war on Germany. As part of the war effort, the Bahamian government established a Central War Committee, with the Honorable A. K. Solomon as chairman. Its task was to manage the reception of children from evacuated areas of Britain. The first group to arrive was from a school in Sussex. A number of wealthy British subjects also escaped to Nassau. By the end of World War II, the Bahamas had also provided refuge for over 100 survivors from Allied ships.

As the Second World War continued, Bahamians once again emigrated from their islands in large numbers. Some joined the British, Ca-

*nadian and United States armed forces. It is estimated that over 8,000
Bahamian men and women, out of a total population of some 70,000,
were involved in the services or in war-time activities in Britain or the
United States. Those who joined the services under British command
went to Europe and north Africa. Bahamians in the United States forces
went to the Pacific. Although the United States offered citizenship to
those who had served, most returned home.*

Joseph Carroll, Long Island

I spent two years in the army during World War II, the Bahamas Defence
Company, North Caribbean Regiment [later known as the Bahamas Bat-
talion]. I were married when I went in the army. But, you know, the young
men, they want to see the world and see everything. I got the world and all
the trimmings! I went to Italy and Africa. We went to the States first. Then
we went to Italy and we spent some time in Egypt, you know. We didn't go
into action because, well, fortunately, the war end[ed] before. I was sorry
I didn't get to fight, but anyway [laughter]. After you train and don't use it,
all the training down the drain. However, I had a family to come back to.
I can't remember how many but I had a couple of children in '43. I was
demobilized in '45.

George Roberts, New Providence

A lot of Bahamians served in the United States military. Myself, Philip
Worrell, Ned Isaacs, Kenneth Sands, Arthur Blakely. But see, I think some
of them were born in the United States. I met them all through tours.
Most of us took training in Fort McClellan, Alabama. That's where we
took the basic training, and from there we separated. Went to the Pacific.
Clark Field was the main base in the Philippines, so they shipped us all
over there and then they distributed us around.

When the war was over, all of us came back home. When I was doing
my basic training, they had a law that if any alien was in the service of the
United States and wanted to become an American citizen, you could sign
up right there. And they would have you sworn in in Alabama. Most of us
were sworn in there. Then we became "Americanized" [laughter]. When
we came back from the services, everybody could go where he want to go.
They gave us enough time to decide. So they said, "You can go to the
Bahamas and stay a certain amount of time and come back and report to

Fort Dix. If you want to reenlist, you reenlist there." My intention was to reenlist. But I got hung up [laughter]. You didn't have to go back. You had a choice. If you didn't report back, you were discharged.

THE CONTRACT

From 1942 to 1966, by an agreement between the British and United States governments, Bahamian workers went to the United States to provide agricultural labor. The "Contract" (also referred to as "The Project") was necessary for the United States, because participation in World War II had greatly reduced the availability of farm labor. It was necessary for the Bahamas, because there was severe unemployment in Nassau. Many of the workers came from the Family Islands, however, further depleting the number of farmers available to work there. Most of the contract workers were male, but some females also went.

The agreement between the United Kingdom and the United States stated that no more than 5,000 Bahamian workers should be in the United States at any time. Many persons rotated back and forth. In 1951, there were 4,000 Bahamian laborers in the United States, with earnings of about $5,000,000. By 1960, fewer than 200 Bahamians continued to be employed as contract workers.

About 25% of the people I interviewed had either gone "on Contract" themselves, or had relatives who did. Since the Bahamian economy was depressed, this arrangement helped provide needed jobs. Some people were able to make relatively good salaries. A few complained that the Bahamian government did not give them the total amount that had been sent home for them. Others never returned home, instead becoming "illegal aliens" in the United States. The Contract was a positive experience for most of the workers. Many traveled to a variety of states throughout the United States. They were exposed to different cultures. And the Contract provided them with the opportunity to save some money.

Benjamin Saunders, Andros

I spend one year on Contract; both my wife and I were working together. Her mother took care of the children. In those days, they send back a certain reduction from your payment every week according to what you make. That come back to the family, home. That was a little help, I mean, to her mother and the children.

Well, according to where you work in the States, some places you go, you make plenty money. I been up as far as Pennsylvania. I worked there. I went from place to place to pick cherries, oranges and apples and beans. All that, I had a part in. And I made good money. I was young and strong and I coulda hustle well.

John Newman, Long Island

I went on Contract. I was there three years. The first place I went to was in Florida. We spent six months there. Then I don't remember how long we spent in Georgia. Then [we went to] Maine and Arkansas. From there I went to Virginia.

You know what happens, sometimes the farmers rush off the laborers picking the fruit so quick, they leave lots of fruit on the trees. And sometimes the fruit is more crowded and it's hard to get. So they try to send to this Project to get men to go there. I was picking apples in Virginia, peaches in Georgia, cotton in Arkansas, beans in Tennessee, and tomatoes in Ohio.

Well, how we worked, I'll say six days. But most of the work was piecework. And you worked to your leisure, but you have to put in those days. The faster you worked, the more money you got. When you weren't working, the foreman, he always look out for a job for you from another farmer. So you never be out of work, still occupied with work.

I went because there was nothing going on in Long Island. Because all we had to do here was to farm for corn, peas, bean, and take care of our sheep and goat. There was not much money in it. Therefore, we see that we have a chance of going to the States and helping ourselves more.

Well, they recruited us and we went over. How long you stay depends on what your contract calls for. It might just call for six months. You extend it while you are over there.

It was some prejudice in Arkansas and Georgia. They were the most prejudiced. Florida wasn't bad at all.

Alfred Love, New Providence

In 1944 I went on Contract. The Contract was during the Second World War. The Duke of Windsor was the Governor. The war caused everything to go down, work and everything. There was no work for the people. Spongers couldn't sponge. Fish was not exported. So after everything came to a standstill, the Duke contacted the American government and said, "Seeing that your men have to go overseas, we have Bahamian workers who can keep your farms going." So under those circumstances, that was how the Contract started.

I went various places. The whole Contract rarely go and stay one place. I don't know if you notice how America is. America have two climates, north and south. The vegetables grow in the winter down in Florida. When the winter season is over, they take the farm workers and ship them north. In the summer, the north grows the same things that they grow in the winter in Florida. I was there in '44, '45, '46 and '47 before I decide to come back home. Some men stayed over longer than me. It was a good experience. Picked peaches, apples, beans and things like that.

Living conditions was satisfactory. To be truthful, you couldn't really expect high-class living on the farm. We used to live in tents in the south, and when you go north you live in wooden shacks, where you could put heaters in them. But we used to mostly live in these canvas tents. Four men to a tent about 20 by 20 feet. When it come to husband and wife, you have two couples in each tent. But anytime they [the women] get pregnant, they had to come home. They didn't let them born their children over there.

Harcourt Stevens, Cat Island

The Duke came and the Contract started. I made fifteen trips to the United States from '43 to '45, '46, round there. Up to '47. I went to Tampa, Florida. I went to Virginia, and I passed 'cross Cape Charles and went to Maxwell, Virginia. Sometime, I stay away six months.

But I had a lot of robbers. When I come to Nassau and the money that I work for, they take from me. So, the merchants, they still owe me now! Every time you go to get your money, the merchant in the States tells you how much you make for the season. But when you come to Nassau, they tell you, "Here's two or three pounds," and say ain't no more money coming. I always tell you that I was robbed. I tell the Bahamas government that we were robbed. You never got what you worked for.

George Roberts, New Providence

The Duke of Windsor started the Contract. They were taking mostly Eleutherans first. At that time I was working in the Water Works [Department]. Well, when they first started, they were giving out I.D. cards, so my job was issuing the I.D. cards to the people. When this Contract came on, they sent people into the United States to work on the farms. So we were only allowed to take certain types. This was word of mouth, of course. But we knew who was qualified to go on this Contract. You had to be that dark complexion. Maybe that's not true, but that's the way we were told to pick these people. They didn't want no white people doing it. You had to be a certain complexion [laughter]. White people who applied were turned down. They took them and sent them to England. They were working on building things there. I guess they were building tanks and planes and everything else. If they had graduated from Government High School, all those people went to England whether you white or black. But the lower-class people, this Contract was made specifically for them. Jack Dillet wasn't lower class, [but] he went. He slipped through, 'cause he had a little pull. They slipped some others through, too.

I think they started with something like three dollars a day. What they did, they gave them so much money, but some of the money came back to the Bahamas government. So the Bahamas government would pay their family that was left here. And keep the rest until you return back from the Contract and you could draw your money.

The American government gave them so much as an allowance while they were in the United States. You see what happened, the Bahamas had inspectors to come into the States and visit all these farms where these people were working. Mr. Wilson, he was in charge of it. He was the chief inspector. He had inspectors under him who came and went from Jersey right down to the Everglades. That's the area that they covered.

So when the workers came home, they collected their money. If they didn't come back, that money went for something else. A lot of them didn't come back. They just disappeared. They still in the United States. Since the Bahamas were allies, United States immigration never bothered them that much.

The Contract was a good thing for the Bahamas. 'Cause there wasn't no work here.

Enid Sawyer, New Providence

My oldest brother went away on the Contract. He was away for thirteen years. He took off from a farm [in the United States] and they couldn't find him for a long time. But when they caught him, they sent him home. He couldn't go back [to the U.S.]. So he came home and he did well for himself. He built himself a house, got married and has children. Now he's retired [laughter]. But he didn't intend to come back. He used to live in Rochester, New York.

Lawrence Smith, New Providence

I grown up until I tell Momma I goin' on Contract in 1943—that's during the war. The riot was in '42 and it was the next year. They [the United States] transporting us. Asking our government to send we [us]. They want help after the war get hot. They recruit us to go to the United States to work. That's to pick fruit. Pick beans, and orange, apple. I went way up north, from New York to Montana—and cold! We gone up there.

Then they start recruitin' womens, you see? And them gotta stay on the southeast coast. So all the young fellas who didn't have no wife, we gotta go up north. We gotta go up to the cold area. We had cushion [heavy underwear] inside our clothes. When we go on the farm, we had to have cushion [lining] inside our glove to pick bean. We only coulda stayed there three months and they had to send us back. It was too cold.

That time, I only stayed one year and three months. Try to battle it out. 'Cause when we come from up north, we had to go down to the south to show them how to work. I enjoy it, because I work with Chick Willis. He was one of the head [those in charge]. After I got from up north, they ship me to Georgia. We had about fifteen men. We stayed together like brothers.

It was hard, but still, we was trying to help, because we wanted the country to have its observance [respect]. They come to me and I got to go, because Hitler say he was going to eat in Buckingham Palace. So we government say, "Oh no, that ain't gonna happen. Send them over. Send them over." You gotta gone. When you read the history, you find out. I couldn't read then and I can't read now.

Olive Ramsey, Long Island

I was one of the women who went on Contract. I was in the States for four years working on the farms. It was hard work.

Some of the people didn't come back. My oldest brother went over there in '47, and he isn't been home one time. He's in New York. And I have two more brothers and a baby sister. They gone in the '50s, not in the '40s. Yeah, they went under contract and they stayed. They married over there.

FAMILY ISLANDS EMIGRATION

A series of government officials have made repeated—and unsuccessful —efforts to reverse the flow of emigration from the Family Islands. The Colonial Reports regularly expressed concern regarding the emigration of Bahamians from the Family Islands to Nassau. This migration was causing reduced agricultural production in the Family Islands, overcrowding and increased unemployment in Nassau. The Duke of Windsor, while serving as Royal Governor of the Bahamas, was known for his opposition to the migration of Family Islanders to New Providence.

As a result of the continuing exodus, there has been an ongoing decrease in the number of Family Islands residents. Less than 20% of the present Bahamian population resides on Family Islands, down from over 73% in 1901. Many young adults have chosen to move to Nassau, New Providence or Freeport, Grand Bahama, in search of better educational facilities, employment opportunities, modern conveniences or health services. From 1963 to 1980, 15,000 Family Islanders relocated to New Providence or Grand Bahama. Others have emigrated to England and to the United States for the same reasons. In 1985, there were approximately 14,000 Bahamians living in the United States.

As a result of these demographic shifts, numerous settlements that I visited on Cat Island, Long Island, and Andros contain boarded-up houses and populations consisting mainly of older people and their grandchildren. The majority of the Bahamian population is made up of young people under 30 years old, many of whom live in Nassau. From 1964 to 1970, the population of Grand Bahama increased over 240% as a result of the creation of Freeport, with its added employment opportunities. These shifts in location of Bahamians have serious implications for the economy of the Bahamas and for the survival of many Family Island settlements. Some are now unable to provide adequate educational and health services.

If the trends of the twentieth century continue, there is little hope that the Family Islands will ever be able again to meet the agricultural demands of these islands. Nor will many of the settlements continue to exist.

Clementina Adderley, Long Island

I don't know why the children go away. But mind, they all home here for the Christmas, but they gone back. They living in town. You see, I believe what caused the children to left from here [leave] [is that] there is not enough things, what you call picture shows and dis and dat and the other for them to see. They go where they can see. Some is worthwhile seeing and some ain't worth for dogs to see. That's why I think they's gone. All the young ones is gone. Every family what had young boys and girls, all quit and gone to Nassau.

Harcourt Stevens, Cat Island

Well, I'll tell you how we could keep the young people on Cat Island. The people today don't want to do work. Even if you gonna pay them fifty dollars a day, they hardly want to do it. But I work[ed] for one shilling. The only thing I could bring them to, if we could find some investors come in and lay down a hotel or so. If I could get me own government to do it. You see, you can't wait on foreigners. You get your own government to build a hotel.

I live in the United States, and the United States government own plenty of hotels and factories. One thing which I told them already, Cat Island right now could take its own factory. Look at what you can do with tomatoes. Let me tell you something. You can make tomato ketchup, tomato paste, tomato juice, and tomato sauce. Tomatoes are the one food you could go into the field and eat. And it don't hurt nobody. I never hear nobody say, "Well, that tomato hurt me." Cat Island grows the best tomatoes ever grown. If you think I'm lying, cut them in half and look and all you see is meat. I mean meat, not skin and seeds. All you gonna see is meat.

I don't see why the Bahamas government don't start factories. They say we got plenty poor people. Those who got a little money, they gonna sit on that. They ain't gonna invest to help the poor. So what the government do? The government get some machines and build one place and start a fire under them. Let them people buy from they own self. You buy your paste. You buy from your own self. You put that San Salvador on it and you could export. We grows enough. Child, if I tell you tomatoes what spoil. Soon as they ripe up there, they don't want it in Nassau. You have to send green ones. These ripe ones we throw away.

So what we could do, if we could get a factory, we [would be] independent. Then the young people stay. You have to try to make yourself independent of tourists. You can't depend on the tourists, because the tourists are fickle. Right now, the economy of the Bahamas is falling so fast. I tell you, it's just like a drum rolling off. That's what's coming down this way. So directly, the government gonna have to devalue their money.

Hazel Newman, Long Island

There are not many young people around, because most of them have gone away to Nassau. Some go for more education; some for jobs. I'm talking about overall. When I was growing up, they stayed on the island. Farming was the only thing. Now we have to be able to offer them something else.

Immigration

As in other countries, acceptance of newcomers to the Bahamas has differed based, in part, on the countries from which the immigrants came, their socioeconomic status and the threat they were perceived to pose to native businesses. Limits on immigration to the Bahamas prior to the late 1920s were not rigidly enforced. At that time, the Bay Street merchants began to seek restrictions, because they viewed the commercial endeavors of Chinese, Greek, Jewish and Lebanese immigrants as possible threats to their monopoly as merchants. Consequently, from 1927 to 1933, the Immigration Act of 1920, which stated that no immigrant would be allowed to enter the colony without the permission of the Governor in Council, was stringently enforced on second-class passengers entering the Bahamas. First-class passengers were exempt from any pre-entry requirements. Bahamian merchants were also successful in having an immigration bill passed in 1928, which prevented the landing of "undesirables." In reality, it was an effort to prevent additional immigrant merchants from establishing businesses that might compete with established merchants. Once again, entering immigrants who traveled in first-class accommodations were exempt from these restrictions.

Chinese immigrants, primarily, had established restaurants and laundries. Greeks tended to be buyers, packers and exporters of sponge. Lebanese peddlers had made inroads in the dry goods trade. Previously, all of these activities had been under the complete control of local merchants.

Sentiment against immigrants from West Indian islands also began to rise. During the 1920s, large numbers of West Indians from Jamaica, Trinidad and Barbados relocated to Nassau as trained workers in the construction industry. This was necessary because there were no provisions for technical education in Bahamian schools. Consequently, there was a shortage of workers possessing specialized skills.

Despite consecutive waves of immigration, foreign-born residents represented a mere 2–3% of the Bahamian population in 1945. By 1970, however, the census reported that 15% of the Bahamian population was composed of nonBahamian natives. During the later half of the 1980s, the immigrant groups with the greatest representation were citizens of the United States, Haiti, United Kingdom, Jamaica and Canada, respectively.

The history of Haitian immigration to the Bahamas predates the twentieth century. Many outstanding Bahamian families have Haitian (French) last names. But most of those early immigrants were professionals or political refugees. In the 1950s, by contrast, Haitians were accepted as ordinary laborers, because manpower was needed in the construction industry for the building of hotels and residences. Due to the demand for farm laborers in 1961, hundreds more Haitians were brought in to work on new commercial farms on Grand Bahama. In 1965, approximately 5,000 undocumented Haitians (who were able to find sponsors) were granted work permits.

But as the number of undocumented Haitian immigrants continued to expand during the latter part of the twentieth century, hostility toward them has intensified in the Bahamas, as it has in the United States.

For the most part, male Haitian immigrants work in menial jobs as gardeners, farm workers or domestic help, while females are assigned the lowliest tasks of home-oriented service and caregiving. A large segment of Bahamians hold Haitian immigrants in low regard, referring to these employees as "my Haitian" or "the Haitian who works for me," rather than by their first or last names. Because they are generally undocumented aliens and, therefore, are afraid to enter the mainstream of Bahamian culture, many Haitians live in squalid conditions in segregated areas of New Providence and are victimized by their landlords and employers.

In 1970, the Bahamian and Haitian governments signed a treaty in an attempt to limit the illegal immigration of Haitians. This undertaking failed to stem the tide of illegal entrants, however. Consequently, in Sep-

tember 1985, the two governments entered into a second agreement. The second agreement provided that Haitians who had arrived illegally after December 1980 would be deported back to Haiti at the rate of 300 a month. It was a five-year treaty that expired in December 1990. Although it is estimated that about 14,000 undocumented Haitians were repatriated from 1985 to 1995, the 1985 treaty similarly failed to prevent continued illegal immigration.

At present, although it is illegal to employ a nonBahamian without a government permit, the law is regularly violated. Because Haitian and Jamaican gardeners, housekeepers and caregivers generally accept lower pay than will Bahamian citizens doing comparable work, these immigrants are in great demand. Many Bahamians frequently ignore the rules.

The current Bahamian Constitution says those persons born of two nonBahamian parents and born in the Bahamas after Independence (1973) "shall be entitled to be registered as a citizen subject to national security and public policy."

During the latter part of the 1980s, Haitians represented 43% of all nonBahamians living in the nation. Further complicating the issue was the fact that approximately 60% of the Haitian population in the Bahamas fell within the 20-to-39-year-old group, compared to only 30% of native Bahamians. The Haitian birth rate is higher than that of Bahamians. Consequently, the percentage of Haitian immigrants served by social services such as educational and hospital facilities is becoming larger and larger as compared to Bahamian citizens.

Joanna Bethel, New Providence

Mrs. Bethel recognized the difference in motivation between Haitian and Bahamian mothers.

Many Bahamians say the Haitian children do better than the Bahamian children in school. They do well, but I think there is nothing unusual about that. The Haitian children do better than some of our children because they are poor and not accepted by many of the Bahamian people. Their only hope is to get a good education.

The Haitian and the Bahamian children have the same brain. But the Haitian children try harder. The reason is that their parents have not had a chance to have an education, so they are going to push their kids. That is very normal. That's what I did.

When school reopens, soon as registration starts, the Haitian mothers are there. They come so early and in such large numbers. When the Bahamian mothers come, there is no more space. There are not enough seats for all of the children in some of the schools, especially the primary level. So that is a big problem. Our parents [Bahamian], if registration starts today, are not going to go on the line from six-thirty in the morning on the first day of registration to register their child. But the Haitian mother wants so much to get her child into the school system that she's willing to do it. And so that creates another problem.

I believe that there is an answer to the problem, but it's going to take a lot of work by the government. It's important, because all of us are going to be affected one way or the other down the road.

We don't have a problem with other nationalities. Americans who have children born here, English Canadians, Europeans, whoever are born here—the kids take the nationality of the parents. It's sad. But I gather the Haitians don't wish to be Haitians. That is the problem. They are not going to want to go back to Haiti.

Fred Ramsey, Cat Island

Mr. Ramsey has a strong opinion concerning the work ethics of Haitians and Bahamians.

We got one Haitian living right up here. He work for someone down the road. We had a plenty, but they was illegal. Didn't have no permit, you know? Good workers. And the government has to call them in. Plenty came here a few years ago. Must have been about six working. Cops bring them down and put them in jail. Ain't got no permit, so the government took them. Government take all of them. But them work more than we [Bahamian] island people. Island people got so lazy, won't work. Them boys do any kind of thing. My daughter have one keep the yard all the time, you know? Come up here to work sometime. Last time he come up here he stay for two weeks, but they let him go back, because people make a talk. People talk too much. When they see you got someone, everybody want him, and it's five hundred dollars to get a permit for them. They don't want to pay that. But don't give the Haitian your permit. You keep that. 'Cause if you give him that work permit, he'll go away.

Tourism

Throughout the twentieth century, the colonial and Bahamian govern-ments viewed tourism as an important element of a healthy economy. In the early decades of the century, general prosperity was predicted for Nassau, because winter visitors had begun arriving on steamships. In 1914, efforts to attract more tourists included the construction of a race course and polo ground. When the original Colonial Hotel burned down on March 31, 1921, it was quickly rebuilt and reopened for tourists less than two years later. (Its present name is the Sheraton British Colonial). By 1926, the Nassau Harbour was dredged to accommodate larger ships, and the Prince George Dock was built to better accommodate tourist vessels. Also, sewerage and water works facilities were improved.

Pan American Airways provided a boon to tourism by introducing daily sea-plane flights from Florida to Nassau in 1929. In 1941, their land planes began arriving at Oakes Field. This operation was increased to include jet service between New York and Nassau in 1958.

During the years in which the Bay Street Boys controlled the govern-ment, most people of colour were denied access to activities and places where white United States tourists were present. As the number of white tourists increased in the 1930s, so did the level of segregation. Hotels re-fused to provide accommodations or to serve blacks in their restaurants. Black musicians were banned from working in hotels, and blacks who were hired were relegated to employment as servants.

The Duke of Windsor, in his July 26, 1941, letter to Lord Walter E. G. Moyne, wrote:

> *The Bahamas, however, which I can well understand from their proximity to the mainland of America, still maintain a very staunch and American attitude towards the coloured problem, and white Bahamians will not al-low their wives to sit down to dinner with coloured people. One of the main local arguments against the inclusion of the coloured element into the social life of the Colony is that it would hurt the susceptibilities of the American winter visitors.*

In 1950, the Governor, Sir George Sandford, appointed Sir Stafford Sands chairman of the Development Board. (The board is now the Min-istry of Tourism.) Due in large part to Sir Stafford Sands' efforts, the number of tourists visiting the islands increased greatly.

The industry received an additional boost in the early 1950s when Wallace Groves, a wealthy American lumber man, developed the city of Freeport in Grand Bahama. Groves changed the mangroves of Hawksbill Creek into a "free port" and industrial center. Freeport is now the second most important tourist destination in the Bahamas and is where people from all of the islands have established businesses and/or found employment.

The Bahamian tourist industry was further assisted, in the 1960s, by the government's large budget for promotion, its modern airport facilities, the introduction of casino gambling and a large amount of foreign private capital invested in the construction of hotels. During the same period, the United States initiated the isolation of Cuba, effectively eliminating United States tourist travel to that island.

During the winter season of '60–'61, Huntington Hartford, the Atlantic and Pacific (A&P) grocery store heir, purchased a large area of Hog Island, including a portion formerly owned by Axel Wenner-Gren, to build a high-quality resort. (Wenner-Gren, a Swedish millionaire, was deported during World War II, because Sumner Welles of the United States had accused him of having ties with the German government.) Hartford changed the island's name to Paradise and opened a luxury hotel there in 1962. He also purchased a medieval French cloister from Randolph Hearst. The structure had previously been dismantled and transported from Europe. Hartford supervised its reconstruction at his estate on Paradise Island. The cloister is presently a tourist attraction and a location where many Bahamian wedding photographs are taken.

It is said that Hartford's personal dream of creating a paradise in the Bahamas was not realized because, politically and financially, he did not support the Bay Street Boys and their government.

As tourism increased in New Providence, Freeport and a few of the Family Islands, the cost of living for the average Bahamian began to rise. Many Bahamians lost interest in agricultural pursuits on the Family Islands, as the financial rewards of work in the tourism industry became evident.

The number of tourists visiting the islands has grown almost continually over the years. In 1951, 76,758 foreigners arrived, according to the Colonial Report. By 1974, annual foreign arrivals had grown to 1,388,040, and 2,325,250 visitors visited in 1984. In 1992, the number of tourists had grown to 3,689,543. Casinos had opened at hotels in Nassau,

Paradise Island and Freeport and no doubt contributed to recent increases.

When the airlines first began making regular flights to Nassau from New York and Florida, a majority of foreign arrivals were by air. In recent years, however, most visitors have arrived by sea. In 1992, this included over sixty-six percent of arrivals. The change has serious implications for hotels and businesses that cater to tourists. Cruise visitors are in the Bahamas for a brief time and consequently spend much less money than those who are visiting the islands as stopover tourists. The latter group tends to stay in hotels, eat in restaurants and shop in the stores on Bay Street. In 1993, for example, cruise-ship passengers' average expenditures were estimated at $54, while stopover visitors averaged $803.

The proportion of tourists who visit the Family Islands has increased in the last two decades. In 1974, a little over eight percent of foreign arrivals went to islands other than New Providence or Grand Bahama. That number has now grown to over twenty percent. The tourist industry presently provides fifty percent of the gross domestic product of the Bahamas.

When a nation has magnificent white-and-pink sandy beaches bordering warm, calm, turquoise waters, it is understandable that tourism is the main industry. But, as Mr. Stevens warned in his narration, "You can't depend on the tourists, because the tourists are fickle." With banking as the only other major industry, a depression in the United States would have a devastating effect on the Bahamian economy.

Carrie Lunn, Nassau

In the twenties, we had three hotels. I worked at the British Colonial and there was the one at Fort Montagu. It's empty and falling down now. The oldest hotel was the Royal Victoria. Have you seen the grounds? They used to be the prettiest yard in Nassau. It's a crime they didn't keep that hotel.

Rich people used to come to Nassau then. The hotels were only open in the winter, from after Christmas to April, because it got too hot in the summer. There were no air conditioners, just those big ceiling fans. The tourists would come on steamships once a week from New York. I think the boat came from England and Canada about once a month.

Before I started the housekeeping job at the British Colonial, I did have in mind to become a nurse. 'Cause I always said when I was a child that I would like to be a nurse, take care of sick people. I really liked that. But when I talked to one of the nurses, she told me, "Child, I just staying there because I can't do anything better." Said all kinds of things, and I never went back to the matron to pursue nursing.

And then, right on the back of that, just shortly after that, this man came and asked if I would like to come and work. I went to the British Colonial Hotel to work. I liked that kind of work. It was decorating and things like that, you see? Working along with an interior decorator, because when she came here to redecorate the hotel, she asked if I would like to work along with her. Different things, you see, matching up the different rooms. I told her I would be delighted. She said, "Well, I'm glad, because I have taken to you and I think we would get along." I said, "Yes, I think we would." I had to go through every room in that hotel and pick out the drapes, spreads and things that wanted renewing. I put the room numbers down and how many drapes to be made and how many beds was in the room, single or double and whether it was a single room with just one bed. I had to put all that, and then I would give her the list.

I would be with her and she would say, "Well, I think such and such a room would look nice painted like this, decorated like this." And I would make certain suggestions to her and she would agree with me. Then, she had her place, and she would have these girls sewing. She would order so many bolts of material, you see? She had a real good upholsteress. So I went along with her and when the things were ready, she would send them in to me and I would have men go around and hang the drapes. Girls make up the beds. I'd have the rooms fixed, and when she come in, I'd say, "Now, look at this room. What do you think about it?" And she would hang pictures to match the drapes and the spread. So I really liked that. I was interested in that, more than nursing.

And I used to have to make out orders, sheets and pillowcases and things. And have to match them to go into the colours of the room. And then my job was to check the staff in, send them to work, check their time, pay them all, fix up the payroll. Fix up that payroll every Friday morning. I had to take that check up and take it to the pay mistress. At two o'clock I go and get the money and pay the people off. Child, what a job. I was happy with that job.

When I started working, we used to get £1, 2 shilling ($5.28 U.S.). A few years after that wages changed and we used to get £5 ($24 U.S.). As the years went on, it depended on how many years you worked there. After so many years, they would increase your salary.

ADASTRA GARDENS AND BAHAMIAN FLAMINGOS

Adastra Gardens, created by Hedley Edwards, is a famous tourist attraction in Nassau. Many of the trees and plants indigenous to the tropics can be found in his preserve. Different types of plants are located in sections separated by winding stone paths.

An added attraction to the tropical botanical garden are Mr. Edwards' trained flock of flamingos. When they used to take flight, at his command, their black flight feathers with a five-foot wing span presented an awesome sight. Although Mr. Edwards is no longer alive, the garden and flamingos still flourish. The new owners changed the name of the garden from Adastra to Ardastra.

The flamingo is the national bird of the Bahamas. On Great Inagua, located in the southernmost area of the Bahamas, between 40,000 and 60,000 flamingos have been sighted. The Bahamas National Trust sponsors the Inagua National Park, a reserve where most Bahamian flamingos live. They are large birds with very long legs and necks and are covered with beautiful vermilion feathers. Their maximum flight speed has been clocked at thirty-five miles an hour.

Rita Wood, New Providence

Hedley Edwards [Dada, her father] was born in Chapelton, Jamaica. He came to Nassau in 1923. He later married my mother, Lillian Allen, who was Jamaican. But she was born in Panama. Her parents went to Panama to help build the Canal. She and my aunt were born in Panama, but the family went back to Jamaica after that stint. And because they were so accustomed to going here and there to help build these countries, they came to the Bahamas to help build the Sheraton Hotel, better known as the British Colonial Hotel. They built the British Colonial Hotel and the Montagu Beach Hotel.

When my dad first came here he was a tailor, but when I was born he managed a bar, a supper club. But Dada always wanted to be his own person. We did not even know that Dada had it in him to create the Adastra Gardens. I was in school in Jamaica for several years and returned in 1945 after the war. Dada was saying, "I'm going to work." So I said to myself, I wonder what kind of work he's doing? Then, it was the building of Adastra Gardens. He bought property from different people. In the end, he had about four acres. It was swamp, all swamp. He filled it in where he wanted to fill, because he had a plan in his mind that he wanted to have a pool where the flamingos lived. He really planned the gardens, beautifully planned. He got his shrubs from different places, but he had special trees, which he got years later from Jamaica—fruit trees. He knew trees that the Bahamians didn't know. So the Bahamians would give him certain trees. They were glad to get rid of them to clear up their property. He got mahogany trees from some people. They didn't know it was mahogany. He got a lot of trees.

When he first started the garden, he had one Haitian working for him, named Joseph. And Joseph is still there. He planned it and Joseph did the work. They even built the club. He had other people to help with that. The club was a nightclub. It was the best thing that ever happened to Nassau. It was crowded every Saturday night. There was a live show with Symonette. He made up and sang Bahamian calypso songs. They had the show, served drinks and had dancing. This was started before he had the flamingos. I think once the flamingos were on parade, he closed the nightclub.

Dada was friendly with the people from Bahamas National Trust. They were responsible for the birds in Inagua. He got about sixty-five flamingos when he started. They were all very young. By the time they were full grown, they were over six feet, from the beaks to the tip of their legs. They were not pink when he got them. He read up on what to feed them and they became very pink. How he trained them was a secret. We didn't know anything about it at all. Not one single thing, until one day he said that he was going to have a show. We didn't give it a second thought. And then, it was unbelievable. First of all, he would say, "Muster," and they would all be in the water. "Muster," and they would all shuffle in a line of twos. And then he would tell them, "Quick march," and they would march out of the water. Then he'd say, "Circle parade grounds," and they would all circle the parade grounds, very stately. He would have eight hundred persons at a time to watch the show. He would give the birds the command and they would follow his instructions, except for one bird he would name "the renegade." He would do the opposite. When Dada said, "Right turn," he would do left. So that became a part of the show, because the tourists applauded. The only reward the birds got was your applause. If you don't applaud, they would peck you.

Most of those birds are still alive. I remember sometime in the '60s, he had an epidemic and some of the birds died. I was really depressed for him. He had special doctors to come to find out why. He found out, in the pool where they lived, everything happened in the pool. Whatever they had to do happened in the pool. In turn, they would put their beaks in there and they got germs. He solved the problem by getting a special machine and he would clean it [the pool] out once a month. He would get new birds from time to time and it's just like everything else, they follow suit. They will follow the other birds. In the end, when he became ill, he made a tape. Then he had a Jamaican man. Although his command was gentle, they knew when Dada wasn't giving them the command.

He had staff walking around wearing colourful skirts and blouses with baskets on their heads. They were just a part of the show. And he had a lot of tourists. They came in droves. They came in taxis from the cruise ships and hotels. They bussed them there.

In the beginning, he made thousands of dollars. Later on, it slackened off. Dada was finicky about the women's attire. He didn't allow them to wear short shorts. You see, he would complain to the tour guides that it distracted the birds. So the tour guides would tell them how to dress. But some women were still defiant, and they would wear whatever they wanted to wear. The wives and husbands would get in a fuss when they got to the garden. The husband would say, "Well, they told you not to wear that." So, in order to continue having his crowds, he would let them wear some of the skirts. He had skirts made to cover up. My husband said, "That doesn't distract the birds, it distracts your father." [Laughter.]

And then he had his signs in the gardens. I remember two signs: "Let it not be said these gardens were more beautiful before you came. Do not touch plants and flowers." Then he had another sign that said, "Only well-behaved children allowed." And this happened because a tourist's child lit the beak of one of the flamingos. Lit it on fire! He got his father's lighter. Most of the tourists respected the garden. They were too much in awe to do any damage.

He had some animals, too. He brought in the crocodiles from Jamaica. And he had a lot of iguanas, lizards. He had hundreds of small rabbits and hamsters. He was a lover of animals.

I liked the gardens. To me, it felt like something to do with the Garden of Eden. Just pleasant, quiet and peaceful. There were a lot of quiet corners in the garden. I remember one Easter, he had a plot of land about three-quarters of an acre, and he developed Easter lilies. There were hundreds and hundreds, sometimes I could even say thousands of Easter lilies. And his special friends, he gave them to. If you were an outsider, they were very expensive. He only wanted to see what the property would yield. The knowledge about plants was just in him. He was a horticulturist. He never went to school for it, but he knew all of the botanical names. He never called anything "a Bahamian bush"; he would say its botanical name. He had a lot of books and he studied at night.

He grew up in the country in Jamaica. He was the youngest of four or five brothers. They were farmers. I have a sister, Valentine, and she can plant a leaf and it grows. She can plant anything and it grows. He had that gift and it was passed on to her.

In the end, the garden was a strain for Dada. It was impossible for the family to run it. When Dada became ill, we still had the shows. Even now, the owners say that they are going to cut it up into lots. The owners mentioned that Coral World has taken away from the gardens. It's somewhere new. It takes a lot of money to keep the garden, just to feed the birds alone. The food for the birds is imported.

Dada has been dead sixteen years. After he died, he received an award for his work from the Ministry of Tourism. I did not attend the award ceremony. I refused it. Why wait until he died to give him an award? My sister went and I think my brother. Dada's work was written up in so many daily newspapers and in the *National Geographic* magazine, October 1957. There were pictures of the birds in action, because at a certain time, he would tell them to run around the parade ground and to spread their wings, so all you saw was the pink and the black. The magazine has a beautiful photograph of that.

One time Dada let people from the United States come in with animals. But, of course, the animals couldn't survive out here. The animals were in these natural habitats that they had created out of things in the garden and thatched huts. Perhaps that was what gave Dada the idea of the flamingos. Before these animals came in, he had the ducks and the pheasants, the peacocks and all kinds of exotic birds. He had to move them out when these people brought those ridiculous animals. They brought all these sixty monkeys and snakes. Dada had always had an electric eel and you knew not to let children go near that. He got so frustrated that these people had messed up his place that he put them out. So some of the animals stayed. I guess the tame ones. I think they owed him a lot of money, because they used a lot of water.

Iris Knowles, New Providence

Mrs. Knowles talks about other aspects of the Adastra Gardens and Mr. Edwards' personality. Her excuse for some of his behavior is that he was "a very eccentric person."

Well, my first recollection of the Adastra Gardens was when Mr. Edwards first came here and was talking to my parents about it, the whole scheme of things. That this area would have been a wonderful place and you had water. Because the area where the Adastra Gardens is, and more recently the Sea Floor Aquarium is, that was all swamp. 'Cause a lot of Chippingham was swamp. So, you know, it lent itself to becoming a garden, because you wouldn't have to worry too much about water. The water level would be very high to keep things going. And I also remembered that, at the time he was laying out the Adastra Gardens, he would bring some of the plants and whatever over to Mommy. That's how we got the palm trees out in the front. Not the royal palms. Mommy had always had them. But the travelers palms, the mango tree in the front, not this one in the back, but the Hayden mango. And I believe the breadfruit tree. And then, of course, some pretty things [other flowering plants].

Mr. Edwards was very friendly with my parents. He exchanged Christmas gifts with them, and whatever fruit they had in the Adastra Gardens, he would bring some over for us. 'Cause he was a very finicky person. A very eccentric person. So he was highly selective as to who were his friends and who he would even give things to. You know, he was that kind of person and liked poetry. He was a romantic. Well, I guess you would expect that with the garden and what have you. I remember we used to go on picnics, because there was a beach house out west called Capricorn. He used to take care of the grounds for the owners. And we used to go out there. These were winter residents, so every summer Mr. Edwards had to keep the grounds maintained.

Prior to his coming here with gifts and plants for Daddy and Mommy, I really didn't know Mr. Edwards. And our first introduction to Rita and those was when Rita was about seventeen or eighteen or so. I guess their mother had died and he brought the remaining children. The youngest one had died in Jamaica. He needed to have surgery and Mr. Edwards said no. It must have been an appendectomy. But you're talking about the days of Noah, when we weren't all that enlightened [laughter]. So then Mr. Edwards brought the three children back from Jamaica. Val, the oldest daughter, went to live with his sister, Aunt Min, a dressmaker, and Rita and Alverstone, the twins, both of them came here.

But then Alverstone left, and I think he went to Aunt Min as well. He spent some time working with Daddy [who was a builder]. He was good at woodwork. 'Cause I remember that he came here thinking that he was doing Mommy a favor. And he sanded down this dining room table and he put a high-gloss finish on it. And Mommy came home and hit the roof. And poor Alverstone had to go and take this high-gloss finish off. He had done it because that's what they do in Jamaica. And he thought that he was giving her a treat! She claimed that the table has never been the same. Because, prior to his doing that, you could put hot, cold, anything on the table and it didn't mark it. Now, you'll note, you get little white circles. And that was him trying to take the finish off. He eventually moved to Grand Bahama and he lives in Eight Mile Rock. I think he does woodwork there, because that was his thing. I think Val did dressmaking like Aunt Min. Rita stayed with us and went to work with Mrs. Cox in Margarita. You know Mrs. Cox had a dress shop, right? So she worked with Mrs. Cox and then she went to work at Armoury. She retired from Armoury. Mr. Edwards was very close to us. He didn't live with us. He lived in a house around the corner, in a house across from the Humane Society. He had a room there with some people. And then that put him smack in the door of the Adastra Gardens.

The nightclub in the garden was nice, because Mr. Edwards had such high standards. So the nightclub was a nice little native exercise. It was built right smack in the middle of the garden. So to get to the nightclub you had to walk through the gardens, and he had nice little lights. It was very romantic. But Mr. Edwards, being the stodgy, staid person, believed in protocol and all the rest of it. He felt that a gentleman had to always be a gentleman. And a gentleman never escorted a lady anywhere unless he had on a coat and a necktie. And so if you came to his nightclub and you weren't dressed appropriately, he didn't let you in. He used to be there. Rita used to work the admission booth, which was to the main entrance. And then he would row [argue with] Rita for accepting the people's money, because once they got to the door, he had a man at the door to send them out. He was always mingling. His eyes were always on the door, and if he saw you come and stand to the door and you were not dressed appropriately, he would beeline over there, and he would also run out to the entrance and chew out Rita for allowing these people to come through without a coat and a tie. I remember this vividly, because my sister Setella's friends would come here to Daddy and they would say, "Well, we're really not going back, because we live all the way up east." And in those days, this was a far distance from anyone living on East Bay Street or Shirley Street. And they'd say, "We're really not going to the dance." Daddy would say, "Well man, Setella and Cyprianna and those are going to be disappointed if you don't come to the dance. So here, use my tie and go back." And just like the ladies who go into the Adastra to see the bird show or just to walk around and what have you, if your knees were exposed—be it dress, skirt, pants—he wouldn't let you in, because he used to say that it would upset the birds. It reached a point, after Mommy and those talked to him, that he just kept some things at the garden. And he'd say, "If you want to come into the gardens, you'll come into the restroom and put on this long skirt or these long pants and then you could go out." Some of the people used to get angry, but then they would turn around and laugh. And they would say, "Oh, that miserable, eccentric man down to Adastra. You better put on your long pants if you want to go in there."

But people continued to go. People continued to go, because the gardens were so exquisite. They were really very nicely laid out. And the flowers and what have you were absolutely gorgeous. He had areas—like he had a fern area and then he had a rose area and then he had a chrysanthemum area. He also had a wishing well. He had a Japanese garden where you could walk. He had the little streams and the little bridges going over and you could stand over and look down. He was before his time.

The new owners are working to bring the gardens back to the way he had them. They're also making changes. They changed the name to Ardastra Gardens and Zoo. And they have many more animals. They even have two Central American jaguars. When I was there, they took harmless Bahamian snakes and let the tourists pose with them. Mr. Edwards' peacocks are still there, and they have lots of Bahamian parrots and birds.

SMALL HOPE BAY LODGE

One of the first tourist accommodations that I visited on the Family Islands was Small Hope Bay Lodge. Not only was I dazzled by the beauty of the site, I was thoroughly impressed by the level of commitment, on the part of the owner and staff, to assure that all visitors' needs were met. Most tourists come to Small Hope Bay to dive, fish or snorkel. Although I wanted to do none of these, when I explained my project, Mona Birch graciously extended herself to suggest and locate seniors.

Israel Saunders, Andros

This passage was included to show the relationship between Mr. Saunders and Mr. Birch and to demonstrate Mr. Saunders' understanding of the importance of keeping his receipt!

I ain't got no currents in my boat. The current went bad. That's why I was come up to Small Hope Bay Lodge. This is the place I was supply with fish and I come to him [Dick Birch] to say send for the fuse. He test the fuse, say, "It ain't the fuse, so go back and check the line." That's what I want to do now. I wanta go back and get them lines check[ed] up to see what wrong with the line and get 'em fixed. I can't get the motor down. I was paying $65 for the insurance. When I get it fixed, they'll have to give me the money it cost to fix it. I got the receipt on it. When I go back home, I'm gonna get the mechanic and carry him and check that line.

Rafaleta Williams, Andros

Mrs. Williams' relationship with Mr. Birch and his family began when she, Mr. Minnis and Mr. Pindling made it possible for Small Hope Bay Lodge to exist.

You see, at Small Hope Bay Lodge, the black land which Dick Birch got there, that what he dumpin' in? That was my daddy's property. And only was three of us, three girls—me and my sisters. After Dick was looking for a piece of place to buy, he couldn't find any. George Minnis asked us if we wanted to sell it. I went to my sister—she's the eldest—and we get together and sold him that. That days, when that sell, that wasn't worth nothing. See, Prime Minister Pindling was a lawyer then. He what sold that to Dick for us. Right out that, it sold so cheap to Dick.

Dick promise me a lifetime job. I spent five seasons working out there at Small Hope Bay Lodge. I was a dishwasher, head dishwasher out there. From then, they friend me [were friends], you know? I can't find no fault of Margo, Dick's oldest living daughter. The oldest one is dead. And I tell you, Miss Margo treat me like I white. She take me as a mother. They always call me Mommy anyhow. And I spend five seasons out there. Then I tell Rosie, his first wife, that I can't make it. I was sick.

Bob Dean, Andros

Mr. Dean has been working with Mr. Birch since the very beginning of this endeavor. As we walked along the property, he told exactly how the plants, trees, wells and cottages were achieved. From his description, I could actually see how it must have been then.

I was working across the creek mixing concrete before I came to work for Dick Birch. Me and the other boss man fall out, and after we fall out, I get in touch with Mr. Minnis. Mr. Minnis say, "Sure, you'll have a job down there to Small Hope." So I've been down here from then until now. Don't find no fault with my boss. He was nice to me and still nice to me. We's nice to one another. So if anything go wrong, we get together and sit down and talk it out. No hard feelings against one another. Anything I want, he try to help me with it.

Dick cut this road through here. Right from that road out there you have twenty-five feet across the road and the further back you go this way, the wider it come. I gonna show you the end of it. This where he gets his water. He uses the water from here now for the kitchen, the toilets. We using the city water for drinking. When we just start up the business, that's the windmill we used to pump the water into that tank. Mr. Birch couldn't do without me in them days. He had to keep me beside him. When we first started, we grow all of this [a vegetable and fruit garden]. When we run short, we used to come up here and get vegetables. We used to get plenty bananas, pawpaw. We got some trees now.

I been here ever since Dick Birch been here. Buy the place [the other acres of land] from a man called George Minnis. So after he done bought the place, he went back home. He lay out that same big place right there, the dining room. When he come back, then we start to work on those small cottage[s]. And I been here from then to now. Back then you coulda stay here on the beach and look clean to the road. None of these big trees been here at all. They spring up of they own. All of these high mangroves, none of them been here. Little things, you coulda look straight in the road out there. In those days we only had a little track road [a path]. But you had plenty of these things which we call bird grass. But we didn't have no guests then. We was just building up. We needed more water and things to make up the concrete, so we dig three wells. Well, the three wells we dig, one was twelve feet deep and the next one was five feet and the next one was three feet.

They didn't spring enough water for me to use to mix the mortar with, so we just have to use salt water. We use sand off the beach. That was good for the construction. You need to let it dry. Let some of the salt get out of it before you mix the cement. That's if you use a tractor and push the sand exactly out of the sea. You know what I mean, not out the sea, right near the sea. You have to let it drain a little bit. But if you get it up top of the beach, you could use it just how the truck dump it. What most cause cracks in your walls ain't salt sand. It's according to your mixing, you see? Some you mix strong and some you mix weak and that will crack your walls. But the salt don't crack your walls. It causes a little rust in your pipes, but you can always spray that and the rust gone.

When Mr. Birch bought this place, no house been nowhere around here. Only up in there what you call Small Hope, way up in the point there. So, one day he was loading up the truck and he said to me, "Bob, what you think I gonna name this place?" Well," I say, "you take from out there and come back down in here, all that is Small Hope." He say, "Okay, so I'll put the bay onto it, Small Hope Bay." And that was a nice name.

Dick Birch, Small Hope Bay Lodge, Andros

Dick Birch is the founder and owner of Small Hope Bay Lodge. He chose a magnificent stretch of beach on which to locate his resort. When the name Dick Birch is mentioned, one immediately thinks of cave diving, blue holes, snorkeling and bone fishing. As he relates the history of Small Hope Bay Lodge, it becomes obvious that Mr. Birch has been an important pioneer in the study of blue holes and has made a real contribution to scientific research.

In the beginning there was only my hope. My hope for a simple place, healthy life and lots of friendly people. I think my hope has been realized.

Then there was Small Hope, the bay. Named, some say, by the pirate

Morgan, who said it was a "small hope" that anyone would find the treasure he had buried there. It never has been found. People are still looking.

Finally, in 1960, there was Small Hope Bay Lodge, the place that grew out of hope and was built on the bay that hid the treasure and became the place that Dick built. Mine is the oldest dive resort in the Bahamas. Many famous divers have visited us.

We have twenty cottages. Bob Dean and I built them using coral rock and Andros pine. Each cottage has the necessary amenities and is decorated in our own island batik colours. Each is situated right on the beach, shaded by pines and hugged by the ocean. All are designed with relaxation in mind—no phones, no TV, no distractions.

Small Hope has a central lodge with a large living room rather than a hotel lobby. Checking in means having your name hung on "Panacea," the old fishing boat that serves as a bar. Nobody puts on airs here. In fact, hardly anyone even puts on shoes. Your friend Lyla's luggage was lost for three days. But she didn't have to worry. You don't need a suitcase filled with fancy clothes here.

Small Hope is home for Mona and myself and for you as long as you are here. We want you to feel part of our family. Meet our kids, pet our dogs and share our lives.

Diving is a specialty at Small Hope. The magnificent Andros Barrier Reef is the third longest in the world and is just one mile offshore. The marine life is fantastic! For sheer drama and variety, it's absolutely second to none. We have been diving here ourselves for over twenty-eight years and we still don't know all the caves and ledges, shallows and deeps of this 142-mile reef that makes up our front yard.

We have protected our reef from spear fishing and collecting, and the result is a tremendous variety of fish and corals. Our dive sites feature jewel-hued shallow gardens and a spectacular blue hole, ten fathoms down. Our over-the-wall dive to 185 feet looks down a sheer vertical drop 6,000 feet into the Tongue of the Ocean. Wall diving as a sport was actually started at Small Hope Bay. Canadian diver Dr. Joe McGinnis and I first "discovered" the Andros wall. Blue hole diving also had its inception at Small Hope Bay Lodge. Blue holes are deep blue waters with underwater cave systems, which probably developed as sea levels changed over thousands of years. Andros is riddled with them. Jacques Cousteau, Dr. George Benjamin and I were some of the early penetrators of the Andros blue holes.

If you don't want to dive, that's okay, too. We have great places for snorkeling. Libyans Point is one of the prettiest shallow sites. You'll find lots of colour and small tropical fish. But these fish are for observing. Your son, Alan, can't take any home with him.

If you're curious about the natural world around you, we'll set you up on a bush walk with Bob Dean, our local bush doctor, who will help you discover the native plants to cure everything from common colds to broken hearts. Bob has been with me since we started the Lodge. He knows everything about bush medicine.

Andros Island is the bone-fishing capital of the world. Why don't you go fishing? Give yourself a chance to relax and enjoy the tranquility of Andros.

6

Opinions and Reflections

In general, the present concerns of those living on the Family Islands are different from those of people living in Nassau and Freeport. Most Family Islanders with whom I visited continue a traditional way of life. Many support themselves by farming and fishing. Electricity, telephone communications and satellite dishes for television transmission are the exception rather than the rule. When a person becomes ill, the choices are to go to a local clinic or to travel to Nassau to be treated. Church activities, visiting friends and attending funerals, weddings and family reunions are major forms of recreation. Parents of teenagers are understandably concerned that, with no hope of further education or challenging employment, young adults will inevitably leave home to pursue employment in Nassau, Freeport or the United States. Most of those who leave, return only for holidays, vacations and/or regattas.

Many Family Islanders proposed solutions to their specific island's economic problems. Some suggested the development of packinghouses and canning factories in their settlements as ways of keeping young people at home. Some believe that tourism to their island will increase, bringing with it additional jobs and money. For most, the presence of natural beauty, tranquility and an unhurried lifestyle seem to compensate for the lack of modern conveniences.

Most Nassauvians' lives bear little similarity to life on the Family Islands. Nassau has all of the amenities such as doctors, hospitals, electricity, telephones, television, shops of every description, movie theaters, fast-food restaurants and public transportation. Most importantly, the tourist and banking sectors provide a myriad of jobs. There are also opportunities for higher education. But Nassau also has a high rate of teenaged pregnancies, the affliction of AIDS, crime and violence. Countless children come from homes with two working parents or a single parent. Because the support systems that exist in settlements on the Family Islands are rarely present in Nassau, many parents are challenged to meet the needs of their children.

Political Opinions

Public interest in politics tends to run quite high in the Bahamas. During the months leading up to an election, almost everyone has a prediction of the outcome and a justification for their revelation. Similarly, most citizens have an opinion on government actions and theorize concerning government policies. Whenever I asked the question, "Tell me your opinion of what the government has been like through the years," I was guaranteed to receive an authoritarian, biased, emotional answer.

Rafaleta Williams, Andros

The government in them days was mostly the Bay Street Boys. There was no PLP then; there was no party then. They do what they feel like and if they care for you [like you] and you keep around them, and you tend to them, they gonna tend to you. 'Cause if you was a police, and you keep around the people in town who were big shots, you could manage. And if you ain't for me, I ain't help you.

Wasn't no pension in them days. When they did pick up the pension, it start in the Bay Street Boys time. [It] was late. That's the same time when Pindling and them was wrestling so great in the house [Black Tuesday]. Then they start this pension. When Momma and them was getting pension, was still Bay Street Boys time, only was ten shillings [$2.40 U.S.]. But when I started getting pension, I was getting twenty-six dollars. And then it grow from that. Still right now, we grumbling, but I does say, "Thank you, Jesus."

Alfred Love, New Providence

Mr. Love was on the winning side!

I had, from the inception of the PLP, supported it, but it been years before I took out membership. Paul Adderley caused me to take it out. But last election, I vote for the FNM.

Israel "Bubba" Saunders, born on August 6, 1919, Behring Point, Andros

It was obvious that Mr. Saunders is an activist.

Life today around here is pretty better. We have somebody what you could talk to. Mr. Charles Thompson is our representative. You can talk to him when he's not in Nassau. The Prime Minister, before he became Prime Minister, used to be the representative. And we could talk to him. He would listen.

Most of the people here vote. You ain't never gonna get the cooperation in the United States like in the Bahamas. A Jesse Jackson could win here. I watch him on TV a couple of times. The black people should do it [vote]. Make a change. Suppose we wouldn't make a change, you think we woulda had it like today?

Andros is the mother of the PLP. This the first island made the change. You know why? Because they want a chance to get equal rights. Those other islands just come along after they see the change was made. They took two years to get the current [electricity] down from here. We got it. I see light, water and telephone. We have that. Everything.

But Pindling is that kinda man that he's for everybody in the country. More like me, I'd punish the ones who did wrong, you know? I'd a punish some of them. But he wouldn't. He got somebody for when he get tired. I believe if he quit, he gone turn it over to Rolle [Darrell E. Rolle]. He from down north. He is good. He been in all the fields in government. But he build them up before he leave.

I done been to [the] commissioner when he don't do right. We make him go. Oh yes, only the PLP, I vote. All through this government, I wouldn't put Pindling down for nothing. See, this whole country owe him a gratitude and lot of them don't like it.

I know when the UBP time, I had one sailing boat. Now I got two speedboats. You understand? In days gone by, where I coulda got that? That engine on that boat cost $8,000. Where I coulda got that? God bless Pindling. I pray for him every day. God may keep him and his wife. People find fault with them; I can't.

Harcourt Stevens, Cat Island

Mr. Stevens described the "big difference now from UBP times."

But after my government [PLP] get in power, and I say my government, then things pick up. We could see light. So I don't mind what wrong they do, I ain't going against them. 'Cause they bring me from no way. I come from no way to something now, because my children don't have to eat corn now. They eating rice now [laughter]. In them days, you couldn't see rice.

There's a big difference now from UBP times. I tell you. They used to run the whole Bahamas with one million dollars. So, you know, some of the islands got to be deficient. My boy what was a policeman in Nassau, he went to Arthur's Town and get £10 [$48 U.S.] what they find out in the books they owed me. Well, after we started, what did they do? They burned the place down [destroyed the records]. They destroyed so that the man couldn't search up to see how much they owed. Man, they'll never see power no more.

Ain't nothing sweeter than the Bahamas. You see, we have the right government in this country now. Before, when it was UBP time, we didn't have no say. You see, this government do in one month what the UBP ain't do in twenty years. 'Cause you find electricity from Behring Point straight down. The last place on this island to be electrified is Mangrove Cay. Yeah, Pindling done great. See, the man ain't got stake in money. He not greedy for money. He greedy for his people. You see, people got equal rights. He don't stop. You call him any hours, he ready to move and do. We have some crooked set in the PLP and as soon as the Prime Minister [Pindling], he find them out, they'll get it. Get rid of them quick.

Best man we ever had is our Prime Minister. Lord, let him live. Lord, let him live. The best! He try to put a little bit in everybody's mouth. Just like a mother with the breast. All the nice babies, let me give you a little bit.

That's what Pindling is doing. He can't do everything. He got all his ministers doing that. You know, they're grown men. He can only say what he wants, what he hopes. Pray for him. We want him to live as long as he can, so that he could govern us well. Anyhow, I know I won't live to see. He gonna outlive me, 'cause I gonna be dead. Well, I hope he gonna outlive me. Let me be out the way.

Herman Sawyer, New Providence

Mr. Sawyer, in spite of the fact that "People always call me Uncle Tom," has not changed his basic philosophy.

We know what we been through. So I can only hope that this government, the FNM, do better. If they go worse, there's no hope. Bury 'em up. They try to dig into everything.

Say you run this guest house. If people come and complain and it [the guest house] get me as a new manager, I should try to counteract what you did. 'Cause I know what you did. Well, say you running this guest house and turn over five thousand dollars a month. I come here, I want to carry some of that five thousand dollars just like the next person. What more you expect? So things will be the same. Since we know the mistake the other ones [PLP] made, it's up to us, the people, to do it. Can't say the government must do it. It's the individuals. Since our eyes are open now, if we sit down and let them do what the last government did, well [laughter]. People always call me Uncle Tom, but nobody change me [laughter]. The only thing I change from the time I was born was my clothes [laughter], and sometimes I change other people's mind. I saw how life was going ahead.

If you go up to where you meet the right type of people, you be on a certain level. You stay with the right type of people, you be on a high level. If you go with the level down there, you gonna go down. Always elevate yourself and go up. Elevate yourself. Some people worry that man down there making all that money. They say, "I on this higher level, I ain't making any money. Should I go down there and thief [steal] money?" But I ain't going down to thief it. That's what I believe spoil the Bahamas today.

Just like the whole world, everything has changed. The black man was rising in the fifties. And since the Bay Street Boys moved out of government, they've [the blacks] gone higher. They gave the coloured people something. We always had coloured men in the House of Assembly. I remember a fellow called Leon Young. He was as black as my shoe. Those white boys going to the House of Assembly respect Leon Young. The black man always the brain. He used to be a member of the House of Assembly. He, Toots, Gerald Cash's daddy, were all coloured people on that level. The white man had the money. That's the only difference. Leon Young had the experience. He always looked out for the country in general, not white or black.

Let's go further. I can speak more about Paul Adderley's daddy. Now that was a brain! He was a gentleman. The Bay Street Boys used to go to him and they would get together and know what is best to do for the country. He was a man of dignity. I could tell that to everybody. He was one of the best qualified men we had.

Rita Wood, New Providence

Mrs. Wood detailed a unique experience as the wife of the ambassador to the United States. As she related events involving Presidents Carter and Reagan, I had the feeling that she must have been perfect in her role. "We were primed" expressed a fabulous degree of confidence.

After the PLP came in my husband, Reggie, was in the diplomatic corps. I had always wanted him to get a position like that, the ambassador to the United States representing the Bahamas. We were in Washington for five years. I had my fourteen-year-old daughter with me. The others were grown up. I enjoyed the living, really enjoyed the living. I didn't mind the winters. I did not think that I would enjoy the winters, but I enjoyed the four seasons. My two best seasons were spring and autumn. The falling leaves and the growing back. I thoroughly, thoroughly enjoyed it.

My husband presented his credentials to President Carter. But he was on his way out. Reggie presented the credentials. Carter was in high spirits when we went. That was another experience I will not forget, never. We had outriders [men on motor bikes] taking us to the White House. One flying the Bahamian flag came to our residence for us and one flying the United States flag. They took us to the White House. There were six ambassadors presenting their credentials, but we did not see each other. President Carter saw each of us separately. And there were the armed forces lining the route wherever we were going. My head was this big [laughter]. They all presented arms. You know, it was so beautiful. And President Carter was in good spirits, because this was the time when they were supposed to be releasing the hostages [in Iran]. That's when it failed;

they were supposed to helicopter. It didn't spoil the day for us or for President Carter. It was beautiful and nice.

And then we went to the inauguration of President Reagan. We had to be to the Capitol for seven-thirty in the morning, because they had to close the area. So all the dignitaries had to be there for seven-thirty in the morning. Well, of course, we were served breakfast. They were very nice and very kind to all the ambassadors and their families. They were very kind to us. I would not say they were not.

Our government provided the housing. My husband bought the house, never knowing that one day he would live in the house. I'm homesick for Washington right now. I've been there twice since I left, but, you know, I miss the things we used to do. We had a hospitality program. They invited all the ambassadors' wives, and I met other people. I went one day and a woman was there. She had a house in one of the islands. We became best of friends. She was invited to all of our functions. She had another friend—a couple. They were always invited to our affairs.

We had the Ambassadors' Wives Association and you would have tea parties to your house. The chancellery was where you lived. And at those special occasions there were not more than twelve or fifteen of the ladies who attended. This month it was the Bahamas' time. It was our turn. And we had over a hundred. We had enough food, because they had already replied. It was RSVP. The British came; the Canadians came; New Zealand came; Australia came—all of the Commonwealth wives came. The Africans came. That was another beautiful experience. When you went to these lavish dinners and whatever, they always wore their national costume. It was really beautiful. I wore regular clothing. You even had the Arabs. They came in their dress. It was beautiful, really. Because at the first inauguration, they had it out on the Capitol steps and I sat beside Bob Hope, and Reggie sat beside Elizabeth Taylor. You were never left out of anything. And that night, they had ten balls. Well, the ambassadors and their wives and dignitaries were always placed on a separate floor. They were able to do this, because they were responsible for us if anything happened. You never went downstairs to dance.

We had two chauffeurs. This was what I enjoyed, too. In the end, I knew more places in Washington than either of our chauffeurs.

For July Tenth, our [independence] celebration, so many Bahamians came. Our house used to be the hotel. Once, we had fifteen guests at our house. When Bahamians came to Washington, they would call us and we would entertain them. They never lived at the residence. It's for the people, but it's still our private place.

One of our daughters was living in Washington. She worked with the airlines, and so she always had time off and she spent her time with us. All summer we had nothing to do, because the whole area people were on holiday. And the end of October was United Nations Saturday. They invited us to the opera or special entertainment, because the Kennedy Center was set aside for that. And, you know, it could be hot, hot, hot, but on that Saturday, you had to bring out your furs. It was cold, windy and cold. You know, the Kennedy Center is on the waterfront. It was windy and cold. And we were all dressed up and you went to the ballet or concerts.

I was always comfortable and dressed appropriately. Because, although Nassau was small, I sort of grew into that because of my husband's job. When we were children we always dressed properly. Even my children wore gloves and silk socks to church. The way we were brought up, my aunt was one of the best dressmakers in Nassau. We were primed.

Bootlegging

In 1919, the United States passed the 18th amendment to its Constitution. That amendment prohibited the manufacture, importation or selling of intoxicating liquors within United States borders. Thus, the Prohibition era was born.

During this period, the Bahamas became a center for the transshipment of contraband English and Scottish liquor to the United States. Supply depots operated primarily from Grand Bahama and Bimini. The economy of the Bahamas experienced a huge boost as a result of this trade.

The Bahamas Assembly controlled taxes and, through the Customs Act of 1919, imposed a duty on each case or barrel of liquor arriving on Bahamian shores. With the revenues derived from these taxes, the public debt was wiped out and millionaires were created. By 1922, the Treasury surplus was £265,000 ($1,272,000 U.S.). The government spent much of this money on improvements in Nassau public utilities and visitor accommodations. Frank Holmes (Holmes, 83) reported in 1923:

It is pleasant to be able to add that, owing largely to the adoption of Prohibition in the United States in January 1920, the consequent large increase in the importation of beer, wines and spirits into the Colony and *the establishment in Nassau of bottling and rectifying plants by foreign capitalists, the finances of the Colony have undergone the most remarkable improvement.*

Predictably, the United States' repeal of the 18th amendment in 1933 had a devastating impact on the finances of many Bahamians.

Joanna Bethel, New Providence

As Mrs. Bethel was telling the story of the Prohibition era's effect on Grand Bahama, I could envision a movie showing before, during and after the period. She is a wonderful storyteller.

Bootleggin' started in 1920 when America went dry. An old man by the name of Hitchcock—I can't remember his first name—used to come on pleasure trips to West End. After America went dry, people [Bahamians] used to have a bottle of rum or things in the house for sick purposes. They always kept something like that for medicinal purposes or for Christmas. He [Hitchcock] went around to the different neighbours and buy up all he could get. And then he took it over there [to the United States]. He sold it for good money. He kept doing that. He had people to come to Nassau and pick up the liquor for him. He would come over [to Grand Bahama] and take it back.

He was a nice old man. I had a cousin Joanna, that's who I named after. She was married to one captain. He used to pilot his boat around in the waters in Grand Bahama. Mr. Hitchcock liked them so much he took the whole family to West Palm Beach. They lived over there until now. Some died over there. That's how the bootleg start.

After the natives find out, a man by the name of Horatio Wilchcombe, a cousin of mine, he built a bar. Another man from Eight Mile Rock, Augustus Hepburn, he always used to run a shop. He came down and he built up a little bar. And they were prospering. People began to find out. Those fishing boats kept coming over from the States. West End and Bimini had the whole thing. People got rich! Rich! Horatio was a millionaire and also Augustus [laughter]. They bought it in Nassau and took it back to their bar in Grand Bahama.

People from Grand Bahama didn't take the liquor into the United States. That fishing boat would come over and pick up the liquor and go back the same day. They would get over there at nightfall so that they could sneak in. And then it grew. Sometimes they get those speedboats.

These people were coming from Jacksonville, Daytona Beach, all over. Used to come over there for liquor. The natives used to make money loading these boats. If the Americans have to remain overnight, the natives would take care of the boat while the others would go around having fun [laughter].

So it lasted until some Abaconians—John Murray lived in Abaco and his son-in-law, Mr. Roberts—came there. They bought property and built bars. They built kitchen, dining room and everything to entertain the bootleggers. Took the business right away from the natives, you see? The natives used to get the job to cook for them [the bootleggers]. They used to bring food from the States and they would get people to cook it and pay them good. But after that the people in Grand Bahama didn't make much. That's how the Bahamians are. They're too—I don't know—just let other people come in and take everything.

Then the Norths from Nassau bought property and the Claridges. They bought property from my father and they built bigger houses and they sold wholesale. The people, like the women folks, the natives, used to get a job from them to bake, use crocus [burlap] bag to make small bags big enough to hold a case of liquor, half case. And they take it out of the box and they pack it in these sacks, make it easier for the bootleggers. Get a penny or four cents for it. They sewed the bags by hand. So that was to help out. Glad to get that little job. It ended in 1930.

Once we had a hold-up that cause the police to come. An American boat came across with gangsters and came on the island and held up every barkeeper. Went from bar to bar and held up every one. They weren't on their guard against anything, you know? The Americans went around holding up every barroom keeper and tied them up and leave them there. Some of them like to died. Take all the money. That was in the early '20s. My brother and another boy went down there [to the dock] to see if they could take care of the boat for the Americans. They didn't realize what was going on. But after the robbers went in such a hurry, the boys thought they better not stay around there. They figured something was wrong and they left the boat. Those American gangsters had left the motor running and everything. They just take money, no liquor, from the storekeepers, because they leave the boat way up at West End and they had to walk. So they just take money, 'cause it was easy to carry.

After that, the government sent police down there [to Grand Bahama]. Had police barracks. Alcohol became a problem at West End for plenty of the young people. After the people from other islands found out they could come there and get drunk, they started coming from Nassau and these other islands, Long Island and all. And then the girls started being prostitutes. That's how prostitution began in Grand Bahama. A few of the native West Enders were doing the same thing.

Once liquor became legal in the United States, the drinking and prostitution in West End stopped. They had to stop, because the barrooms then began closing down. There was no sale. People began moving out in 1930. Other than that, the neighbours carried on as normally as usual. They make a little money here and there.

George Roberts, New Providence

Mr. Roberts' narrative surprisingly told the story of some of those who transported the contraband into the United States.

Mommy was involved in bootlegging, because Mr. Beeson was her boyfriend. He was involved with Al Capone. Mr. Beeson used to run on the *Managua*. That was the biggest boat they had. It ran between Nassau, Miami and New York. So he would come to Nassau and carry back cases and cases. He transport things up and down. Wasn't no interference in Nassau, because it was legal here. But when you get in Miami, the immigration check you. With him, he didn't have to leave the ship; only leave the ship when he feel like it. He take a bag and go about his business. Everybody know him. I just got rid of the trunk where she hid all the money she got from this bootlegger.

Alfred Love, New Providence

Mr. Love even mentioned the government's role in rum-running.

There was certain people what was involved in rum-running. You hear about R. T. Symonette? That's where he made his start. Quite a few more Bahamians used to run liquor into the United States in those days, from Nassau and Grand Bahama as well. 'Cause I know they used to have a government shed or something up by Western Senior School. Women was there and used to sew whiskey in burlap sacks and pack it away. They carry the liquor like that. Coloured people didn't make lots of money out of rumrunning. The coloured people ain't had no boats. The whites had motor boats. They carry liquor from here to Bimini and Grand Bahama. The coloured Bahamians were in the crew and went along, but they didn't make the money. It was mostly the Conchy Joes took part in rum-running.

Herman Sawyer, New Providence

"Everybody want that fast dollar" expressed Mr. Sawyer's attitude about the illegal activities of smuggling liquor and undocumented aliens into the United States.

I remember after Poppa got married again, we went down to Berry Island at Gun Cay right off from Bimini. That was the main route for bootleg-ging. West End was only about five miles away. That was big money, but it was more or less like the dope. It was illegal to take it over to America. Bahamians did it just like they do today, transferring Cubans and Haitians [smuggling undocumented aliens into the United States]. [Laughter.] People are losing their lives and everything. It's nothing changed. Only change is a bigger way. Everybody want that fast dollar. Regardless, they don't care who they kill.

Cat Island versus San Salvador

At the time when I visited Cat Island, many residents were engaged in debates concerning the true location of San Salvador. Most current his-torians designate San Salvador (Watling's Island), one of the southern-most Bahamas Islands, as the site of Columbus' landfall in the New World. But it was important to these residents of Cat Island to establish that their island was really the correct location, because they assumed that they would receive publicity and that tourists coming to the 500th anniversary of Columbus' arrival in the new world would then come to Cat Island and spend large sums of money. As it developed, the anniver-sary did not bring fame and fortune to any of the Bahamas.

It's interesting to note that the argument concerning the original loca-tion of Columbus' landfall is a longstanding one. Stark, in 1891 (Stark, 22–23), stated:

Cat Island was supposed until recently to have been the land first seen by Columbus, and called by him San Salvador . . . This decision is now re-versed, and the reason for this change seems conclusive. Lieutenant Beecher, of the British navy, proves conclusively that Cat Island cannot be San Salvador, and that Watling's Island answers the description better than any other island laying in the track of Columbus. His two strongest reasons are that Columbus states that he rowed around the northern end in one day. The size of Cat Island makes this physically impossible, while it is quite feasible at the other island. He also speaks of a large lake in the interior. There is no such water in Cat Island, while such a lake does exist on Watling's Island.

In 1986, the National Geographic Society further complicated this debate by suggesting that Samana Cay was the most likely location of the first landfall of Columbus. Samana Cay is uninhabited, nine miles long and about twenty miles northeast of Acklins Island.
Despite these theories, many Cat Islanders are determined to retain the name San Salvador and the claim of being the first landfall of Columbus.

Rufus Hepburn, born 1902, Industrious Hill, Cat Island

Mr. Hepburn is a ninety-year-old gardener at Fernandez Bay, Cat Island. He had agreed to be interviewed but referred most of my questions to Mrs. Olive Ramsey. One of his only firm comments occurred when I raised this topic.

When Columbus came, he saw a cat and when he saw the cat, he called it Cat Island. So there ain't no use in they telling you different. [Most references say that the island was named after a pirate named Arthur Catt.]

Harcourt Stevens, Cat Island

Mr. Stevens assumes that there would be an advantage, during the 500th anniversary of Columbus' landfall, for Cat Island to be designated "San Salvador." He concluded his argument with the statement, "My parents' birth certificate say San Salvador."

This is not Cat Island, this is San Salvador. I knew it from twelve years old. They must be know what they doing. But this never was Cat Island. This was San Salvador from the time I was born. My old people, their marriage paper called it San Salvador. Everyone up here is from Bluff, San Salvador. Somebody got the history of what happened. They are working on that right now. That other island [now called San Salvador] used to be called Watling's Island. That's what I know.

They change our name from San Salvador to Cat Island. Cat Island now got three names. The people in the former days, before 1919, their birth was in San Salvador. All were born before that time; their birth was in San Salvador. We have Columbus' statue right up there now. Show you how to get up there. The bulldozer done tear the place down now [made a road], so when the two years are up, they can come and look at Columbus' island, Salvador.

Little San Salvador is right here. That's nine miles on the west. It's a little island. Now, what they gonna do? Put some more cays between Cat Island and Watling's? So that it will grow and by that time it ought to be big enough and it'll be big San Salvador [laughter].

You see, by losing that name, we lose a lot of things that would come here. The island name from creation and they change it and give it to another place. They should go by the people. That government in '32 or '36, somewhere around there, they didn't tell nobody. From 1926 down, they changed the name. My parents' birth certificate say San Salvador.

Olive Ramsey, Long Island

Mrs. Ramsey quoted her ninety-one-year-old father as her source in this debate.

See, I thought they called the area up there San Salvador [northern part of Cat Island]. There are two San Salvadors. The onliest [only] thing I can tell you, Miss, is that when I was growing up, they tell me that little island is Little San Salvador. But I hear them now, since one of the teachers, Mr. Moncur, came from Nassau and talked here, he's saying that this is San Salvador. I don't know nothing about that.

I know this as Cat Island all of my days and I'm going to be fifty-six. When I was growing up, my parents told me it was Cat Island. Little San Salvador is the island up the creek. And big San Salvador, we used to call Guanahani, better known as Watling's Island. That's what my teacher told me. Since that other teacher come and spoke, the children tell me that this was San Salvador. My children told me that. My boys, you understand? They say, "You know anything about that?" I say, "No." All I can tell them is my father is ninety-one. He's living in Nassau with my sister,

Sophie. He knew this as Cat Island. When I was a kid, my father say Cat Island. No, that's all he knew.

Family Islands vs. Nassau

Those who remain on the Family Islands have strong feelings about the advantages of their settlements as compared to Nassau. In general, they like the feeling of community that exists. Everyone knows the others who live in the settlement. The two narrators quoted here disliked Nassau because of the pace, the killings and the crowds.

Joseph Carroll, Long Island

I don't like Nassau. I don't like city life on the whole. I go to the United States for two or three days and that's it. And that's why I'm living here. After I got out of the army, I couldn't see myself raising a family in Nassau, so I came up to Long Island. It was only me. All the family was in Nassau. We have plenty property and everything there. Some of the pressure that you have to endure in the city is terrible. And what I learned in cities, you haven't got a place to go in the world and you find yourself going as fast as they're going. You got to go with them.

Kathleen Thurston, Cat Island

I don't go to Nassau. Momma, how you gonna manage in Nassau? I hear every day they kill the children; they kill the people. I does cry. Oh, I does cry. It ain't gonna get better, because I just hear two—no three—take this woman and shoot her. And some run into one big tree. They buy these vehicles and they wouldn't take time. They just speeding along the road killing they self.

Offspring

Many of the people I interviewed wanted to talk about their children and how many "grands, great-grands and great-great-grands" they had. On the Family Islands, it was obvious that most of the young people had left the island and headed for Freeport, Nassau or the United States. Although I made no effort to interview people whose children were achievers, most of their offspring seem to have done well.

Even though I did not raise the question, men frequently reported that they had children with their sweethearts (women other than their wives). This practice continues among younger Bahamians and has a detrimental effect on many families. None of the women mentioned this behavior. Nor did I raise it with them.

Clementina Adderley, Long Island

I in my ninety-one year. I never had no trouble. I had one daughter and she married and she living up at the Turnquests. I have two sons living here and two in the States. That's one of my sons living on that side [next door] and the other one living right round here. I got twenty-six grandchildren and sixty-six great-grandchildren and six greatty-grands.

My daughter, she got five children. Her two daughters, one teaching, one is a head teacher to Freeport. The one named Arrie, she married to a schoolteacher. She been all over the islands teaching, and now they in Nassau teaching. And my grandson's working for the government. Teddy, he is a lawyer and he's in the House of Assembly. Denizen is a lawyer and his wife is a lawyer. And the other one, he does work in the House of Assembly. He does do the books. Every one of Arrie's children working in the government. And Ollie, he only got one. That's Bernard. He working up here in the station at BATELCO [Bahamas Telecommunications Corporation]. He was working there now for quite a long time. That's all. All the rest of his own is away.

Only two I got away, one in New York and one in Virginia. I don't expect the one in Virginia to come back, because he got too much over there. When I was there, he had his first home what he built. Then he had a club built. And when I went back again, he had another big building built. It was like he was living in the country then. But when I went back, he was out in the city. After he was out there, the people who go all about to pick apples in Virginia, they didn't have nowhere to live. So he bought plenty of these old homes, you know? He repair all of them and he put them on rent. He got five of those on rent, different from his first home and the club. He running that hisself downstairs, but upstairs, people living in that. And then he got his own dwelling house right in there. So he ain't coming back. But I had a letter from him [on] Christmas. He said, "Momma, I'm coming out for the regatta. Let me know what time that the regatta gone be." That be in May every year. And all what is away, they does come, you know? They come and go to the regatta down at Salt Pond.

N. Granville M. Major, Long Island

I have ten children altogether. I didn't mean to get married. You see, my name bothered me. N. G. M.: Never Get Married [laughter]. I think they named me that at Rum Cay. My wife has four. My wife is from Long Island, right down the road. She was a Turnquest. We raised our four children. Leo, my oldest son, he is on the boat *Leander*. He is assistant to the mate there. Sharon, my oldest daughter, she is in BATELCO. She's been there ten years. Gail, the third, she is on the Defence Force. She has a degree and she's in the accounts department. And the last one, she works at Trixie's beauty parlor in Nassau. Does manicure and pedicure. Two in Nassau, one on the boat, and one here. The others, Val teaches in Nassau. Glen, he's over in Atlanta. He's still in school.

Fred Ramsey, Cat Island

All my children are in Nassau, Alabama and all about. I had seven in the home and eleven outside. None of them are here. One of the grandboys gone from here the week before last. Sometimes they come and spend two or three weeks. I had a wife, but she died nine years ago. I live by myself. It isn't that lonesome—you got people coming around. Friends in.

Joseph Carroll, Long Island

I have thirteen, the baker's dozen. Nine boys and four girls. I have a boy, you probably heard of him—Frank Carroll. He have a band called Hit Squad or something like that. He's in Canada. Yeah, well, he was out here sometime ago. He played in some of the hotels. I have one boy in Canada. I have two in Nassau. Freddy is on the police force and Terry is an electrician in Nassau. Then, I bet you would know Norris Carroll, the lawyer, in Freeport. I have another son, Forrester. He's in the brokerage business in Freeport. He even want to sell his home down here. That's his home over there. He has everything tied up in Freeport. He's doing very well. My last boy, Kevin, is in medical school in Jamaica now. I have another boy who's on a boat, Peter. There's Clarence—he's down in Freeport. I got one boy who died. Sometime I can't remember them all, you know. There's Clarence, Norris, Freddy, Terry, Kevin and Peter. That's all the boys. Then I have Linda, Carolyn, Val. Carolyn is in Freeport; she works for Syntex [a multi-million-dollar pharmaceutical plant]. Carolyn went to school in the States. The other girls, none didn't go to college. And Val is the only one here.

Well, you know, nobody was interested in my business. Because, a couple of the older boys, they went to school. They went to college and all that. I guess they wasn't interested in my business. I told them already, I'm just marking time, you know? I'm just trying to keep up with it until somebody take over. But if I die, they'll take it over then. Come home then. Nobody wants it. Well, I would be fair about it. Norris, he studied law. Clarence is about the only one eligible. He could retire now—four years ago. But his heart is in education, you know.

The first kids had it tough, you know what I mean? The first ones, they're the more dedicated ones. The other children are okay, but they take everything for granted. You know, they think it was always like this. In fact, the majority of young people think that.

Enid Sawyer, New Providence

Herman and I have eight children, seven boys and one girl. I needed to work, because we had two or three in high school at the same time. Tuition was high at that time and now it's much higher. But we made it. Rudy went to St. John's University. Marcian didn't want to go to university. He was a good basketball player. He was a high-jump champ, too. He could have gotten a scholarship. He went to Taylor's Industries. He learned how to do engineering just from going to work. He's really an electrician. Now, a certified electrician has to sign when he does work. But what I'm telling him is to go to night school and get a certificate. Then he could work on his own. Julian is a chemical engineer. He worked at Burke when he finished high school and they gave him a full scholarship. He started at Florida A&M. But he didn't get what he wanted, so he went to Southwest Louisiana. He got everything he wanted down there. Tyrone is the MBA. He's in tourism. Barry works in the law field, Francis works in a brokerage business, Trevor works at Freeport Power, and Janice is a secretary at Purity Bakery.

They're never without work. All we make, we spend giving them a fairly good education. Every one of them is holding a post. We worked hard to make sure that our children would have an education. Wanted them to have an easier life. Thank God the time and energy paid off!

Hazel Newman, Long Island

My eldest son is in Florida with the North Scope Company. He works on heavy equipment. Crane operator is really his post. I think he's in Nassau now. He could be on some other island building a dock or something. And my second son, he's a sergeant with the police force. I think right at the moment, he's assigned to a court—prosecutor or magistrate's court. My third child, my eldest daughter, she is presently the manager of Scotiabank, the bank of Nova Scotia branch on Bay Street. She was employed for many years in Palmdale. Before that, she was a stewardess with Bahamasair. My fourth daughter, she's the one who is with BATELCO.

If I had the chance, I would tell young mothers to see that their children get as much education as possible. And that they make use of that education. It seems to be a difficult task today, with drugs and so many things. That's what I'm so worried about with my grandchildren. Children go to school and they be doing well. When you look, they've been involved with bad company and they go. You try with them and still they throw it all away.

We're so concerned about the schools. All you can do is just keep on trying. Try to involve the children in other things outside of school, community work. My children were involved in ball games and stuff like that. Try to keep them busy, as much busy as possible.

Rita Wood, New Providence

I worry about the young people. I'm always in touch with young people. You see, I think we are too materialistic. They want everything now. They don't wait. I don't think it will ever be the same as it used to be. With my children, I didn't wait for things to happen. I told them what would happen if they did certain things. I would threaten them [laughter].

I have a daughter who is a character. And she wore a tie to school. All schools wear uniforms. Her tie was threaded, because she bit on the edge of the tie. So I said I would make her a tie of the grosgrain ribbon as a new tie for the new school term. She did not like it because it was not the original. So she came home one day without the tie. And I said to her, "Natalie, where's your tie?" She got all startled. "Oh, the tie." I noticed she was feeling for words, so I said, "Now look, girl, just don't come home without it tomorrow." So the next day she came home with the tie. She was wearing the tie. She didn't say anything about finding the tie. I said,

"Natalie, you found your tie?" "That's something, hey Mommy?" she said. "George found the tie and thought this got to be Natalie's tie." Oh, sometimes I hit them, but they know when I say something, I mean it. That same daughter, when I would punish her, would say, "When I have my children, I'm going to let them do what they want to do." So I remind her about it now. And she says, "Mommy, why don't you be quiet!"

You have good young people. But there isn't enough for young people to do. And too many of our families are without a head of the family. And the children from these families want to have the same things that better-off families give their children. And this is when we get our violence. Sometime last year or the year before last, it was given to Bishop Gomez as something to think about. What kind of plans we could have. And the report came out three or four weeks ago. He thought they should have this or that and whatever. First of all, whatever we're going to do for the young people, we'll have it in church halls. So it would be for this area, that area and the other area. We had this years ago at St. Francis, you know.

Olive Ramsey, Long Island

I stayed on Cat Island and I married here and lived with my mother and father. I lived in a settlement called the Cove. I have ten living children, and four boys died. Two of my daughters, they married in Nassau and they are maids at Cable Beach. Two here. They get their education right here. They started out at the school in Knowles, and after which they went to high school at Old Bight. They finished get their schooling there. Each of my children, you know, before they have GCE [General Certificate], they have BJC [Bahamas Junior Certificate]. Some have nine subjects; some have eight. Only two I have now in school. My last boy is fifteen. His name is Abraham. His older brother is eighteen. Hopefully, he get a good job. If he get a job at that building across the street, he might stay. Other than that, he'll leave Cat Island.

Health

At the beginning of the twentieth century, a government hospital was constructed on a twenty-acre site in Nassau. Its accommodations included a "poorhouse" for indigent patients, an asylum for the mentally ill and an asylum for lepers. Health needs on the islands were significant, especially among low-income residents. In 1915, the Colonial Secretary

reported that tuberculosis continued to be "rife" among the poor. In addition, he reported, the annual summer outbreak of typhoid continued to
occur. Because Nassau lacked a municipal system of sewage and a water
supply, germs spread rapidly among the needy. Affluent citizens possessed
septic tanks and wells and, as a result, received some protection from
contamination-related diseases. By 1929, water supplies in Nassau
had been chlorinated and pipe borne. This did not prevent a serious
influenza epidemic in 1929, however. Nor did it reduce the growing incidence of tuberculosis.

The Colonial Report of 1946 defined the chief health problems during
that period as malnutrition, syphilis and tuberculosis. By 1959, tuberculosis and hypertension had been identified as the most serious health
problems. During the early '60s, malnutrition caused a number of protein deficiency-related diseases among the poor.

In 1974, Clifford Darling, a member of the PLP and the Minister of
Labour and National Insurance, introduced the country's first national
insurance program. The system provided benefits to qualified contribu-
tors for retirement, disability, sickness, maternity, funeral expenses and
survivor's assistance. In addition, noncontributory assistance programs
maintained old age pensions, sickness and survivor's assistance to persons
who had no other meaningful source of income.

By 1990, the country had 948 hospital beds and 218 physicians, most
of whom practiced on New Providence or Grand Bahama. A total of 107
clinics were operated by the Ministry of Health and Environment on
the Family Islands in 1996. There were also 21 government and 7 private
medical doctors serving the Family Islands. The vital statistics report for
1991 listed as the four leading causes of death: heart diseases, malignant
cancers, cardiovascular disorders and pneumonia. Despite a public
awareness program, the incidence of AIDS is increasing.

Clementina Adderley, Long Island

Mrs. Adderley has a successful prescription for longevity.

I still could wash and I still could cook. And I still could do anything what
I could manage to do with my hands. I got a walker. I got sick and I can't
get in the house and I can't get out. My dear, my two legs. If nurses come,
they come. I got arthritis. If I get up, I've got to hold on. Now, when I get
out here and stand up a little while, I could manage. I could still take a

cutlass and go out there and cut weeds. I use my walker. Take the cutlass and hold onto my walker and I go out there. I can't sit down much. Must be I was used to work [laughter]. But come right down to it now, pain. If it wasn't for my two legs, my dear, I could go out here and just work. Old as I is, I could go out here and just work.

But one good thing, I never drink a drop of liquor in my life. I never had a pipe or a cigarette in my hand in my life, not in my life. All these people I does see what drink liquor, I don't know nothing about it. I'll tell you the truth, the doctor even put me off of soda. I used to have indigestion so bad. He tell me don't use it. He say the soda got too much acid. And I put that down. I don't have indigestion like I used to have it; only, if I eat a little bit of greasy food, it will, you know, repeat on me. I don't eat mutton. And I only use corn out of the can, beef out of the can and fruit cocktail. Now I use fish. I like fish. And I like pork, but no mutton. I don't cook that at all.

Joanna Bethel, New Providence

I could easily picture it when Mrs. Bethel said, "We had a battle over that."

I have arthritis. My hand is so soft and achy, I can't hold the broom. I have a girl that come every other week, clean up good for me. My neighbours here at South Beach are nice. The ones right out to the beach have taken me on like a mother. She and her husband both come. They brought me Valentine roses. And those in the next house were over here last night.

My arthritis is the reason I can't drive now. I had a slight stroke, so I don't drive. I hated giving up my freedom, I'll tell you that [laughter]. We had a battle over that!

Rafaleta Williams, Andros

Mrs. Williams' reaction to the possibility of regaining her sight was depressing.

I blind and I got some children livin' with me and people come and do for me. I manage. I crawl in there. I hold onto something and feel along. If I want water, I go feel for the bucket and I get water they left for me. Sometime, well, I be alone all day.

Now I glimmer outta this eye. I manage to glimmer, but I can't glimmer nuttin' outta this one. Just like darkness all the time. The doctor say cataract. Can't get it off lessen [unless] they operate, they say. But I wouldn't take no operation, 'cause I too old. I hear a couple of people had operation on they eye and they coulda see. But I wouldn't take it.

John Wilson, Cat Island

I observed that some of the people in the settlement helped compensate for his loss.

I blind, so I don't do nothing. I lose my sight. It's glaucoma. I use drops that just keep the heaviness out. Keep the pressure down. I read until I couldn't read no more. I looked at a book until I couldn't look no more. I tell you, it's gone altogether. I used to read in my church every Sunday of the year. It's all gone now. I can't see no letters now.

Then Compared with Now

Many of the Family Islanders with whom I spoke were nostalgic about the past, while recognizing the conveniences that time and progress have produced. They acknowledge that life was different in their youth, when work opportunities were few, roads were nonexistent or poor, and their government did not truly represent them. Nonetheless, some are wistful about "the good old days," when people were much more willing to cooperate with each other and to aid their neighbours when necessary. Life was less stressful, and children showed adults a much higher level of respect. Several spoke of the high levels of honesty and low incidence of crime that existed in the past. The fact that settlements have lost so many residents was a major concern. I was surprised that some Family Islanders said that it was "fifty-fifty," meaning that the advantages and disadvantages during each period balanced out.

None of those living on New Providence wished for the "good old days." No one remembered Nassau before the telephone and electricity systems were available for those who could afford them. Most complained about downtown traffic, but only two did not drive on a regular basis. Some felt that life is more difficult now. Most narrators had been victimized by some form of theft, but said they felt safe where they were living.

Rufus Hepburn, Cat Island

Mr. Hepburn explained why "Only my wife and the McCoys stay in our settlement."

Cat Island was better when I was growing up than now, because it had plenty folks here, many settlements. There were a lot of people. Now the island just kinda exists. Some industry and the people are in Nassau. Only my wife and the McCoys stay in our settlement. Two McCoy and one Hepburn. All is dead, and who ain't dead is staying in Nassau.

They leave, 'cause it wasn't like now. They could make the money now. At that time, they couldn't make nothing, just farm. Raise sisal and ship it on the boat. They have the mailboat. When I was growing up, we didn't even have a mailboat. The mailboat stopped in New Bight and Arthur's Town, only two stops. But the more I grow up, in the '60s, we had mailboats starting in October 1960. That was the first time the mailboat stopped in the Cove. We have a dock there. But eight or ten years back, the mailboat stopped coming to Cove.

Ivy Simms, Long Island

Salted meat and levels of stress and safety are the criteria Ms. Simms uses to evaluate changes.

Gracious, Long Island has changed in so many ways. I mean, in those days we never knew what refrigeration was. You know, we had no Frigidaires. We had fresh meat when it was first killed. After that it was salted, the same as fish. So you got it fresh one time. Then you had the salted one. It was very nice. You had to soak it to get the salt out. So we did that with meat, I mean with mutton, pork and fish. After you served it, you would not know it wasn't fresh. So life has changed in that way.

And, of course, things were harder to get. But I don't think people felt as much stress. Now I lock my door. I want my key, because when I turn my key I want to know that when I come in there is nobody in here.

Benjamin Saunders, Andros

Mr. Saunders talks about how the cooperative spirit in the settlement has changed and the fact that he doesn't have anything to worry about in these times.

Those days, we used to cooperate a little bit better than they doin' now, because we helped each other. If I going to my farm and I want something to be done, why then, I could have a farm within three or four hours. If I need, ten men get together, take the machete and cut down my farm within that space of time. Well, that ain't so today. They'll see you working your nails off and very few you will find to come and give you an assistance. Now you must pay. Well, it wasn't so in them times. In my early life that I'm saying, you could hardly pay nothing to go to Nassau. My wife take £1 [$4.80 U.S.] and she went to Nassau and she come back with a full stock of groceries—for £1.

Of course, it don't make no difference to me. When it's smooth weather, I go in my dinghy. I don't have nothin' to worry about, not now, not in these times. Catch fish for my own self. I own my home. I retire this December past. I write in my resignation then from the postmaster service. I get pension from the police—small pension, nothing much.

John Newman, Long Island

To quote Mr. Newman's evaluation of the changes, "It's a fifty-fifty thing."

To me, I would think it's a fifty-fifty thing between the old days and these times. 'Cause in the old days, there wasn't much money. The money was small. These modern days now, the money is kind of plentiful. But what you could buy with the money you made in the old days, you can't even buy today. So to me, I think it's just a fifty-fifty.

Joseph Carroll, Long Island

Mr. Carroll, too, says that the cooperative spirit in the settlement has changed, as has the level of prosperity

Oh, Long Island has slowly but surely changed, The people changed. I know when I were growing up, if somebody wanted to build a home, everybody joined in and helped them to build that home. All you had to do at that time was find a couple of shillings to pay a carpenter. And he probably charged four shillings [96¢ U.S.] a day. But, it was hard to find four shillings. However, people used to chip in. Now, as a little prosperity come along, all that vanished. That's one change, you know.

Well, it's obvious: everybody for themselves. Another thing is when you didn't have anything, everyone used to visit one another in the evening and talk. Now, you don't have the time to visit. That's another change. I'll tell you, in my case, I'm so tired at the end of the day, I just want to go and throw myself in the bed. But then, it isn't that way with everybody, you know what I mean? Once in a while, we get out, before church, on a Sunday afternoon and visit some people, like that.

If I had children here, it wouldn't be so bad. But I have to do everything. Val, my daughter, and her husband up here, because they ain't doing well in Nassau. Paying rent and all you never get anywhere. Since she been here, they built a nice home and everything. They couldn't do it in Nassau. And she's a tremendous help, but still, that's the only one here.

Harcourt Stevens, Cat Island

Mr. Stevens gave a scathing evaluation of the honesty of young people.

Things have changed on Cat Island. Now you have to lock your doors. They will steal. Well, they'll clean your house out. Empty it. We never had a taste of that growing up, you know. It's the youngsters. They want money. They don't work, yet they want money for food and liquor.

But you can still walk in the street. Nobody bother you. They won't bother us. If the sand flies and mosquitoes don't get you, you could sleep right out there on the porch. No one will worry you at all. No, we don't have anything to fear, not yet.

Life is fifty miles different. When I was brought up, I had to do what my parents said if I like it, if I didn't like it. In those days, we had to know what we were going to say in front of our parents and today the kids can say anything. In those days, we were told that there were certain things we couldn't do and should not say. If we made a mistake one time, we wouldn't say it a second time.

People used to be honest. I know as a young man growing up, you passed by houses along the way, you don't see any lock on the door. I know an old man; we used to call him Captain. He had a barn where he kept all his farm produce, you know? And I never see a lock on that door. All he had was a stick to keep that closed. Day and night, for years and years, he never had a lock on that door. You could go out in the field and just close the door. When you come back you meet the house. But now. you better know you have something to keep them out.

There was this man, Mr. Barber, used to live up at Fernandez. I think he living in Eleuthera now. He looked to me like a German or something.

And he been here, must be about fifteen years. He had his house and he been here. After he had some thief broke into him, steal some of his goods, he get mad and he sell his property. He gone. He was right in there where Briscoe live now, on the north side.

I know when I could have gone to Nassau and leave my house open. We don't trust that now. We could have gone to Nassau and leave our house open, no lock, no key. Just put a wood stick to hold the door close. And if that wood blows down, some of the neighbours would come and put it back and we ain't gonna miss nothing. But you don't trust it now. They ain't broke in mine yet, but I won't trust it. We does lock it. That's my house across the road. This one belong to a neighbour. Their children is in Nassau. The neighbour died a long time. Only the children now and they in Nassau. It empty, 'long with plenty others.

Alfred Love, New Providence

Mr. Love remembers, "Love thy neighbour as thyself."

I look at changes in this light. In time gone by, it was little possessions you had. It didn't cost much to live. But today, it costs a devil of a lot to live. If you are not working, you suffer more. Your neighbour would help you in time gone by. If they cook a meal and they know you over here [and] ain't in position to help yourself, they take up a plate of food and bring it to you. It ain't like that anymore. Number one, first thing they gonna say, "Well, I have trouble to get money to buy this. So I'll try to make use of it myself." In time gone by, whatever little they had, they share it. When it come right down to it, there is more money in circulation. But at the same time, it is very burdensome to some people. And it is more difficult for them to exist than it used to be.

Israel Saunders, Andros

Mr. Saunders was quite positive in his discussion of change.

It's better now than when I was young, because we have a better government, see? The government looking into everybody's future. Yes, the people live better. You can find a dollar better. And years gone by, you couldn't do it. I tell you the truth, I like our government. I never—from the day they came into being—I never decide to change to nothing else [to a different political party]. And whether that suit anybody else, I ain't nothing to do with the next person. Pindling is my man as long as he live!

Enid Sawyer, New Providence

Mrs. Sawyer suggested one possible reason for the increase in crime.

Things have changed in Nassau a lot. Right now, we want the economy to go up to help the people. The economy has gone down so much and there's a lot of crime. It seems crime came in gradually. Like the young people, watching TV, imitating what they see other people do, copycats getting the wrong impressions. I think they should really cut that violence out on TV. They should not show it on TV, because the young mind is very impressionable. They could be influenced easily.

Herman Sawyer, New Providence

Mr. Sawyer shared his perspective and why he feels he "made something out of nothing."

I came through these last seventy-two years and saw a lot of changes. I know when things were down; I know when they came up; I know when things start flourishing during the wartime. Just before that, things go to bottom. People really poor. And then the tourist business start. But if I go back, I can remember years gone by, when we used to have the sisal business going ahead. Most people used to make it off of that. But sometime you had to go on the side of the road and crack rocks to fix the road [laughter]. They used to sell it by the bag for three pence, which has no value now. They would fill these ordinary cement bags and put them on the side of the road. They pick them up and get three cents or something like that. The rocks were used for building, foundations and like that.

About my life, I did something with nothing. They say you can't get something out of nothing. But I tell them, I did. I gave my family a comfortable home to live in. I educated my children. I don't have millions [laughter]. Everyone figure if you don't have a quarter of a million dollars or a couple thousand, you can't be happy. But I tell them I'm happy with nothing. I hardly had to go to the doctor. I went to the doctor twice, because I had two operations for hernia. Almost everybody have that.

Kathleen Thurston, Cat Island

Rastafarians are people who practice mystical beliefs that hold that the now-deceased Emperor Haile Selassie I of Ethiopia is the living God. Mrs. Thurston saw them as a criminal element.

Those were the good old days. The good old days was be then. In them days we didn't have no trouble, no worries with these Rasta [Rastafarians] and all. You know them? And trouble killing people. But home here, I don't want to hear about that Nassau. Boy, we have it good here.

Lawrence Smith, New Providence

According to Mr. Smith, both Adelaide and Jesus have changed.

Yeah, ma'am, Adelaide change plenty from when I come first. And it still change now. The changes is the people. The village ain't changed; it's the people. They changed, and they react bad with each other, ma'am. If you live in the village we coulda gone to you and said, "Please come and help." Now they turn you away. They change.

I believe my Jesus, He change, too. Because that's the only explanation I can say to you for now. If they change, God change with them, too. You see, the reason for this, they got a Hitler reaction against one another, that's all. That ain't good. The Good Book tell you, "Love ye one another, for ye shall be loved." But they ain't doin' that. 'Cause if you go ask that, they gone turn you away just like that. I don't think that's right.

Hazel Newman, Long Island

Mrs. Newman not only communicated the changes that have occurred, she offered a concrete suggestion to improve the Long Island economy.

Long Island has changed, because people now realize that education is very important. I think in my days, like my mother, she took me from school. They didn't give a thought that you could have continued on. At that time, there wasn't any high school or anything like that. Had just started one in Crooked Island. I think it was the first Family Island to have a high school. Anyway, education-wise, people are aware now that it is important for children to attend school.

I notice that the young people don't have that background of farming—some of them, I should say, particularly in Clarence Town. Some of them are employed in fishing here. They go fishing and some again, they just don't farm and they don't fish, so I don't know how they support themselves. That's what I'm so concerned about. It's only the older men who still farm. The young people can't do things like farming and stock raising. That was the big thing in those days—mostly sheep. Now here, they go into fishing. They fish for crawfish and groupers. There is a crawfish season and a grouper season.

When I was growing up, everyone farmed when they finish school. Now the trend is go to Nassau. We need something to attract the young people back to the islands [Family Islands]. The government has a packinghouse here. The produce that people have, they can sell it at the packinghouse. We need something to preserve the fruits. The fruits, that's just a loss. Like in the mango season, the packinghouse can only take so much. The rest of it just spoils. Get too much rain or something like that, and the pineapples rot.

What happened, like I said, when the children stayed to school, more or less, they didn't bother with farming. Or their parents wouldn't bother them to say, "Learn this." But the younger people, some of them who went away, are back and building larger homes. Well, I was speaking generally all over the island—south and north. Some come back and they settle home.

Ena Major, Long Island

Mrs. Major shared some of her valuable parenting skills.

Well, I would say that Long Island has changed a lot, because when I was a child, everybody was given a job to do and the parents would see that it was done. But here, today, nobody is given a job to do and no one sees whether it is done. Everybody do what they feel like, that's what it appears to me.

I think that the younger parents don't seem to have the energy, or put out the energy that the older ones did. I lived with my grandmother most of the time, right? She raised me as a child. And when she say go, you gotta be gone! But today, you talk to a child three or four times and they couldn't care whether they move or not.

I didn't have a problem with my children. 'Cause I would be at the store and they would come home and I would come home and get their supper for them. I tell them, you do such and such. When I go back, it's done. I used to get up at five o'clock in the morning, hang a lamp in the tree. Wash my children's clothes and make sure that I get to work on time and they go to school. No one does that anymore. I guess you say we live in a changing world. But I do think that the parents are not taking their responsibility serious enough.

They do go to church. Some of the children go to church, too. Sometimes they go. Sometimes the parents go. But still I feel that they should have their children do something constructive, you know, and keep them busy. Give them something to do and make sure that they do it. I think we could get more done out of the young people. Because they always said, "An idle mind is the devil's workshop." And, I believe, give them something to do and keep them busy and they won't have time to get into trouble. Give them something to do.

When I came from school as a child, I always had my work to do. I had the clothes to wash. I had homework to do, and then you do the plaiting [of sisal]. But these children, they don't have anything to do to take up their spare time. They ride a bicycle up and down the road. When nighttime come, nobody know where they are. It is a big change. And I'm sure that every parent of yesteryear will say that the way children are going, they couldn't have done it before. But they do stay in school and get an education now. So I have hope for these children and the future of the Bahamas.

Glossary

ACL lodge *n.* A group of individuals who are members of an association made up of people from Acklins, Crooked Island and Long Cay.

admire *v.* To like.

all-age school *phr.* A school that includes all grades.

aloe *(Aloe vera) n.* A plant whose succulent, spikelike leaves are used medicinally to prevent scars from burns and to improve the looks of skin and hair.

Asue *n.* The cooperative savings system primarily used by working-class black Bahamians.

back of the bush *phr.* Away from other settled areas.

banana hole *n.* A deep natural hole found in limestone where bananas are frequently planted.

BATELCO *n.* Abbreviation for Bahamas Telecommunications Corporation.

bay gerina *n.* A seashore vine with small leaves used medicinally.

Bay Street Boys *n.* Politically and economically powerful white Bahamian merchants of Nassau.

be bo ben *phr.* "The old story is ended."

benne *n.* Sesame seed.

bight *n*. A narrow inlet or bay.

bird pepper (*Capsicum minimum*) *n*. A plant with tiny, red, extremely hot seeds.

biter *n*. The large claw (pincer) of a crab or lobster.

black crab *n*. A land crab considered to be a delicacy.

black land *n*. Rich inland soil containing humus.

Black Tuesday *phr*. April 27, 1965, the day Lynden O. Pindling challenged the authority of the government by throwing the House of Assembly mace out of the window.

bob *n*. Slang for a shilling, 24 cents U.S.

bootleg *v*. To sell alcoholic liquor to United States citizens during Prohibition.

Boukee, B'o' Boukee *n*. The gullible character of many folktales.

bright *n*. Light-skinned.

bully-net *n*. A net on a round wire frame attached to a long pole, used to catch crawfish.

Burial Society *n*. An organization whose members contribute money to provide for their funeral expenses.

bush doctor *n*. A practitioner of herbal remedies; a practitioner of Obeah.

bush medicine *n*. Herbal remedies usually prepared by boiling the leaves of one or more plants and drinking the tea.

buzzard *n*. A kind of hawk.

cassava (*Manihot esculenta*) *n*. Also known as *manioc*. A plant whose starchy root is eaten.

cay *n*. A low, sandy, very small island.

coloured *adj*. Referring to a person having skin other than white; people of mixed ancestry.

commissioner *n*. The representative of supreme authority on a Family Island.

conch *n*. Gastropod with a foot and large shell. A favorite Bahamian food.

Conchy Joe *n*. A white Bahamian.

Contract *n*. An agreement between the United States and the British government whereby Bahamians worked on United States farms for a stated period of time. Also referred to as "The Project."

crawfish *n*. Bahamian spiny lobster.

dada *n*. Father.

fair-skinned *adj*. Referring to people who have a light-brown complexion and wavy hair.

fetish *n.* A material object believed to have magical powers.

five-finger (*Potentilla*) *n.* A shrub with five leaflets and a brown pod.

Fox Hill Day *n.* A festive holiday held in Fox Hill on August 1.

Friendly Society *n.* A social organization whose members contribute money to be used to aid the sick and elderly.

Goombay drum *n.* A drum made from a discarded wooden barrel with goatskin or sheepskin stretched or nailed over one end.

Government High School *n.* Located in Nassau, it was the first high school sponsored by the government. Students were required to take an entrance examination. A fee was charged.

grant-in-aid school *n.* A government school in which parents were expected to contribute to teachers' salaries.

greasy bush *n.* A shrub whose leaves act as a detergent.

guava tree (*Psidium guajava*) *n.* A tropical tree bearing small, yellow, oval fruit with many hard seeds.

guinea corn *n.* Small ears of corn with black and white kernels.

guinep tree *n.* A tropical tree bearing small, green, sour fruit with large seeds.

gumelemi tree (*Canarium commune*) *n.* A tropical tree with aromatic leaves sometimes used for medicinal purposes.

hard accent *n.* Standard English dialect.

haunt, hant *n.* Restless spirit that comes back to harass the living.

high yellow *adj.* Having a light-brown complexion.

Hopping John *n.* The native dish of pigeon peas and rice cooked together with seasoning and a small amount of salt pork.

Indian corn *n.* Large ears of corn with red kernels.

jackmada *n.* A shrub used medicinally as a cure for "sweetness of the blood" (diabetes).

Johnny Cake *n.* Bread made of wheat flour, shortening and baking powder, usually cooked in a heavy skillet.

jokey *adj.* Fond of a joke.

jook *v.* To yank, poke.

juju (*Zizyphus jujuba*) *n.* A sweet yellow fruit from the jujube tree.

Junkanoo *n.* A festival in which masked paraders dress up in brightly coloured costumes and rush to the music of drummers, cowbell ringers and horn players. Junkanoo takes place in the early hours of December 26 and January 1.

lodge *n.* The local branch of certain societies or clubs.

lodge brother *n.* A fellow member of a lodge.

Lignum vitae n. Tropical tree having very hard, heavy wood.

lose his nature *phr.* Become impotent.

love vine (dodger) (*Cuscuta gronovii*) n. A leafless, twining, parasitic plant having thread-like orange-yellow stems.

mace *n.* A club carried by an official as a symbol of power.

mainland *n.* A large island close to one or more cays.

mistletoe (*Viscumalbum*) *n.* An evergreen plant of the Loranthaceae family, with waxy, white, poisonous berries, growing as a parasite on certain trees.

monitor *n.* An older student who assists the teacher by "teaching" the younger students.

The Mud *n.* Shallow sponging waters west of Andros.

Obeah *n.* Not a religion like voodoo in Haiti, but the two do have elements in common, including a belief in the power of magic, witchcraft, and charms to affect an event or person.

old-story *n.* A folktale, often with animal characters.

onliest *adj.* Only one.

outside child *n.* A child born out of wedlock.

over the hill *phr.* Referring to the settlements separated from the commercial part of New Providence by a rocky ridge.

packinghouse *n.* A building where produce is stored.

parch *v.* To roast, toast.

Penny Savings Bank *n.* Bank established by black businessmen to provide services to poor black Bahamians.

pigeon pea (*Cajanus cajan*) *n.* A small, reddish brown bean contained in flat pods used in peas and rice.

plait *v.* To braid or weave dried strips of palmetto leaves or coconut fronds.

pothole *n.* A deep hole in rocks, usually filled with soil.

pound *n.* Previous basic unit of money in the Bahamas, equal to 20 shillings.

The Project *n.* A term used by Nassauvians to describe the construction of the airfields in Nassau during World War II and/or the practice of going to the United States to work on various farms for a given period of time.

quarry *n.* Crushed limestone.

Rabby, B'Rabby *n.* The cunning hero of many folktales.

raffia *n.* Fiber from the leaves of certain palm trees.

Rastas (Rastafarians) *n.* People who practice a complex set of mystical beliefs, which hold that the now-deceased Emperor Haile Selassie I of Ethiopia (whose given name was Ras Tafari) is the living God.

relish *n*. The part of a meal having a distinctive flavor, in contrast to starchy foods.

rock oven *n*. A free-standing, mound-shaped outdoor oven, about four feet high, made of stones and cement.

rush *v*. To dance quickly and rhythmically in a Junkanoo parade.

sapodilla tree (*Manilkara zopota*) *n*. A tree in the Sapotaceae family, with small, round, brown, sweet fruits.

scale fish *n*. A fish with scales.

scorch *v*. To score, to cut slashes.

scrap gang *n*. An informal group in the Junkanoo parade.

settlement *n*. A small village.

shilling *n*. A silver coin equal to 1/20 of a pound, 24 cents U.S.

silver-leaf palmetto (*Sabal serenoa*, family palmae) *n*. A small palm tree.

sisal *n*. A natural fiber contained in the leaves of *Agave rigida sislana* plants.

stone crab *n*. A white crab with large, meaty biters.

sloop *n*. A sailing boat of native design with a fish well.

sour orange *n*. The Seville orange, frequently used in seasoning fish and conch.

soursop (*Annona muricata*) *n*. The large, dark green, slightly acid, pulpy fruit of a small tree in the custard-apple family.

sponger *n*. Person who fishes for sponges.

straw work *n*. Goods made of woven strips of palm fronds.

sweetheart *n*. The lover of a married man.

tote *v*. To carry.

trans *n*. A means of transportation; a ride.

white land *n*. Land near the sea consisting mainly of coral sand.

white magic *phr*. Incantation that is practiced for good purposes or as a counteraction to evil.

you pass seven if you pass six three times *phr*. Since schools did not have a curriculum for seventh form (grade), students were required to take and pass the sixth-form examination three times to get credit for passing the seventh form.

Bibliography

Albury, Paul. *The Story of the Bahamas*. London: Macmillan Education, 1981.

"Anglicans Divided over Women Priests." *Bahama Journal* 7, no. 28 (March 19, 1994): 1, 3 and 7.

Bahamas—Census, 1891, 1901, 1911, 1921, 1931, 1943. Woodbridge, Conn: Research Publications, 1981. Microform.

Bahamas Handbook and Businessman's Annual. Nassau: Etienne Dupuch, Jr., Publications, 1978, 1990, 1991, 1995, 1996.

Bahamas Reference Annual 1985. Volumes 1 and 2. Nassau: Interpress Public Relations Consultants, 1986.

Bethel, E. Clement. *Junkanoo Festival of the Bahamas*. London: Macmillan Education, 1991.

Bloch, Michael. *The Secret File of the Duke of Windsor*. New York: Bantam, 1988.

Cash, Philip, Shirley Gordon, and Gail Saunders. *Sources of Bahamian History*. London: Macmillan Caribbean, 1991.

Chibwa, Anderson K. "Internal Migration in the Commonwealth of the Bahamas 1960–1970." Master's thesis, University of Miami, 1979.

Collingwood, Dean W., and Steve Dodge, eds. *Modern Bahamian Society*. Parkesbury, Iowa: Caribbean Books, 1989.

Courlander, Harold. *A Treasury of Afro-American Folklore*. New York: Crown, 1976.

Craton, Michael. "Bay Street, Black Power, and the Conchy Joes: Race and Class in the Colony and Commonwealth of the Bahamas, 1850–2000. In *The White*

Minority in the Caribbean, ed. by H. Johnson, 71–94. Kingston: Ian Randle, 1998.

Craton, Michael. *A History of the Bahamas.* London: Collins Press, 1968.

Craton, Michael, and Gail Saunders. *Islanders in the Stream: A History of the Bahamian People.* Volume 2. Athens: University of Georgia Press, 1998.

Crowley, Daniel J. *I Could Talk Old-Story Good: Creativity in Bahamian Folklore.* Berkeley: University of California Press, 1966.

Department of Archives, Ministry of Education and Culture. *The Bahamas During the Early Twentieth Century 1900–1914.* Nassau: 1982.

Department of Archives, Ministry of Education and Culture. *The Boat-Building Industry of the Bahamas.* Nassau: 1981.

Department of Archives, Ministry of Education and Culture. *Settlements in New Providence.* Nassau: 1982.

Department of Archives, Ministry of Education and Culture. *The Sponging Industry: A Booklet of the Exhibition of Historical Documents.* Nassau: 1974.

Department of Research and Statistics, Ministry of Tourism. *Bahamas Tourism Statistics.* Nassau: 1984, 1992.

Department of Statistics, Ministry of Finance. *Selected Economic and Social Indicators: The Commonwealth of the Bahamas.* Nassau: 1989, 1992, 1993.

Department of Statistics, Ministry of Finance. *Vital Statistics Report: Commonwealth of the Bahamas.* Nassau: 1995.

Dupuch, Etienne. *Tribune Story.* London: Benn, 1967.

Edwards, Charles Lincoln. *Bahama Songs and Stories: A Contribution to Folk-lore.* Boston: Houghton, Mifflin for the American Folk-lore Society, 1895.

Eneas, Cleveland W. *Bain Town.* Nassau: Cleveland and Muriel Eneas, 1976.

Eneas, Cleveland W. *Let the Church Roll On.* Nassau: Cleveland W. Eneas, 1984.

Glinton-Meicholas, Patricia. *Talkin' Bahamian: A Useful Guide to the Language of the Islands.* Nassau: Guanima Press in association with Counsellors, 1994.

Great Britain, Colonial Office. *Colonial Report, Annual Series on the Social and Economic Progress of the People of Bahamas, 1907–1908.* London: His Majesty's Stationary Office, 1909.

Great Britain, Colonial Office. *Colonial Report, Annual Series on the Social and Economic Progress of the People of Bahamas, 1917–1918.* London: His Majesty's Stationary Office, 1919.

Great Britain, Colonial Office. *Colonial Report, Annual Series on the Social and Economic Progress of the People of Bahamas, 1926.* London: His Majesty's Stationary Office, 1927.

Great Britain, Colonial Office. *Colonial Report, Annual Series on the Social and Economic Progress of the People of Bahamas, 1929.* London: His Majesty's Stationary Office, 1930.

Great Britain, Colonial Office. *Colonial Report, Annual Series on the Social and Economic Progress of the People of Bahamas, 1932.* London: His Majesty's Stationary Office, 1933.

Great Britain, Colonial Office. *Colonial Report, Annual Series on the Social and*

Economic Progress of the People of Bahamas, 1934. London: His Majesty's Stationary Office, 1936.

Great Britain, Colonial Office. *Report on the Bahamas, 1946–1947.* London: His Majesty's Stationary Office, 1948.

Great Britain, Colonial Office. *Report on the Bahamas, 1948–1949.* London: His Majesty's Stationary Office, 1950.

Great Britain, Colonial Office. *Report on the Bahamas, 1950–1951.* London: His Majesty's Stationary Office, 1952.

Great Britain, Colonial Office. *Report on the Bahamas, 1958–1959.* London: Her Majesty's Stationary Office, 1960.

Great Britain, Colonial Office. *Report on the Bahamas, 1960–1961.* London: Her Majesty's Stationary Office, 1962.

Great Britain Central Office of Information. *Commonwealth of the Bahamas.* London: Her Majesty's Stationary Office, 1973.

Griffiths, John. *We Live in the Caribbean.* New York: Bookwright Press, 1985.

Hannau, Hans W. *The Bahama Islands.* New York: Doubleday, 1969.

Higgins, J. Kevin. *The Bahamian Economy: An Analysis.* Nassau: Counsellors, 1994.

Higham, Charles. *The Duchess of Windsor: The Secret Life.* New York: McGraw-Hill, 1988.

Hill, Christopher. *The Century of Revolution 1603–1714.* Edinburgh: Thomas Nelson, 1961.

Holm, John A., and Alison W. Shilling. *Dictionary of Bahamian English.* New York: Lexik House, 1982.

Holmes, Frank. *The Bahamas during the Great War.* Nassau: The Tribune, 1924.

Hughes, Colin A. *Race and Politics in the Bahamas.* New York: St. Martin's Press, 1981.

Johnson, Doris L. *The Quiet Revolution in the Bahamas.* Nassau: Family Island Press, 1972.

Johnson, Howard. *The Bahamas from Slavery to Servitude.* 1783–1933. Gainesville: University Press of Florida, 1996.

Johnson, Howard. *The Bahamas in Slavery and Freedom.* Kingston: Ian Randle, 1991.

Johnson, Howard. "Friendly Societies in the Bahamas 1834–1910."*Slavery and Abolition: A Journal of Slave and Post-Slave Studies.* 12, no. 3 (December 1991): 183–199.

Meditz, Sandra, and Dennis M. Hanratty, eds. *Islands of the Commonwealth Caribbean: A Regional Study.* Washington, D.C.: Federal Research Division, Library of Congress, 1989.

Ministry of Finance, Commonwealth of the Bahama Islands. *Report of the 1980 Census of Population.* Nassau: 1981.

Moore, James E. *Pelican Guide to the Bahamas.* Gretna, La.: Pelican Publishing, 1984.

Orde-Browne, Granville St. John. *Labour Conditions in the West Indies.* London: His Majesty's Stationary Office, 1939.

Parsons, Elsie W. Clews. *Folktales of Andros Island, Bahamas.* New York: American Folk-lore Society, 1918.

Patterson, Orlando. *The Sociology of Slavery: An Analysis of the Origins, Development, and Structure of Negro Slave Society in Jamaica.* Rutherford, N.J.: Fairleigh Dickinson University Press, 1969.

Popov, Dragan, ed. *Island Expedition: The Central and Southern Bahamas.* Miami, Fla.: Graphic Media, 1988.

Saunders, Gail. *The Bahamas: A Family of Islands,* 2nd edition. London: Macmillan Publishers, 1993.

Saunders, Gail. *Bahamian Society after Emancipation.* Kingston: Ian Randle, 1994.

Saunders, Gail. "The Peoples and Cultures of the Bahamas." *Festival of American Folklife.* Washington, D.C.: Smithsonian Institution (1994): 61–66.

Saunders, Gail. "The Role of the Coloured Middle Class in Nassau, Bahamas, 1890–1942." *Ethnic and Racial Studies* 10, no. 4 (October 1987): 82–95.

Saunders, Gail. "Social History of the Bahamas," Master's thesis, University of Waterloo, Ontario, 1985.

Saunders, Gail. "The 1942 Riot in Nassau: A Demand for Change?" *Journal of Caribbean History* 20, no. 2 (1985–1986): 117–146.

Saunders, Gail. "The 1958 General Strike in Nassau: A Landmark in Bahamian History." *Journal of Caribbean History* 27, no. 1 (1993): 81–107.

Sealey, Neil E. *The Bahamas Today: An Introduction to the Human and Economic Geography of the Bahamas.* London: Macmillan Caribbean, 1990.

Smith, Anastasia E. D. *Aspects of Bahamian Culture.* New York: Vantage, 1978.

Stark, James Henry. *Stark's History and Guide to the Bahama Islands: Containing a Description of Everything on or about the Bahama Islands of which the Visitor or Resident May Desire Information.* Boston: J. H. Stark, 1891.

Symonette, Michael A. *Discovery of a Nation.* Nassau: Management Communication Services, 1973.

Symonette, Michael A. "UN Drug Report Praises the Bahamas." *The Bahamas Financial Digest and Business Today.* Nassau: Management Communication Services 21, no.2: 31–32.

Taylor, Henry. *My Political Memoirs.* Nassau: H. Taylor, 1987.

Tertullien, Mizpah. *Old Stories and Riddles, Bahamiana Culturama #1.* Nassau: Tertullien, 1977.

Trager, James. *The People's Chronology.* New York: Henry Holt, 1985.

Weather Labs, Inc. *Historical Hurricanes,* 1996 http://www.weatherlabs.com.

Whittier, Sara. ed. *Insight Guides, Bahamas.* Hong Kong: APA Productions, Hans J. Hoefer, 1987.

Williams, Patrice. *A Guide to African Villages in New Providence.* Nassau: Department of Archives, 1979.

Wisdom, Keith G. "Ecstasy in Junkanoo: A Public Celebration of Freedom." *Festival of American Folklife.* Washington, D.C.: Smithsonian Institution (1994): 76–79.

Ziegler, Philip. *King Edward VIII—A Biography.* New York: Knopf, 1991.

Index

ciency, 121; then versus now, 259–260;
United Bahamian Party, 237–238
Stevenson, Cyril, 171
Storekeeping, 153–156
Straw work, 139–146
Subsistence farming, 111, 114–123

Taxi union strike. *See* General Strike of
1958
Taylor, Henry, 171
Telephone and electricity services, 193–
194
Then compared with now, 256–264
Thurston, Kathleen Dawkins (narrator),
71–73, 121–123, 203, 248, 262
Tourism, 218–233
Turnquest, Sir Orville A., 176
Turtullien, Mizpah, 87

UBP. *See* United Bahamian Party
Ugly Woman, 103–104
United Bahamian Party (UBP), 171, 173–
175, 236–237

Watling's Island. *See* San Salvador
West End, 6, 10, 68, 186, 243–244
Williams, Eva Augusta McPherson (narrator): color, 77–78, dressmaking, 148–
149; early life, 18–22; murder of Sir

Harry Oakes, 169–170; school, 187–
188
Williams, Rafaleta "Goddie" (narrator):
Bay Street Boys, 235–236; drugs, 200;
early life, 12–14; health, 255; holidays,
95; religion, 68–69; sisal farming, 112;
straw work, 140
Wilson, John (narrator), 113, 116–117,
124, 256
Windsor, Duke of (formerly King Edward
VIII): emigration, 208–209, 212;
Junkanoo, 91; letter to Lord Walter E.
G. Moyne, 218; murder of Sir Harry
Oakes, 170; riot, 161–162, 164–165,
168; strike, 172
Wood, Rita Edwards (narrator): Adastra
Gardens, 222–225; color and class,
81–82; early life, 47–51; Emancipation Day, 96; government structure,
172–173; Guy Fawkes, 94; hurricanes, 197–198; Independence Day,
97–98; Junkanoo, 91–92; offspring,
252–253; role of ambassador's wife,
239–241
World War I, 76, 126, 205
World War II: Contract farming, 207;
crawfishing, 129; Duke of Windsor,
161; enlistments, 205–206; refuge
from, 205, Wenner-Gren, Axel, 219

Olga Culmer Jenkins received her Ed.D. from Columbia University and her B.S. and M.Ed. degrees from Temple University. A former Fulbright-Hays fellow, she taught at Temple University and Hofstra University. She is currently a curriculum consultant.